A Forger's Tale

Confessions of the Bolton Forger

A Forger's Tale

Confessions of the Bolton Forger

SHAUN GREENHALGH

ALLEN&UNWIN

Originally published in a limited edition in 2015 by ZCZ Editions
Hardback edition published in Great Britain in 2017 by Allen & Unwin
This paperback edition published in Great Britain in 2018
by Allen & Unwin

Allen & Unwin
c/o Atlantic Books
Ormond House
26–27 Boswell Street
London WC1N 3JZ
Phone: 020 7269 1610
Fax: 020 7430 0916
Email: UK@allenandunwin.com
Web: www.allenandunwin.com/uk

A CIP catalogue record for this book is available
from the British Library.

Paperback ISBN 978 1 76029 528 8
E-Book ISBN 978 1 92557 524 6

Printed and bound by CPI Group (UK) Ltd, Croydon, CR0 4YY

10 9 8 7 6 5 4 3 2 1

For my Mum and Dad

Introduction

by Waldemar Januszczak

Y OU ARE ABOUT to read the story of a man who grew up
differently from the way most people grow up and who was
waylaid by forces bigger than him. The forces of art. You have
probably heard something of Shaun Greenhalgh already because
back in 2006 he was, briefly, front-page news. In 2006, following
a police raid on his parents' home in Bolton, Shaun was arrested
and eventually charged with producing a large number of fake artworks. According to media reports at the time, the Greenhalgh
family – Shaun, his mum and his dad – had formed a kind of
fakers' Cosa Nostra, a forgery ring operating out of a garden shed
in Bolton. From there they had fooled some of the world's most
important museums. The British Museum in London was one. The
Chicago Art Institute was another.

While Shaun was acknowledged as the maker of most of the
fakes, his parents were presented as the deal closers – the pretend
pensioners who cobbled together the provenances and approached
the museums. The 'Artful Codgers' they were dubbed on the
telly, the oldest criminal masterminds in Bolton. Though their
crimes were serious, there was a sense of working-class rascality
about them. From my distance – from far away – the whole affair

1

had a humorous tinge. You could imagine someone making an Ealing comedy out of their story, starring Alec Guinness as Shaun's dad, and the young Jim Dale as Shaun himself. With their Lancashire Leonardos and their garage Gauguins, the Bolton forgers should never have got as far as they did in the posh environs of the art world.

But this sense of working-class mischief was well and truly stamped on in June 2007 when a judge at Bolton Crown Court sentenced Shaun Greenhalgh to four years and eight months in gaol. How long? If Shaun hadn't spared them all the cost of a trial by pleading guilty it would actually have been seven years. His parents were sentenced, too. But because of their great age their sentences were suspended. Hah! As I write this, the captain of the cruise liner the *Costa Concordia*, which ran aground off the coast of Tuscany in 2012, has just been given a sentence of 16 years for the crime of killing 32 people. A ship captain kills 32 people and gets 16 years. Shaun Greenhalgh sells some objects to a museum that were not what they appeared to be and gets four years and eight months, reduced from seven years. What kind of a world sees things that way?

I came into contact with Shaun a bit later. For my sins, they let me on to the telly occasionally where I make films about the artists I love and in whose footsteps I happily stumble. One of the artists I have most wanted to make a film about was Gauguin, the stockbroker turned painterly genius, best known for his escape to Tahiti. I have always enjoyed the Tahiti pictures with their dreamy fibs about Tahitian life and their magically coloured seashores. But just as much, or even more, I admire the art Gauguin made before he left France on April Fool's Day, 1891. He was multitalented. He could do many things really well – painting, sculpture, prints, ceramics. He was also a skilled fencer, a fine billiards player, a boxer, a musician. So he was one of those rare people with magic in their hands who can pick things up and do them. Like Shaun Greenhalgh, as it happens.

One of the best exhibitions I have ever seen was held in 2002, in Amsterdam, in the prestigious Van Gogh Museum. It was devoted to the wild and fruitful relationship between Gauguin and van Gogh, his art-buddy, whom he briefly visited in Arles in 1888. This was the disastrous artistic houseshare that culminated in the notorious ear-cutting. Van Gogh and Gauguin were together in the south of France for just a couple of months, but they churned out enormous amounts of great art. Seeing it all together in a show called *The Studio of the South* was unforgettable. As I was making a Gauguin biography for the BBC, it was a show I had to film.

Among the objects on display in *The Studio of the South* was a ceramic I had never seen before that had been lent to Amsterdam by that fabulous American museum, the Chicago Art Institute. It showed a faun, a follower of Pan, half man, half goat, sitting naughtily on a ceramic mound. The cheeky ceramic was signed 'PGo', the shorthand signature that Gauguin sometimes used, derived, apparently, from the nautical slang for a penis. A typical Gauguin joke. Wanting to make a point about this signature, I settled on the Faun as the clearest example in the show. Peering closely at it, particularly at its familiar hooked nose, I fancied, too, that I saw something of Gauguin himself in it. So when it came to do my piece for the camera, I introduced it on film with obvious enthusiasm and added some clever remarks about its possible autobiographical meaning. What I didn't know then was that, back in Bolton, its maker was watching me on the telly with some pals in a pub and probably thinking, 'What a plonker.'

In the past, I have been reasonably good at spotting fakes. When William Boyd published *Nat Tate: An American Artist 1928–1960*, in 1998, I knew within a couple of pages that Nat Tate had never existed. It was all a clunky hoax. Whenever somebody finds yet another stash of lost Jackson Pollocks in yet another Long Island garage, I can usually tell from the first newspaper photo that they were made in China. So I'm not always easily fooled. The fact that

3

the Faun was on show at the Van Gogh Museum, that it had been lent by the Chicago Art Institute, that it was included in one of the best exhibitions I had ever seen, all served to make it unsuspicious.

So when it came out at Shaun's proceedings that it had actually been made by him in his shed, I wasn't angry. Yes, I'd been made to look like a twit on national television, but that was my fault for opening my mouth so quickly. Besides, whoever made this thing was a faker of impressive cunning. The Faun was unexpected, but not impossible. At some point, it could well have existed. There was even a tiny drawing of it in a genuine Gauguin sketchbook. Instead of hating Shaun Greenhalgh for fooling me, I immediately liked him for pushing my button and being such a clever rogue.

The day after the Greenhalghs were sentenced, in the autumn of 2007, I sent off a proposal to two commissioning editors I knew who dealt with arts subjects on television asking if I could make a film about the Bolton Cosa Nostra. One of them quickly replied that I had been beaten to it and that such a film was already commissioned. Eh? There were, in fact, a couple of films made about the Greenhalghs in the end. And as you can now read in this book, both were massively inaccurate. I never met Shaun in gaol, but remained fully fascinated by him, and having the chance to work with him later on a series I made about the Dark Ages – he created an Anglo-Saxon brooch for the film, using all the original methods – I got my hands on a manuscript he had written in prison which a researcher for another TV company, Clare Duggan, a true hero of the Shaun Greenhalgh story, had persuaded him to attempt. It took me a few months to get round to tackling the mighty memoir. Once I started, I binge-read it in a couple of days.

A Forger's Tale works on various levels. If you're a nerd, like me, who's interested in techniques and methods of making art, you will find here several garages' worth of useful nerdish information. If you're a crime buff, here are some very tasty and very subtle crimes to relish. If you're a museum professional, I'm afraid these admissions are an indictment of much of your profession and a serious questioning of your levels of knowledge. If you're a policeman, you might be thinking: why the hell didn't he tell us all this at the time?

Through my agent, I sent Shaun's manuscript on a tour of the publishers with an underlined demand that its contents remain confidential. Eventually, they all rejected it. Among the comments that were made, a common one was that the manuscript was 'self-justificatory'. Which made me laugh. Of course it is, here and there, self-justificatory. This is a man who has spent a significant slab of his life in prison for crimes of which many others are also guilty – in many instances, more guilty than him. Of course he wants his side of the story to be heard and understood. The real wonder here is not that these confessions are, occasionally, self-justificatory, but how often they are not. Most of the time, in these pages, Shaun Greenhalgh is funny, charming, self-deprecating, warm-hearted and, above all, instructive.

The detail lavished on how it was all done is sometimes close to delirious. Shaun knew the methods inside out, especially when it came to the making of ceramics – from pre-Columbian pots to fake Barbara Hepworths; from brand-new eighteenth-century Chelsea ware to that damned Gauguin Faun; from the mad birds churned out by the Martin Brothers to the delicate porcelain of the Emperors of China. Some will read these accounts and mistake them for a forger's guide, an instruction manual on how to make copies. I prefer to see them as the expression of an ecstatic interest in art, bulging with knowledge and expertise. Here's a forger who can disguise all kinds of things – except his own obsessive fascination with making things.

Is there too much of this technical ecstasy in the book? Again, some will probably think so and, again, I do not. Too many of us are too used to letting such information slip. When we look at a van Gogh painting or a Chelsea pot, we admire the image but ignore the methods, as if art arrives before us by magic. It doesn't. In Shaun Greenhalgh's world, the making of the objects is what really counts. In this joyously detailed account of how it was all done, with its alphabet soup of technical terms, we have a resource that is valuable and shape-shifting.

Art has always attracted the crazies – off-centre people who see things differently. I'd like to think I am one of those, but Shaun definitely is. His life story is an extraordinary blossoming of passion among the dark satanic mills. Against all the odds, a northern lad from a Bolton comprehensive manages, somehow, to fall prey to the addictions of art and, without anybody's help, turns himself into an Egyptian granite carver, a Venetian bronze caster, an Impressionist sculptor, an American watercolourist, a second L. S. Lowry and a one-man Renaissance. The real subject of this book isn't the forgery or the unmasking. It's not the ever-present warning, 'buyer beware', or the detailed record of a particularly unlikely Lancashire life. The real focus here is the power of art to bewitch and change, inspire and transform.

Reading these pages, it's tempting to conclude that some societies might, however, be better off without it – our own most of all. Without art, there would be less deception, less pretence, less deviousness in the West End of London, less crashing of values at the Frieze art fair. The world would be more honest. But it would also be duller and less tasty. A sponge without its jam. When we step off the hamster wheel of history, art is the best evidence we leave behind. What would we know of the Egyptians or the Greeks or the Romans if they had not left behind their art? It's our memorial, our gift to the future. That's assuming, of course, that some of it is genuine. These days, who knows?

Is Shaun a scoundrel for filling our antiques shops and museum walls with so much that isn't what it purports to be? I suppose so. He has made it harder to know what Gauguin really created and that is an unhelpful act, at best. This entire memoir is studded with pleas of innocence and complex moments of dissembling as we range backwards and forwards between copies and fakes, real truths and imaginary ones, mirrors and their reflections in other mirrors. To my mind, Shaun was more aware of what he was doing than he usually admits. But while there are reasons to doubt some of his suggestions of innocence, there are no reasons at all, I believe, to doubt his basic drives.

This is a man who was enslaved by art. Every time he tried to get away from it, it hunted him down. He fell in love. It hunted him down. He joined the army. It hunted him down. This is not a book about art as a hobby or a sideline or a profession, it's a book about art as a motor force. The only thing. For all the flimflammery and dissembling that comes with the territory of being Britain's greatest ever forger – a regrettable title, yes, but one that Shaun surely holds – what is most often expressed here is an addiction. Compared with the tepid art dealers who tiptoe furtively through these confessions, or the blundering curators, or the frantic Keystone Kops of the Art & Antiques Squad, Shaun's passion for art is a volcano next to some molehills.

In contrast, the art world's role in the saga is dismal. Too many of the incidents remembered here, too much of the detail, is too scary. Those of us who have dipped our toes already into the world of art dealers, auctions and museum purchases, but who have previously had no overwhelming reason to doubt art's seductive surfaces, are in for a slapping. You will decide for yourself, reader, if every word in this memoir tells it exactly as it happened. But I guarantee you will emerge from the read substantially less ready to trust the demonic modern entity, fashioned from desire and mirrors, that is the art world.

I've been an inhabitant of it for a long time. I've known for a long time that it is full of mountebanks. For a long time I have been particularly suspicious of 'new discoveries'. But it turns out I only suspected a fraction of what really goes on behind the closed barn doors of the Cotswolds or inside the converted mills of Bolton. Now that you mention it, that head of Nefertiti in Berlin does look like something the Art Deco era might have come up with, doesn't it? And 'La Bella Principessa', by Leonardo da Vinci, really could be 'Sally from the Co-op', by Shaun Greenhalgh, couldn't she?

At the end of the book, there's a glossary. Nerds speak their own language and we part-time nerds need some translation tools. Theseus had his ball of silken thread when he descended into the labyrinth. You and I have the glossary.

Preface

Most of this book was written whilst I was in prison several years ago. Originally, because this book is essentially about me and my life making and faking works of art, I intended to write it by starting logically, at the beginning, on the day I came into the world – the 21st of June, 1960, the Summer Solstice. Having written nothing substantial since boring school essays – something now almost 40 years ago – I thought that would be the best and simplest way to go. However, thinking further about it before putting pen to paper, and not wanting to send my reader off to sleep before turning the first page, I have decided to cover the consequences of my time faking works of art first. Then onwards in due course – forwards to the past, so to speak. This part of my life seems to be what people most want to know about.

Also, there's been so much rubbish in the press, that I thought it time to say something on the subject myself. Many of those articles were laughably inaccurate. I've been described as some kind of class warrior fighting that old chestnut, the North–South divide. As the little man against the Establishment. Others have me down as a disgruntled artist out for revenge. But, having never been to art school or ever been interested in an artistic career, revenge against whom? Some even said I was a nutty recluse, which is good for a laugh, I suppose. Never let it be said I haven't got a sense of humour. All of it is more exotic and complicated than the actual reality of things. So this is my story, told in my own way. I just hope it doesn't have too much of the snooze factor about it.

I have also described some elements of my life which aren't really related to art or fakery. Originally, I thought not to include them, but those events have had a bearing on my life as it turned out, so they are part of things, I suppose. In most cases I have not used the real names of the people within, sometimes for personal reasons, other times to protect the innocent and, lastly, so as not to get embroiled in any legal tangles. I've had quite enough of the law. This is just my side of things. For the record.

I.

A knock at the door

F OR DRAMATIC PURPOSES, I'll start with a knock at the
door – 8.30am, the 15th of March, 2006. That date, the 15th,
was already in my mind. Then I remembered – the Ides of March!
A most inauspicious date for the ancients and a bloody awful one
for me as things turned out.

By this time, I'd been back at my mum and dad's for some
years. They were into their eighties and I was their paid carer. Well,
40-odd pounds a week doesn't really cover the effort, does it? Not
much more than a kid's paper round. But it's the government's
going rate for a stressful and full-time occupation for legions of
relatives and friends of the sick and vulnerable in what passes for
society these days. I'd better climb down from my soapbox for now
and get back to the story of my Waterloo. Please forgive me if I
occasionally climb up on it again and feel free to skip those rants
if you wish, with my blessing. I've been talking to myself on such
things for years, so doing so in print will carry on the tradition.

To continue. Standing there at the door, peering past me whilst
shouting loudly, was a little fat man with a red face, dressed like
a downmarket stockbroker, but doing his best impression of a
TV cop – hooking his foot around the door, as if resistance was

expected. The next thing, he, his foot and his followers were all crowded into the lounge, all speaking at once, so I couldn't make out a single word. What followed during the day is still a pretty vivid memory for me, even though that experience is now all of four years ago. Looking back, much of it seems a bit Laurel and Hardy and would, but for its consequences, be quite amusing, even to me.

The detective in charge introduced himself and informed me that they were from Scotland Yard's Serious Organised Crime Unit, and that their bit of it was known as the Art & Antiques Squad. Whilst offering this information, the others dispersed all about, upstairs and down, going through drawers, cupboards, scattering everything as they went.

A particular memory is of a detective sitting cross-legged on the floor, with the contents of my dad's glass-topped fossil cabinet scattered all about him, a hobby my father took particular interest in. There was nothing particularly valuable in it. All the specimens were always neatly laid out with handwritten descriptions, something he would get out and show to his grandchildren whenever they called, showing his latest pieces and explaining all about them and their place in the great scheme of things to enchanted little faces. The detective was now sat in the midst of them like a monkey sorting nuts. What he was looking for still isn't apparent to me. When he'd finished, he simply scooped up handfuls of them and dumped them in a heap in the drawer. Others were trod underfoot. I decided there and then that co-operation was, for the time being, out of the question.

The day dragged on, searching and more questions, occasionally finding various items, some greeted with a squeal of delight. Another peculiar incident occurred when my sister arrived to help out Mum and Dad whilst I was, for want of a better word, 'helping' the police with their enquiries. My sis had just put a chicken in the oven to cook for teatime and was closing the oven door as a female

DC came into the kitchen from the garden. The DC suddenly took it into her head that this was something sinister and proceeded to unwrap the bird from its foil, probing it in a most unladylike manner. Raking through the drawers for a pair of scissors, she proceeded to cut the suspect chicken in half, almost mincing it in the process. What she thought to find is a mystery.

By now various detectives were busy looking for and collecting all sorts of materials, equipment and discarded work. Some things came from the loft, including a bust of the second president of the US, John Adams, which had been sold in auction some years earlier for £100,000. Finding he couldn't sell it on, the purchaser had later requested a refund. Never wanting to draw attention, I was quite willing to refund the discontents and move on to the next project. The bust joined a growing collection in the back of a police van, one of many parked outside. I think the neighbours were expecting bodies in the garden or something, such was the hive of activity. I thought then, as now, that it was all a bit over the top for an amateur artist armed with a paintbrush and chisel.

Next on the scene were the firearms experts who arrived to great effect in two large vans – all blue lights and wire grills – and in marched several large gents in jumpsuits and body armour. The police had discovered a deactivated old revolver and a toy rifle, left by my six-year-old nephew some weeks earlier. One of the firearms officers took up the revolver, looked under his eyebrows at the detective proffering up the deadly weapon and dismissed it as a 'wreck'. The toy gun was picked up with a loud sigh and a despairing sideways glance at me. Then, 'Out lads, there's nothing for us here.' And off they went, much to my relief.

As I stood there looking about me, I noticed several DCs rooting around outside, all in animated conversation. They were handling some pieces of alabaster, cut into slices, sawn off the back of a large panel that I had been carving into a copy of an Assyrian relief of a winged deity from the Palace of Ashurbanipal, one-time king

15

of the seventh century BC Assyrians. These relief panels, depicting scenes from palace life, were mostly about half life-size and originally lined the walls of the king's mud brick palaces in a place called Nineveh that's now in Iraq. They were mostly dug up in the mid-nineteenth century by British explorers, the British Museum being the main repository of them. Others were taken by members of the expedition and are now in museum collections worldwide. My effort purported to be just such a piece.

I had first looked at these Assyrian scenes, so full of life, when I was about 10. Horses and men, fighting lions, kings and gods, all presided over by the great god of the Assyrians, Ashur. In the guidebooks I'd found an even better-sounding name – Ahura Mazda. I hope what springs to your mind isn't what I pictured as a 10-year-old reading this name in a British Museum guide – Lieutenant Ahura of the Starship Enterprise driving a shiny Mazda sports car through the desert sands, with lions in pursuit! Perhaps I should have been a surrealist back then.

Those alabaster pieces were particularly damning as they had been cut from the back of a panel presented for inspection just four months earlier to the Keeper of the Middle East collections at the British Museum. I originally intended to dispose of them, but, due to the cost of the original block, I had decided to keep the offcuts with a view to doing some fragmentary pieces at a later date to sell through the trade. I never liked to discard materials which are all the while becoming more difficult to source. Even in my own time, some things still available 30 years ago can no longer be found. So off to the ever-growing pile in the back of a police van they went. And on to the garden shed went the DCs.

'Shaun, can you come upstairs and tell us something about this?' Another half-forgotten object had been found at the back of a cupboard. Then in came the detective in the stockbroker's pinstripe suit, now partly coloured orange. He'd picked up a bag of iron oxide that I used in my glass and ceramic work, without putting his hand under the old paper bag in which it had come from Stoke-on-Trent, a few years before. Now he looked as though he'd been Tangoed! I said something bland to the effect that he'll probably need to get his suit steamed, but he seemed upset at this and retorted that he could get another one on expenses – the implication being that it might be a while before I had the opportunity to acquire another suit myself!

The old shed proved to be a goldmine of finds. Over the years I'd produced some of my best work in that place, which seemed to amuse the detectives. One of them gave it the title of 'the northern annex of the British Museum'. That got a laugh all round and even squeezed a smile out of me on a decidedly unsmiley day. Some of the stuff in there had been kicking around for years – a sandstone head of the pharaoh Akhenaten in a white crown, a red sandstone female figure in the Hepworth style, an old kiln in which I'd fired the Gauguin Faun, marble blocks, marble points, chisels and mallets, enamels and glass, diamond saws and burrs. All of it was being carried through the kitchen and out into the aforementioned vans, which were now rapidly filling up with enough to hang me for sure. Gulp!

The day turned into the afternoon. More questions, more comments, but very little from me. These people come in here storming about, I thought, making the place look like it had been ransacked by burglars – and, incidentally, overlooking a great deal that might have been of interest to them, if only they had possessed a better understanding of the materials and methods used to make art! I say this not to poke fun at anyone. I'm sure the detectives are very good at what they do. After all, one doesn't get to work for Scotland Yard, whose reputation speaks for itself, without being the best! At that time, and still now, I'm of the opinion that if they had come in peace, sat down and talked to me calmly, explained their presence and asked to be shown what I might have in the way of 'fakes', and the means of their production, they would have had my co-operation from the start. It would have sorted things out 12 months earlier than was the case. Some high-placed collars might have been thrown in as well.

By now I was getting a bit concerned for my mum and dad. They had been sat in the midst of all this for hours, so I told the Tango man that I needed to get them something to eat and drink, both being diabetic. Off I went to the kitchen with a DC following. What they expected me to do, I can't say. 'Drinks only,' the DC ordered, 'we've got some more questions for you yet.' I protested, to no avail. It just served to harden my attitude.

Not until 4pm, or thereabouts, did they decide to call it a day. I returned to the living room to see a man who didn't introduce himself, but who I took to be the boss, putting the sofa cushions back and generally attempting to tidy up what his underlings had scattered throughout the day. I made it clear to him that we'd had nothing to eat and no time or opportunity to do so. At this, he reached for a plastic bag and handed it to me with a mumbled apology. He seemed genuinely upset. The plastic bag held the remains of their lunch – two scotch eggs and a partly eaten chocolate bar. I've heard rumours that police suffer more than most from piles and ulcers. If that's what they live on most days, no bloody wonder! I just put their actions down to bad manners and left it at that.

The most curious incident that first day was the disappearance of an old business ledger I'd had since I was a kid – the type used for bookkeeping in times past. Made in 1921, it was backed in calf-skin and had beautifully marbled paper. I'd got it from a dealer at the Last Drop Antiques Fair in 1971, swapped for several of my bottle digging finds. From the age of 11 or so, I had used it to keep a record of every single thing I'd ever made. Even the destroyed or recycled ones. How and with what I'd made them, kiln firing times, mould burnout cycles, alloy recipes, paints and all sorts of other things. I last saw it on the kitchen table that afternoon, obviously put there by one of the detectives, and presumed they'd taken it with them when they left. This can't have been the case, for if they had, why so many questions? All the answers were in that book. So that's a bit of a mystery.

As they left the house, they informed me I would be required to attend Bolton Police Station the next day, but that my mum and dad could be interviewed at home on account of their age. I thought that was very decent of them. They said I should get my solicitor to come along and off they went. I duly rang the solicitors used by several family members over the years, only to be informed that due to the nature of the case I needed the services of a good criminal lawyer. A couple were suggested. The first one was in court that day. The next one turned out to be the gentleman who was to act on my behalf, for better or worse, for the next two years.

I don't think he would mind me saying that he was definitely of the old school – softly spoken, obviously well educated, clever and cultured, with an interest in and knowledge of art to boot. Much later, long after the court appearances, and even after the completion of a substantial part of my sentence, I would receive letters from various media people who had been in contact with him about some projects in which they wanted me to participate. Most had been sent from his office with a flea in their ears. All I can think is that he had either had quite enough of the whole affair, lengthy as it was, or, as I prefer to imagine, he was looking after my best interests.

Before going on with what happened after that day, I would like to say something about how I first came to the attention of Scotland Yard. I mentioned earlier some fragments of alabaster from the back of a fake copy of an Assyrian bas-relief panel. This was the object that proved to be the 'one too many'.

This Assyrian relief was my main project for 2005. Over the previous few years, I'd started to do considerably fewer pieces of work than before. Money had never really been the driving force for my artwork and, in any case, by this time I was secure enough financially to do pretty much as I pleased. Quite a lot has been said in the media about my motives for doing the fakes. Things like me wishing to expose and deride a particular art expert's abilities or have a go at the art establishment in general. Others have claimed it was some kind of one-man crusade against the supposed art snobbery of the south, as if art had regional loyalties and traits. It doesn't. In common with music, art is one of those rare things that speaks to all people, and includes and involves all. Somehow it found me. And from the time I was a kid, it just seemed to be what I was interested in. Whenever I tried to walk away from it, it would search me out and wind me in again, like a puppet on a string.

It was a visit to the Manchester Museum, in late 2004, that had brought the Assyrian thing to mind. I had gone to look at this great collection with nothing particular planned, just an afternoon's wander through the galleries. Whilst walking around, I saw this particular stone relief of an Assyrian figure. It was pretty standard stuff – a standing figure in side profile, walking to the right, with wings and the head of an eagle, carrying a libation pail and a palm leaf. I had seen many such figures at the British Museum years earlier and, through my wide-ranging amateur art interests, I was quite familiar with all things Assyrian.

Apparently, these winged deities were actually priests of the court in costume and not, as I had presumed as a child, something mythological like you see in classical art – hippocamps, centaurs, satyrs and the like. Across the bottom was a band of cuneiform inscription. This script was used at various times across Assyria – modern-day Iraq – and usually consists of the king's titles and his achievements in war and lion hunting, a particularly popular pastime of kings and widely illustrated in the art of Assyria. These inscriptions consist of groups of what look like, for want of a better description, little paper darts.

Having never cut such a thing in stone before, I spent a long time perfecting the manner of their appearance, even going to the trouble of taking an impression in white Plasticine from a panel at another location, so I could look under high magnification at the direction of cut used by the ancient craftsmen. Such small details can prove decisive in attributions. After several attempts at copying a plaster cast of that impression, I was confident enough to have a go.

In making a successful copy of any artwork, no matter in which medium you are working, fluency of line is everything. Also, it's best to keep in mind that the artists and craftsmen who made the originals did these things every day of their working lives, and that only the finest work would be acceptable to their patrons. So being up to scratch, without the job looking laboured, is a must before setting about the copy.

You may have noticed that I refer to it as a 'copy', when, considering my past, you might think 'fake' would be a better description. Copying in art is as old as art itself, something most artists, and certainly all of the most proficient ones, have done throughout art's history. Buonarroti after the Laocoön. Rodin in the manner of Bernini. Moran after Turner, and so on. A 'copy' only becomes a 'fake' when it is knowingly misrepresented as being a work by a particular artist or age, when, in fact, it is no such thing. Misrepresentation is something I mean to cover later, so for now, if I may, I'll call it a 'copy'.

Early January, 2005, saw me back at the British Museum, reading up on the mid-nineteenth-century expeditions to Nineveh, and taking mental notes of old illustrations and anything else that may have helped in the project I had by now decided upon and which, for various reasons – some reported, some not – led to my present situation. Speaking of my present situation, I need to get back to the story of the arrest before the trail goes cold.

The night after the police visit, I didn't sleep much. Eight in the morning. A ring on the doorbell. Standing there were two of the detectives from the day before. 'We've just called to remind you that your presence is required down at the Central Police Station at

9.30am, if you remember?' As if I could forget! They were making sure, of course, that I hadn't done a Ronnie Biggs in the night. At least that was my take on it.

I'd arranged to meet my solicitor at the station, but he was fashionably late, so in I went. Gulp again! The Central Police Station in Bolton was, at that time, in its final days of occupation. A new one had already been built at a location on Manchester Road, close to the site of the old Bolton Wanderers football ground, which had been bulldozed and moved to the Reebok Stadium at Horwich. So, as you can imagine, the old station was in a grotty state. The actual building, though, was quite a grand affair. Housed in a neoclassical crescent, to the west of Bolton Town Hall, it had the museum and art gallery at one end, and me and my captors at the other.

I informed the desk sergeant of my name and that I had an appointment for 9.30am. 'Please take a seat if you will,' he replied. I sat there, watching the clock, as people with sheepish looks and their own troubles went in and out. Then I was called to go through to the police station proper, where Sergeant Tango was standing, all smiles, rubbing his hands together. Forward stepped the youngest female DC, rather nervously I thought. A formal arrest came squeaking forth. I informed them that my solicitor had not yet arrived and that I didn't wish to proceed without legal representation. So they searched me, put my watch and other belongings in a bag, took my details and put me in a cell.

I hadn't been in a police cell before. The first thing I noticed was the cold. The smell wasn't great either. I was expecting shouts and groans from the other cells, but it was perfectly silent and quite eerie. I don't know how long I waited. It seemed a long time, but in reality it was probably less than an hour. Finally, the spyhole in the cell door flicked open and I saw a beady eye at the aperture, looking like a piss-hole in the snow. Sergeant Tango. (The 'piss-hole in the snow' line isn't original. It's something I'd heard earlier at the station.)

Tango informed me that my solicitor was here. So off I followed to meet him. He introduced himself and explained that I would now be formally cautioned and a recorded interview would take place. A bit of small talk. And in we went. As I walked in, piled 3 feet high against the wall, was what I took to be the contents of their haul from yesterday. I later found out it was just a selection. I've always been pretty prolific. But quite a lot of the piled-up work was stuff I thought had been destroyed or recycled. Had I realised there was this much lying about, I would have had a jumble sale!

Before the proceedings got underway, my solicitor addressed the gathered ensemble: 'There are solicitors and solicitors. I can assure you that I am the real thing. So we'll have things done properly.' The assembled all nodded at this and then they read out my rights, each speaking into the tape as it buzzed into life.

One by one, the sculptures, pictures, materials and all were described for the record. They asked me if I had seen them before and did I have anything to say about how they came into my possession? All through that first day, I denied that I or anyone known to me had anything to do with their production. As I saw it at the time, it was my turn to be awkward and to make them earn their pay. For the record, my denials were nothing to do with trying to wriggle out of my predicament. I was well aware that the material evidence was damning. My actions were purely a response to the over-the-top treatment I had had, and – more than that – to the disgraceful disrespect shown to my mum and dad. For that, I was of a mind to give them a run.

Initially, they assumed several people were involved in the production of the artworks. Months later, when I decided it was finally time to co-operate, it was with difficulty that I managed to convince them I alone was responsible for all the work, wide-ranging as it was. My interest in art has always been non-specific and I could never have imagined myself as just a painter, sculptor or any other single discipline. I always prefer to try my hand at everything. Trying different things helps me to understand the methods used and, in some small way, improves my next effort.

During the day, the conversation wandered about from piece to piece, with me feigning ignorance about everything. This went on into the evening. So I didn't get home until 12.30am, bailed until further notice, while the police pursued their enquiries.

For some time after, I heard nothing more from them. Next up, however, was the media interest, something I found more trying than the police investigation. Throughout my life I'd always preferred to stay out of the limelight, so having a gaggle of journalists and photographers hanging about from dawn to dusk was something to get used to. A particularly persistent duo were from Germany. How they came to hear about all this, I haven't a clue. They looked to me like the comedians Little and Large from back in the seventies. By now, I had started to leave the answerphone permanently on and every morning, without fail, at around 9am, on would come a German accent asking, very politely, if I or my father would like to give them an interview, and if we could discuss some ideas they had for German TV along the lines of the things done by the art faker Tom Keating.

I didn't know much about Tom Keating on TV. I vaguely remembered that he too had been convicted many years ago for selling copies with false documentation. Eventually, I told them that in my present situation it would be inappropriate for me to comment, but that when this was settled I would be happy to discuss things with them. That seemed to do the trick. Now all I had to do was put up with a bashing from the British press.

After my conviction, a lot of hurtful and untrue things were said in the press about me and my personal circumstances. Hopefully, I can set the record straight in the pages of this book. Having heard it straight from the horse's mouth, you can then make up your own minds as to the degree of my villainy.

In early May, I heard again from Scotland Yard. A letter from my solicitor informed me that I must attend another interview at Bolton Police Station. Between the first and second interviews I'd had quite a torrid time of it and was feeling pretty low. To top it all, on the 23rd of April, St George's Day, my dad had a bad fall whilst coming in from the garden. He'd been out to feed the birds, something he did most days. From the position of his foot, which was lying flat outwards, I could see he had broken something. My understanding of anatomy was finally of some use – other than in the impractical world of art. I called the ambulance and off to hospital we went. Sure enough, he'd broken his leg, and the break was awkwardly situated just below the hip socket. The doctor explained he would need an operation to fix it. The op was done the next day and the following weeks were a mix of sidestepping journalists, hospital visits and dealing with solicitors.

By this time I hadn't picked up so much as a pencil in months and decided it was time to have a clear-out of what remained of my artist materials. First, I checked with my solicitor that doing so wouldn't constitute the destruction of evidence. I was already deep enough in you-know-what without digging deeper! Over the next few weeks I binned the accumulated tools of 30 years' work and took down the old garden shed that had been my 'studio' and was now in a pretty wonky state.

Also, at this time, some of my best and most expensive equipment seemed to disappear. I presumed the police had taken much of it, but, apparently, that wasn't the case. Some 18 months later, my solicitor sent me a list of all the confiscations, and most of what I was missing wasn't on the list. So that's a mystery not to be solved.

Another sad loss was a box of pictures and Plasticine models I'd done as a lad, some from as early as six years old. Unbeknown to me, my mum and dad had saved them until my arrest. Those weren't on the police inventory either. Heaven knows what happened to them. As things stand, I've little of my past work left, or the means to make any more. However, looking at it positively,

I've still got what any artist needs – two eyes, two hands and what passes for a brain. So I'm still a going concern. Before that's taken the wrong way, let me add immediately that, without any doubt, I have had my fill of fakery!

The day of my next meeting with the art squad came round sooner than I wished. I can only suppose that during the interval they had been busy little bees, building their case against me. There's not much hope for you when Scotland Yard is on your trail, is there? Two months earlier, on leaving them at Bolton Police Station, I had already decided that at our next meeting I would put up my hand to everything and get things over with as soon as possible. However, the day before our meeting, I had been to see my dad, who by this time had been moved to a nursing home. The doctors had decided he wasn't fit enough to go back home yet, so he was in a bit of a state and wanted to go home. This was in my thoughts as Sergeant Tango and his crew entered the room. So I changed my mind about co-operating.

The second interrogation followed mostly along the lines of the first, only this time all the material evidence had now been photographed and described on individual files. On walking into the interview room, the only thing there 'in person', so to speak, was a Lowry picture leaning against my solicitor's chair. Conscious of being watched for a reaction, I pretended not to notice it, though I did instantly recognise the picture for what it was – a pastel drawing in the manner of L. S. Lowry, done by me several years earlier, one of hundreds of such things I have copied.

This particular 'Lowry' was now reframed in some style and at obvious cost. I had only initialled it L. S. L. and, as in most of my productions, it contained a fault, a skew in the perspective, something Lowry himself would never have done. He was a draughtsman of the first order and would never have made this type of mistake in the geometry of a townscape with which he was so familiar. And so expert at depicting.

My copies were always purposely designed to contain such faults. They were meant to be decorative pictures, sold to dealers by me or my father for reasonable sums. If those dealers took the picture to be a genuine Lowry, then the prices they offered to pay us were nothing short of theft on their part. I suspect that on seeing what they took to be a turkey ready for plucking, they took some pleasure in thinking their birthdays had all come at once. The proper course should have been to make the seller aware of any potential value and to point them in the direction of a reputable valuer. This, without exception, they never did. So to all of them I would say – buyer beware. And the next time something looks too good to be true, it most likely is!

This particular 'Lowry' had been sold to an antiques dealer not far from Bolton. He bought it with the express understanding that its authorship was questionable. If that is disputed, I point to the fact that a few hundred pounds hasn't been the going rate for a Lowry since before old Lowry started shaving. Some days later my dad answered a call from this same dealer. He said something to the effect that he'd had someone in to 'look' at the picture and that if my dad would write a note and post it off, he would pay an extra £900 for it. The note had to say that the picture had been in the family for X number of years, as this would enable the new owner to insure it and prove it hadn't been stolen.

Throughout my time dealing with these people, these types of things were commonplace. I knew full well that he had found a customer for the copy and was in the process of giving it a provenance and, in all probability, a huge price hike. I eventually found out that he had, indeed, sold it on to another party as a genuine Lowry for £7,000. At the time of my arrest, it was in the process of being sold again, this time for a sum I believe to be around £75,000. How all this could have been discovered by the police in such a short time, considering what a minor work it was compared to other things I had done, was a mystery to me.

During the summer, the police informed us that six people had been arrested in connection with this 'Lowry', and that it had apparently been accompanied by a letter of provenance. This letter was less genuine than the picture, which at least didn't carry a fake signature – unlike the letter which was in my dad's name! Much later, when I had been sent to prison, I received an anonymous note from someone who seemed to be in the know and who claimed that the reason no charges were ever brought against those arrested in connection with the Lowry was that it had been the property of a person involved in my case. This fact had not been declared as it should have been, so to proceed against them at that time would have compromised the case against me. If at all possible, I hope to make some headway in this regard and hope to expose the 'Lowry' man in due course. Maybe I will hear from the letter writer again.

After going through all the photos and written descriptions, still denying all knowledge of them, I was bailed to appear again at a later date. All that summer, I heard nothing more from the police. Dad, I'm happy to say, started to show signs of improvement, due in no small measure to the fine nurses at Thicketford, the support of all the family and the pester power of his grandchildren. They simply wouldn't allow him to give up. My mum, in the meantime, had a pleasant summer being taken on trips, treated to some new outfits and generally looked after by my sisters and brothers. This, I must admit, was a timely break for me, too – a chance to get back to some normality.

So this is a good place to get back to the story of the Assyrian relief that I mentioned earlier – the one that led the police to my door. I made it in the summer of 2005, in the shed at my parents' house. Since the casual look at just such a panel at the Manchester Museum in late 2004, I had been researching it and, for several weeks after, I'd tackled some Limoges-style enamelling in the manner of the ancients, just for practice, trying all the time to improve my attempts. The actual enamelling isn't the problem. The difficulty is cutting the design in copper without a slip and achieving a convincing artistic style and fluency. I'd also been doing some sculpture, mostly horses, usually about half life-size, so as to be manageable in the confines of my studio – the shed.

Having settled on the Assyrian design, next came the problem of finding the stone in which to cut it. The stone used originally was a calcite alabaster commonly called 'Mosul marble', on account of it coming from Mosul in present-day Iraq. Given recent world events, you can see my difficulty in getting hold of a large block of this material. Unfortunately, I don't know any US Army generals! So it would have to be done in something closely resembling it. Eventually, I settled on a calcite alabaster that I knew I could work with, having used it before.

There are two types of alabaster. The calcite one is harder and more durable. Being crystalline and translucent, it was used by the Egyptians and throughout the ancient world. Some magnificent examples have been found in the tombs of the New Kingdom pharaohs in the Valley of the Kings. The other type, more usually found in nineteenth-century work, is the softer gypsum alabaster. This was famously used in English Medieval church work, carved into the figurative groups known as 'Nottingham alabasters', an allusion to a major source of this material throughout the period.

Having ordered and paid for a block of suitable dimensions, I went down to the stone yard to collect it. It was enormously heavy. When I finally got the slab home, I transferred the image of the winged deity onto the stone with a pencil and then went over the pencil marks with a stylus, scratching the image into the surface so it wouldn't be lost during the cutting. Gypsum alabaster is much softer than Mosul marble, so I decided to cut it with wood chisels.

The first task in doing any relief work is to cut away the background – in this case to a shallow depth of 10 or so millimetres. With the figure standing proud of the surface, it can be rounded at its edges and the detail easily rendered with a chisel and rasp. This cutting back the surface, without being able to use the mallet in case it bruised the stone, was the arm-aching bit. It took a couple of days' hard labour. I could have removed the stone more quickly with a router, but didn't fancy getting silicosis! After polishing the sunken background, I traced on the detail of the figure – face, fingers, feathers and all. Carving the detail is the best bit. When I was satisfied as to the correct form, I set about the cuneiform inscription.

There have been some sneering comments in the press about this, saying I made a fatal mistake in the execution. This isn't the case. The fact is that in all ancient inscriptions – whether they be cuneiform, Egyptian hieroglyphics, Greek, Hebrew or Latin text, or even early Chinese characters – the artisans charged with the task were almost without exception skilled but illiterate stone-cutters, following the marks inked in by the scribes. These marks were not always followed to the letter, as you see time and again on ancient monuments of undoubted authenticity. As an eminent archaeologist said to me many years ago: 'If an inscription is perfect, it's suspect.' So I cut the script as I saw fit. And moved on to putting some 'age' into it.

This was, and usually is, as difficult as producing the piece in the first instance. Often, it's more difficult! In this case what was needed was a soak-bath large enough for the relief. This was achieved by means of a plywood frame, a couple of inches larger and deeper than the panel, inside which I fixed some pond liner. Primitive but practical.

Depending on the type of stone being worked, a wide range of ageing techniques can be employed. For this piece, the first thing I needed to create was a layer of 'weathered' surface to receive the colour. This was done by soaking the panel in a strong alkali bath. The solution reacts quickly with the calcite and, at a point decided by trial and error, the bath is drained gently so as not to disturb the fragile corroded surface. Next, it's rinsed repeatedly to return it to neutral pH and then gently heated. If too much heat is applied the stone becomes opaque, a definite giveaway! So care is needed at all stages.

On this particular piece, the 'ancient' surface wasn't quite as critical as it would have been in other circumstances, as I'd decided to treat it to a 'Victorian' makeover. It's a trick I'd used before to give the experts something to discover for themselves. Many of the reliefs that had been in private collections were poorer quality pieces that were not required for the official collection destined for the British Museum. These were often damaged or unattractively stained or fire-damaged. Some of them had been recoloured, and, in some cases, waxed or even shellacked. For this piece, I decided to recolour it with tannin and iron stain, and added some light beeswaxing to reflect its Victorian makeover. This was pointed out at its inspection by the experts – to my feigned surprise!

So that was how I made the Assyrian panel which ultimately led to my arrest and conviction.

II.

A mention in passing

B ACK IN BOLTON, after that relatively peaceful summer, it wasn't until September that I was informed by my solicitor that the police wanted to speak to me again. By this time my parents were mostly back to themselves, or as near as they would get, and because of this I was now prepared to answer the detective's questions – something I had hoped to do earlier. Better late than never!

My solicitor was already at the station when I arrived and after the usual formalities with which I was becoming familiar I asked to have a private conversation with him and told him I was prepared to co-operate with the investigation. At this, he left the room to inform the Yardies. He seemed relieved, and I was too. I was never comfortable with my previous behaviour. In retrospect, I wish things could have been more decent all round. But I've always been of a mind that bullies must be resisted, and state-sponsored bullies resisted most of all. Rightly or wrongly, this was the impression I had of them from day one.

The detectives had once again travelled up to Bolton from their base at New Scotland Yard. They were apparently staying at a place called The Last Drop, a hotel and conference centre half a mile from my parents' home, up on the moors above the town. When I was a kid, The Last Drop had been Headley's Farm, somewhere we would pass on our Sunday walks with my dad, home to a gaggle of bolshy geese that would follow us hissing and snapping at our ankles. My dad once put one of them in a sack and wrung its neck. We got our revenge on it by having roast goose for Christmas dinner.

The farm had been bought by a family of well-known Bolton businessmen – owners of the now defunct Walker's Tannery, once one of Bolton's major employers – and turned into a country hotel, a small concern then, but now much enlarged and owned by a multinational. I knew many of the staff and had worked there myself during school holidays. I hope the detectives enjoyed their stay. I'm sure they would have been well taken care of.

They certainly looked bright-eyed and bushy-tailed that morning. A quick reminder that I was still under caution and on went the recorder. This time, instead of getting them to believe my denials, something they were never likely to do, my new problem was to get them to accept that I was the sole author of the various works they had managed to identify over the last months. Even my own solicitor moved the conversation round to marble-cutting, telling me of his own attempts and giving me the impression he was trying to draw me into describing the process, presumably to satisfy himself that I knew what I was talking about. So I duly obliged. His scepticism, which I have experienced on many occasions, is quite understandable, I suppose. I put it down to the fact that I don't usually come across in conversation as a particularly well-educated or cultured individual, and probably the last person you would think of as an artist. It's true that I have no formal qualifications in art, being mostly self-taught and gaining what measure of proficiency I have by sheer effort and practice.

During these latest interviews I did gradually manage to satisfy the sceptics that I was the maker of everything, so we moved on. Various items were shown to me, followed by a written description, usually stretching into several pages. I only wish I could manage to say so much about so little in order to fill these pages. I'd have this finished in a blink! It also occurred to me that those prepared documents, or at least some of them, must have taken longer to make than the objects they described.

This puts me in mind of something said to the press by one of the DCs, after my conviction. He talked of me boasting during one of my interviews, something along the lines of it only taking me a few minutes to produce a work worth thousands of pounds. Anyone who knows me knows that I'm not a boaster – quite the opposite in fact. These comments related to a watercolour after one of my favourite artists, the American landscape painter Thomas Moran. I had sold a small watercolour, 'Cliffs of the Green River', to the Bolton Museum in 1993 for £10,000 and during the conversation one of the detectives asked me how long it took to do. Seeing as I was now fully co-operating with the investigation, I told them, 'About 10 to 15 minutes.' He seemed to disbelieve this. I was actually trying to explain that a watercolour is a spontaneous thing and works very quickly or not at all, as any artist reading this will know. Anyhow, I think they got the wrong end of the stick on that one. Maybe it was my fault for not explaining myself well enough. My articulation is akin to my typing. I am reminded of the words of another American artist, C. M. Russell, painter and sculptor of the Old West, who was also an author of some repute. He said – I don't know if originally – 'the pen and the pick are alike to me, both bloody hard work'. To which I would add – as is talking to Scotland Yard detectives!

The day dragged on into the evening, again, with more photos and more questions, along with some comments suggesting that I was holding out and telling them just enough, and no more. I can say with a clear conscience that I told them everything my fuddled mind could recall. Even to the point of enlightening them about a particular piece they had missed, a copy of a late antique Roman silver plate, known as the Risley Lanx, which had been found under a plough at a place called Risley Park, Derbyshire, in the early 1740s. They had probably missed it on account of it having entered the British Museum's collection not with that alarm-bell-ringing tag 'acquired from the collection of a Mr Greenhalgh', but by way of a London antiquities dealer. This dealer had bought the plate from me in 1991 for £5,000 as a copy, and it was described as such on the receipt the police had.

The conversation then moved on to some of the other items they had identified during the intervening months as probably done by me. One such object was a small ceramic figure of a classical 'faun', a Roman wood-spirit, half man, half goat. This purported to be by the post-Impressionist artist, Paul Gauguin, whom most people will know from his association with van Gogh. Gauguin wasn't particularly celebrated as a sculptor, but during the 1880s he'd dabbled in ceramics and some of his pots are in museum collections. It was also known that he had, at some point, made a sculptural Faun. A thumbnail sketch of it in an old publication gave me the basic form to work with, and the resulting piece was now the subject of my conversation with the detectives sitting opposite, who, it seemed to me, were also angling for a convenient moment to halt the interview for a tea break. One of them said he thought I was telling them the bare minimum required for co-operation and that I was holding out on them. This, I suspected, was all part of their amateur psychology. The upcoming break would give me time to work out how to give them more facts to satisfy their demands. On cue, up came the break.

While they went off for their elevenses, I was taken to a cell with a cup of water. A couple of hours passed by, though my estimation of time during my questioning was always a guess because my personal effects, including my wristwatch, would be put in a bag as a preliminary and left with the custody sergeant. All standard procedure I believe. I did consider a T-shirt and shorts next time!

I had always imagined a police station to be a hive of activity, and all bustle and noise. But on every occasion I was in there it was almost completely silent. During those silent days I rediscovered a pastime from my childhood – making shadow-figures with my hands in the light cast by the sun. Dogs, birds, profiles and such. I thought, if someone was to look through the spyhole in the door they might conclude that I needed the services of a good shrink. Still, it did help pass the time.

At the resumption of the interview we continued on the subject of the Gauguin Faun. I began to relate to the detectives the circumstances of my dealings with it. I had made this in early 1994 and, months later, sent a photo of it to a well-known London auction house. After some delay, they wrote back to me requesting that I bring it to London so they could have a look at it first-hand, explaining that it was not their policy to give an opinion from a photo, something of which I was already well aware. The photo in the post was an ice-breaker I often used.

I then took the sculpture to be examined by the Works of Art department of the said auctioneers, along with an 'unprovable provenance', which, as the description implies, should not have been taken seriously as a provenance for a piece by an artist as prominent as Paul Gauguin. With my bag containing the sculpture, I walked into the imposing HQ on Bond Street and informed the girl at reception that I had an appointment with Mr Anon. She rang the office and I was shown into a small room to await the expert. He came in, introduced himself to me, shook hands and, after a few polite words about my journey and such, took the Faun from its holdall and placed it onto a baize-topped table, sat back in his armchair and proceeded to look at it with his critical eye.

At the time, I myself always made sure to do the same. Over the years, I gained more insight from these observations into what was important to the expert in his assessment of an artwork, be it picture, sculpture, metalwork or whatever. First of all, he sat back to take in the overall effect of the piece. Then he turned it to another angle and looked again from a distance. This was similar to my own actions when working on an original model, so as to make sure the fundamental structure is accurate before moving on to the detail.

Next, he moved in closer, to look at the finer points. For ceramic work of any date, be it sculpture, art pottery or factory work, the actual body of clay from which it is made is distinct in every instance. Having apparently satisfied himself as to its 'rightness', I was told that he would like to show it to others, so could I possibly leave it with them? This I agreed to, signed the appropriate forms, picked up my receipt, which described it as a 'ceramic for further investigation', and left.

None of this gave me any cause for concern as it is usual for the auctioneers to be cautious, and rightly so. I have found London auction houses – except on rare occasions, such as those attributed to myself – to be among the most diligent establishments in the matter of attributing artwork to the original authors. If this is doubted, I would point to the fact that they handle thousands of lots every year, almost all of correct attribution, many of them only returned to the market through being recognised by the auction house experts.

At this point in the recorded interview, the detective directing the interview suggested we leave the Faun, as they were aware of its fate, and go on to the next item. As a final question on the subject, however, he asked me to describe it. I thought this a strange thing to ask, especially as they said they already knew its fate. But, in my new attitude, I went about describing it as a statuette in brown stoneware, approximately 20 inches tall, depicting a seated faun on a domed base, inscribed with pastoral scenes. This, it seems, was different from what the auctioneers had said. They, apparently, had described it to the police as 'an inscribed bowl'. How the auctioneers could have mistakenly identified it as 'a bowl' is something of a mystery.

I also told them I knew where the Faun was now. It was in a

major US museum collection. I had only become aware of this because, some years after the sale, I had been watching a TV programme about Gauguin, just as a matter of interest. I'd been in the pub some days earlier and the landlord had asked if I was going to watch it. I wasn't aware that such a programme was on, but as he and some of the regulars often talked of art and artists, I thought I would have a look at it, if for no other reason than to have something to talk about on my next visit to the watering hole. That night, as I watched the TV, there staring back at me out of a glass case surrounded by walls covered in post-Impressionist masterpieces, was my Faun at the elbow of the presenter. I was rather surprised to see it there, and you can be sure I didn't mention it in the pub the next time I called in.

Most of the pieces which the police were asking about had been done years before, some of them almost two decades earlier. Yet they seemed to expect me to have instant recall of the most tiny of details. This was something I found most taxing during those long interviews, each lasting all day and sometimes past midnight. I can say with honesty that I did my best to fill in as many of the details with which they bombarded me as I could. The only occasions on which I was not as forthcoming as I might have been was when they wanted to know how and with what I had simulated the age of a particular piece. My reasoning for this was that my efforts in this respect weren't, as I saw it, relevant to the investigation into the alleged fraudulent sale of fakes. As far as I was concerned, the techniques I had learnt, mostly by long hours of trial and error, were the product of honest effort, though, admittedly, used to dishonest effect. So I just told them that I used tea or coffee and the household materials used on myriad potboilers by uncaring copyists over the past decades. And left it at that.

One especially strange notion they had – it was reported in the press at the time – was that the Risley Lanx had been made by melting down genuine Roman silver coins. This, coming from detectives of the Art & Antiques Squad of no less a place than Scotland Yard, beggared belief. If they had stopped for a moment to consider that the most readily available Roman silver coin, the late antique silique, a coin of no more than 3g, even in a very poor grade, costs over £50 each, and that the Risley Lanx weighed in at approximately 4.5kg, they could have readily seen that such an expense – to say nothing of the wanton destruction of so many ancient artefacts – was ridiculous and unnecessary. It takes so little effort or time to produce silver bullion for the production of plate.

Whenever I worked on metalwork, I'd always take particular care to use the 'right' metal. One of the first things the experts look at, after satisfying themselves that the style and methods for that particular period are correct, is the make-up of the alloy. These are very distinctive in particular ages and cultures, and a major pointer to authenticity. Nowadays, due to the ever-wider publication of metal analyses, the information is easier to find. But still, if you get this basic wrong, it shoots down the piece right away.

The next object up for consideration was a silver and gilt copper reliquary in the manner of tenth-century Anglo-Saxon church art. The detectives were particularly interested in the Latin inscription on the base in gold wire and blue glass. They said, 'Have you any idea what this means round the base of this piece?' Another stupid question, I thought. I would hardly have put a garbled legend on something into which I had otherwise put such a great deal of effort. So, in sarcastic response, I said, 'No. I'm completely illiterate in Latin. I haven't a clue.' To which one of them replied, with a wise-guy grin, 'I do.' 'So do I,' indicated my solicitor, who by now must have had writer's cramp. He'd been scribbling away for hours, but this, as far as memory serves, was his only verbal contribution for as long as he'd been scribbling.

I'm certainly no scholar in any language, but – contrary to the stories woven in the press to explain away my undoing – I knew enough to make sure of my inscriptions. At the time of my arrest, the most satisfying study I ever did in languages was of Egyptian hieroglyphics. When I was a child I was fascinated by all things Egyptian. I'd stand and stare at the objects in the Bolton and Manchester Museums, but always felt a frustration because I couldn't understand what was written all over them. To me, at that time, the hieroglyphics were just part of the colourful design and totally undecipherable.

For Christmas, 1968, my eldest brother, Edward, bought me a book about Napoleon's adventures in Egypt, describing Champollion's untangling of the Egyptian 'code' and the Rosetta Stone's place in achieving this. I'd seen this stone as a cast in Bolton Museum, and then the real thing in the British Museum's Great Egyptian Gallery, usually surrounded by a throng of tourists. The cast in Bolton seemed more real to me because as a small child I could stand in front of it, at my own eye level, and – after reading the book – try to work out how the Greek script related to the Egyptian.

The interview at Bolton Police Station had now gone on into the late afternoon, and still the photos kept winging their way across the table. 'Is this your work?' 'Yes.' 'And this also?' 'Yes.' Occasionally, if they thought the piece merited it, they would ask more about it, and those which I remembered best are the ones I relate to you in these pages. None of them were particularly significant at the time I made them. Just another project in a sea of such things. I'll mention a few of them for interest, and hope it doesn't start to bore. In later chapters, at the suggestion of others more used to knowing what is readable, I intend to go into greater detail as to how some of them were made. For now, I'm just going to describe them.

Among the items of metalwork traced back to me by the investigation was a particular piece that hadn't been found during their search, but which was now in a private collection. The DC held up a photo of it for me. Some of the artworks I had produced had made their way into the collections of quite notable people, or so I have been led to believe. I myself was totally unaware and, frankly, unbothered by their fate. When they were finished, that was that. Anyway, this piece, I was informed, had found its way into the collection of a member of the Royal Family – who exactly, I can't say.

It was only about 3 inches tall, a silver gilt Christ, or 'corpus', in the twelfth-century English style. A vellum wrap bearing a legend alluding to it was taken from the tomb of King John at Worcester Cathedral. I had read the account of the tomb's opening in 1797, and duly fitted up this cast with an appropriate history. It had been sold at auction in London in 1998, rather disappointingly, as far as I was concerned, for £10,000. I was expecting a good deal more. But this was often the pattern. The purchaser, with better contacts, then passed it on at a multiple. That's life in the art business.

I can't recall any other metal objects being the subject of questioning that September day. Next up was the very first thing to come to light at the time the police first turned up, a blue stone inlay head of an Egyptian pharaoh. It was in my dad's desk drawer where it had been since I carved it out of a lapis lazuli 32 years before. I think it was my very first attempt at hardstone carving. I'd done it with a mini drill from Argos and an amateur set of diamond carving burrs, which I had bought on mail order in the *Exchange and Mart* when I was 14.

The slice of lapis from which it was carved I'd bought from a gem dealer who had a stall at the Sunday antiques fair at the Last Drop, the place where the Scotland Yard detectives were staying whilst on the hunt. It was expensive for my pocket, so I sold my collection of Victorian beer bottles and figured clay pipe heads to another dealer there, got the lapis and turned a profit into the bargain. The bottles and pipes I'd dug up from an old Victorian tip. It was a popular hobby everywhere in the 1970s and something I did with my school friends during the holidays on the rare occasions when I was in an archaeological mood. After this first attempt, I went on to do a wide range of hardstone and gem carvings and engravings over the intervening years. They are amongst the most difficult things to do well, but also virtually impossible to date accurately. If the style and material is right then you're pretty much home and dry.

By this time the pile of photos had been mostly gone through. Some of the exhibits were very obscure and minor – a little pouch of niello here, an uncut amethyst slice there, even the odd bottle of ink or silver foil. Another item they wanted to discuss was an unfinished watercolour of the ship *SS Great Britain*, docked on the Hudson River off Manhattan. The dimensions of this picture had proved something of a problem, as the paper I wanted – a particular weight, thickness and finish – was no longer commercially available. So if I wanted to proceed, I needed to go back into paper production.

Some years earlier, in the late 1980s, I had set up a small-scale watercolour paper-making concern. The product was a success and sold quite well. But a regular supply of cotton linters, the basic stuff from which paper is produced, was difficult to guarantee, so I gradually ceased production. I've reproduced old-style papers of varying types. In particular, I've struggled with getting the watermarks to look right on sheets used in sixteenth- and seventeenth-century Old Master drawings. These are sometimes definitive in the attribution to certain artists or schools by experts in the field, and original sheets are expensive and very difficult to source.

Anyway, this sheet of heavyweight paper was quite a handful. The larger the sheet in handmade paper, the more difficult it is to get an even density out of the pulp tank, which, in turn, affects the sizing and then the laying of paint on the surface. This time, the only fault I encountered was in the stretching. It tore whilst drying, but only around the borders, which could be trimmed on completion. However, I never got around to that as when the police took it on its ride to London, with the rest of my stuff, it was only a ghost image, still taped to the plywood board.

The last photo they passed to me was of a painting I had done in 1989–90, an oil on canvas, in the manner of the Scottish artist Samuel Peploe. Along with Cadell, Fergusson and others, Peploe was a member of the 'Scottish Colourists' of the late nineteenth and early twentieth centuries, a school of painters who were in high demand in the 1980s. This particular picture was a still life of about 18 inches by 20, a pretty standard format for Peploe. On the occasion of its sale, my dad had gone down to London with me and we had an appointment to see a dealer who had already expressed an interest in it. We arrived at the gallery, just up the road from Harrods, to find that we could park right by the shop, quite unusual by London standards, I thought, especially without having to fill a parking meter to the gunnels as with most visits to London.

The gallery was a plush affair, Persian carpets and cigar smoke, something I always took as a good harbinger. Into this emerged a long-faced, hand-wringing man with a look of great disappointment, who informed us that he had been having a bad time of late and could only offer £4,000 for it as the market 'just wasn't there'. I knew this to be utter rubbish. The market did fall some time later, in the wake of the early nineties' crash, but at that time it was about as high as it got back then. This guy should have been a fortune teller if he really believed his own spiel.

A couple of times he disappeared into the back of the shop to have a good look at the picture, closing the door each time. At least he trusts us not to help ourselves to the silver, I thought. If he only improved his offer slightly we had decided to go into the West End around Bond Street reasoning that if he was prepared to pay £6,000 or £7,000 for it – knowing from experience that this guy knew his stuff – there might be a better price to be had elsewhere. As we left the gallery with the dealer following in hope, his last offer was £6,500.

In the West End, we eventually lighted upon a dealer who was unknown to me, but well known on TV, apparently, where he used to do antiques shows. My dad did the deal. It was getting late in the day, so I dropped him off outside the gallery somewhere behind Fortnum's. He gave us £20,000 for it, which I estimated was probably a fifth of its value. Later, there was to be some further wrangling over this picture. At the time, I pocketed the cheque and we set off for home, several hours up the motorway.

With this, the detectives heaved a sigh of relief. My solicitor finally looked up from his notes. And things started to be packed away. The conversation turned briefly to less specific subjects. What had led me into this business of fakery? Who were my favourite artists? How long had I been doing the fakes? Did I have any formal tuition in painting and sculpture? And so on. After all the hours answering their formal questions I didn't feel particularly chatty. In fact, I was more burnt-out than I let them know at the time and very relieved to get out of the police station.

Picking up my personal effects I walked out into the night. Though it was late September, and after midnight, the air was still summer warm. The Yardies had left via another exit and I could see the tail lights of their cars zooming off down Deansgate and away to their rooms at the Last Drop hotel, before they headed off back to London the next day. They had their informants, I had mine.

As I set off for home, the town centre was perfectly still. My solicitor came out and asked if I needed a lift. I told him my brother was picking me up, so no thanks, and at this, he too left for home. I didn't actually have a lift, but had decided to walk home along the Bolton to Blackburn railway line. It's the quickest route. I had used it many times in my teens and early twenties, usually when I'd missed the last bus and run out of cash after a night out. It was a fine night for a stroll and a good opportunity to clear my head of police officers, art and all that crap, which, by that time, had come to fill my every thought.

Walking through the town, past the parish church, I jumped the line and headed for home with my eyes adjusting to the darkness as the tracks plunged into the night. I remembered an old chestnut tree and wondered if it was still standing. Sure enough, there it was, looking not a day older after almost 30 years. I had last climbed it as an 18-year-old and was now fat and mid-40s, so I struggled a bit to get up, but one consolation was that the old tree shook more easily than when I was a 10-stone whip of a lad. With just one wobble from me, the whole crop of chestnuts hit the deck and down I got to fill my pockets. Some of those nuts looked quite familiar. A nice reminder of my day, in more ways than one.

Before I leave this description of the artworks that were the subject of the Scotland Yard investigation and move on to the hurdle I couldn't jump – the judiciary and its consequences – I need to finish the story of the object that got me into this hotspot in the first place: the Assyrian relief. It was the nail in my coffin, so you need to know how and why it got hammered in. When I'd finished carving it and stood it upright for a last look, I was confronted with how heavy it was. Most of the original reliefs were at least a few inches thick, but that varied with the size of the panel. Mine was over 4 inches thick! To make transportation easier and add to its 'Victorian makeover' credentials, I decided to cut off the back, reducing it to a manageable inch or so, something akin to a concrete paving slab. Much easier on the old back. The pieces I cut off were the pieces later discovered by the visiting Yardies.

I finished the panel in early July and put it to one side for the remainder of the summer, spending a few weeks night fishing for sea trout on my favourite stretch of the Eden near Penrith. It's something I've done every year since going on my first night fishing adventure almost 40 years ago. Last year was the first season I've missed, for obvious reasons. I'm writing this in gaol, remember! In August, I had a few invites from friends to some good rivers and shooting days, and also heard from a few people I hadn't seen in years. In my youth I'd been a member of the British Falconers' Club and from September onwards I was able to go hawking with a borrowed falcon. The best day was at a place called Battersby Park, North Yorkshire, which had formerly been an American airbase. Zooming along the concrete runways, standing up in the back of a Toyota pickup truck whilst following the flight and stoops of the falcons, was great fun.

By October, I decided to get on with the hoped-for sale of my labours for the year, so I photographed the Assyrian panel and sent off the photos with a note to the British Museum. A reply came winging its way back quickly asking to see it and if it would be possible to bring it to the British Museum for examination. Ringing the number on the letter, my dad spoke to the Keeper of the Middle East collections and suggested a date sometime in mid- or late November.

Come that day, I arrived at the British Museum at the appointed time and was directed to a place off the visitors' path, an incline into the bowels of the museum at the side of the building. There, waiting for me, was a tall, distinguished-looking gent. He shook hands and introduced himself as the Keeper. With the help of his assistants, I unpacked the panel and they carried it into a cluttered room where a man I took to be a restorer employed by the British Museum was standing, along with several other people. The panel was carefully placed on the table and the experts began buzzing round it.

As far as I could make out their initial response was positive. And after 10–15 minutes of debate it was suggested to me that this was, indeed, at first glance at least, a relief from the palace of an Assyrian king of around the seventh century BC. The debate had apparently been about its non-standard colouring and the fact that it had been cut down from its original thickness. I was told this had been done in the nineteenth century, and that lesser pieces taken out of the ground in a poorer state of preservation were sometimes treated this way to make them more appealing for the commercial market. 'So far so good,' I thought.

At this point it was suggested the Keeper would show me round the Assyrian galleries if I wished. I jumped at this, though I tried not to show too much keenness. A personal guided tour of such a magnificent collection, along with an insight into it by a Keeper of Collections at the British Museum, isn't something to be declined, not by me anyway. First, we had a quick look around the British Museum storerooms, where a multitude of pieces, complete and fragmentary, littered the floors and shelves. One thing in particular lodged in my mind – a pivot of a great door from an Assyrian palace, figuratively carved. The Keeper pointed out its worn centre where the doors swung to and fro. Something to consider for another project, I thought. Quick and easy to do, yet obscure enough to be a discovery by some unsuspecting expert in the future.

What an Aladdin's cave of a place it was. I would have loved to have spent many hours trawling through it but was compelled to look half-interested so as not to prompt any suspicions that I was not as unknowing of such things as I made out. Over the years, I have found that if an expert, dealer or whoever thought they were dealing with a total amateur they were more open and more willing to reveal what they knew. I suppose it stems from their professional instincts – not wanting to add to a competitor's knowledge if it could be avoided.

We went along a short corridor through a door and suddenly we were standing in the Assyria gallery. The door was almost invisible in the gallery wall and we emerged to the startled gaze of a group of Japanese tourists. The Keeper started to discuss the scenes before us in a very interesting and animated way. He also talked about a lost Assyrian relief that had been discovered in the wall of a public school near Bournemouth. Twice as large as my piece, but similar in subject, it had been whitewashed, then covered with house paint. It had, therefore, long been considered a cast of an original. The location, though, was significant. The school had been the home of Sir Austen Henry Layard, the pre-eminent nineteenth century excavator of Nineveh and Nimrud, from where, under his direction, the British Museum's fantastic collection of Assyrian art had come.

It was common knowledge that Layard had also formed his own collection which was acquired from his relatives by the Metropolitan Museum of Art in New York. Anyway, it transpired that the whitewashed cast wasn't a whitewashed cast, and the school later sold it at auction for £7,000,000. The Keeper quickly added that mine wasn't worth nearly as much, but it was still a valuable find. He was obviously a fine scholar, but it was this person who later contacted the police, a course of action which ultimately brought me to my current position.

We returned to the basement where the others had been examining the relief. It was agreed I would leave the panel with the museum for further study. We settled on an appraisal period of two months and I left, with an agreement to return after the Christmas and New Year holidays. What happened over the intervening period was filled in for me later by the Scotland Yard detectives during one of our little get-togethers down at the police station.

Apparently, over the Christmas period, there was a function at the BM at which the Keeper began talking about his latest discovery with a former colleague. Our name was mentioned, and at this the former colleague, who was now a West End dealer, said that he had dealt with us in the past and suggested it would be wise to be careful with the panel. Over the following weeks, suspicion grew, until, after some deliberation between the Keeper and his superiors at the museum, the police were called in. That, at least, is what the police told me.

During the time the panel was at the British Museum, I had also been contacted by an expert from a New York auction house. In anticipation of an auction sale, he needed our consent to come over, look at the relief and value it. This he did. Afterwards, he rang from the US late one night to say he had called at the British

Museum, examined the piece and thought a reserve of £300,000 was reasonable. In consideration of its quality, it would be no surprise to him if it went for a great deal more. There the situation rested until January.

Several days before I was due to return to the British Museum to collect my property, my father received a strange call from the Keeper. He sounded rather irate. He had learnt that we were considering sending the panel abroad for sale and was most insistent that it should be sold in London. He said he would make the reasons for that plain when I went down to collect it. All rather bizarre, I thought at the time.

I arrived at the British Museum almost an hour early and was waved through by security. When I knocked at the door and entered the storeroom – the place I had been in some months earlier – the Keeper was in conversation with another man and looked surprised to see me. I apologised for being early. For some reason, he seemed flustered, but after regaining his composure he rang his assistants and asked them to bring in the panel, which was now carefully wrapped. Then he asked me about my intentions for it, as regards its sale, and what the American had valued it at. I told him the reserve had been set at £300,000 and that I had arranged to deliver it to their London depot that afternoon, prior to its export. That valuation was way off the mark, he said. It could be worth up to £3,000,000. Then he suggested I take it to a rival London-based auctioneer, so the sale, as he put it, could go ahead without the need for an export licence. Good reasoning, I thought at the time. He even offered me the use of the museum's phone, for which I had to dial '8' for an outside line. Against my better judgement I was persuaded, and rang to cancel my appointment.

It was later alleged that by this time the Keeper had already contacted Scotland Yard and that if I had sold the piece overseas it would have been beyond their jurisdiction. Personally, I'd have thought the proper course of action would have been for me to have been met by detectives at the British Museum that January day so the matter could be taken from there. Not for the British Museum to advise me to attempt a sale through a London auctioneer whilst suspecting the piece to be a fake.

Anyhow, I took my leave of them and on their advice carted it round to Bond Street and left it with the auctioneers who, with hindsight, seemed reluctant to take it, considering it had been authenticated by the British Museum and carried the likelihood of a whopping commission. All very strange and not the usual reaction. Such a definite attribution, combined with big money, usually has the auctioneers jumping for joy. Must be a bad day, I thought. How right I was.

During the next few weeks, I had a couple of letters confirming the sale date, the catalogue and such. Then that knock on the door on the 15th of March.

III.

Consequences

AFTER MY LATE-NIGHT walk home that warm September evening, I heard nothing more from the police until the following February. So I just carried on with my life as it had become, though the artist in me seemed to have gone on permanent leave. I think 2006 was the first year since I could remember in which I hadn't produced any artwork at all, not even the occasional sketch. Throughout my life, I've always seemed to go off the boil as far as art is concerned whenever things aren't going well personally. It must be the artistic temperament or something.

The year drew to a close and I for one wasn't sad to see it go. My next meeting with the Yardies, was, as I said, in February. A few days earlier I'd had another terse letter from my solicitor informing me that I must attend and alluding to the consequences if I didn't. Quite unnecessarily, I thought. These letters, six lines long at most, were the only contact with my solicitor throughout my association with him. Looking back I can't help but think I should have asked for alternative representation. Up to that point, of course, I hadn't had many dealings with solicitors, but as an 18-year-old I had been in a motor accident and had more concern from my solicitor then, over a relatively minor affair, than was ever shown by the man representing me now. I suppose it's what they call professional behaviour.

I duly arrived at Bolton Police Station, though by this time the old place had closed. The new station was much lighter and brighter, but still made the butterflies rise in my stomach – strangely similar to the first day back at school. I was shown through to a room where, to my surprise, my solicitor sat ready and waiting. For once, he seemed quite upbeat and told me the police had discovered a few more things that could be attributed to me, so he just wanted a couple of hours with me to run through them. 'OK,' I said. 'Let's get on with it.' I thought it best to answer in kind and be, for now, a man of few words.

He leaned back in his chair and said something to the effect of 'Shaun, do you know of any other US presidents with the name Jefferson?' I presumed this was in reference to a terracotta bust I had once made of Thomas Jefferson, the third president, and answered 'No.' He then added, 'What about William Jefferson?' Bill Clinton came to mind, but, again, I said 'No.' With this he decided to give up the cat-and-mouse game and told me plainly. The bust had been purchased in London and was now the property of William Jefferson Clinton. As far as I know, it still is, and I hope it brings him pleasure. I certainly enjoyed making it, even though I had to restrain myself as it was supposed to have been made by a young artist at the beginning of his career called Horatio Green-ough of Boston, circa 1820, so it had to show this. I read President Clinton's autobiography, *My Life*, all 969 pages of it. The book cost me £10. Much less, I should imagine, than his Jefferson cost him. Sorry Mr President!

I went through to the interview room and thankfully Sergeant Tango wasn't to be seen. The female sergeant detective and the DC were much easier to get along with. Most of the items they ran through were not fakes as such. Most of them were ceramics, mainly copies, unmarked, so unattributable. I had made such things, on and off, for years and sold them on as decorative pieces, mainly through dealers and the odd auction. None of them brought large prices. They went for what they were worth, the time and effort expended on them.

One particular item was described on their list as 'plaster statuette', signed Lalique, the nineteenth-century French art glassmaker. In fact, there were four of them, all cast glass, a technique that was difficult to do but typical of Lalique's personal work. They had been attributed by the Lalique Museum in France after I sold them at a non-Lalique price. The four pieces represented the four seasons, personified in amber, white and green glass, some of my best work in fact. I informed the police of this, but for some reason, unknown to me, the present owner had told them they were plaster.

When the list had been run through I signed the document and that was another day done with. Off I went, out into the winter sunshine. This time it was still daylight and only 2pm, instead of midnight. To me, that was a result, though at my next and, as it turned out, my last meeting with the Scotland Yard detectives, I was decidedly of a different opinion. This was just a few weeks later.

The next thing was to charge us. All of us. Though with what still hadn't been decided. My mum and dad were also required to attend. We arrived at the police station early on a March day in 2007. By this time, Dad was unable to walk without the use of a Zimmer frame, something he had used since his fall the year before. For convenience, I took his wheelchair along to save him any long walks.

The treatment of my parents was, and is, something that has caused me the most anxiety in this whole affair. Their part in it has been greatly exaggerated and, in any case, I don't think in a decent society people of such an age and frailty should be pursued for the actions of which they were accused and later convicted. You're probably thinking 'He's bound to say that, isn't he?' And I fully appreciate that mindset. But come on! An occasional phone call or letter by my mum and dad, in support of a story concocted by me, hardly different from myriad tales on the *Antiques Roadshow*? My granddad was given this Ming vase 100 years ago, ya know. He was best mates with the Emperor of China!

The March day went along differently from my previous encounters. There were no more questions, at least not for the record. The four detectives were in and out all morning. They told me they were in consultation with the Crown Prosecution Service lawyers upstairs in the building, debating with them what charges were to be levelled at us – something they were unsure of, apparently. No decision was taken before lunch. They left for lunch at about 11.30.

After lunch, the Scotland Yard detectives returned and seemed in high spirits. At one time, one of them referred to my parents as: 'Oh look, it's Bonnie and Clyde.' In other circumstances, they'd have got a fat lip for that, but they had the upper hand and knew it. After some time, I was informed that the CPS lawyers 'upstairs' couldn't decide on the nature of the charges we were to face, so outside advice had to be sought. This was the reason for the delay. Eventually, they had the documents typed and brought them down, read out each one in turn and formally charged myself, my mum and dad with conspiracy to defraud. A date in April was provisionally set for the magistrates' court and we were free to go.

The next day we were front-page news, and a new wave of photographers and shite-hawk journalists descended on us so as to make life quite difficult. Thankfully, this state of affairs only lasted a few days before they got wind of another story and buggered off. Our next ordeal was to be an appearance at the Bolton Magistrates' Court in April, only three weeks hence. The last 12 months had been a nightmare. For my part, I was resigned to my fate and just wanted an end to the proceedings.

The morning of our first appearance at court finally dawned and, just as I was about to call the taxi for our journey to the Bolton Magistrates' Court, the phone rang. It was my solicitor. He said that due to my dad's mobility problem, he didn't see how we could attend court today on account of the lift being broken. According to him, it hadn't been working for ages. Why, then, hadn't he informed us earlier in the week?

'Now that we're ready to go, I would prefer to get this done today,' I said. At this he suggested I leave it with him and he'd call back as soon as he could arrange something. An hour or so later, back came the message that we could have the hearing at the court in Bury, but we would need to hurry. They could fit us in during the morning session. I felt as if I was arranging an MOT for the car at Kwik Fit. The taxi picked us up and off we dashed to the Bury court.

Waiting for us at the courthouse was a gaggle of photographers. Whenever they were hanging around at home, I had tried to sidestep them. This time that wouldn't be possible. With me having to set up Dad's wheelchair, I felt like a fish in a barrel, the photographers clicking away at their leisure and all the while me doing a 'Norman Wisdom' with the chair – those bloody contraptions always seem to turn awkward at the worst possible moment, don't they? Having finally sorted it out, we set off for the door of the building, me pushing, with the shutter-clickers following. As we walked in, something came to mind which made me smile to myself. Did it all look a bit like Benny Hill leading his intrepid scout troop?

There was some logic to our solicitor arranging the hearing at Bury. It's a fairly modern building and unlike the neoclassical pile in Bolton, all on ground level with easy disabled access. The solicitor thought we would be finished in an hour or two, but after my marathons with the Art & Antiques Squad of the previous year I took that to mean another long, long day. It was almost lunchtime when he finally reappeared and, surprise surprise, informed us that the court couldn't fit us in until the afternoon. With that, off he toddled for lunch.

With all the photographers milling about in the car park we decided to have our own lunch in the cafe at the courthouse. We got in some sandwiches and coffee, and a middle-aged lady sat down at the table behind us, along with what looked like her son. They seemed rather strange to me. Then I heard a squeaky squiggle of voices – the type of noise a pocket voice recorder makes on rewind. The woman began to eff and Jeff at the lad in a very unlady-like manner, and up they jumped and legged it. All very peculiar. I can only presume they had planned to record our conversation, although heaven only knows what they were hoping to hear.

We were eventually called into court after 3pm – the last case of the day. Most of the previous cases were yobbos on various aggro charges and such. I suppose their need to get home and put their feet up in front of the telly with a can of lager was deemed a greater priority by the magistrates than the welfare of a couple of octo-genarians in poor health. But I digress, again.

Quick formalities, three minutes adjourn and out. That was the magistrates' hearing sorted. As we left the court my solicitor's voice boomed out: 'This could go to the Old Bailey.' For what reason he said this, I haven't a clue.

We went out to the waiting taxi accompanied by the rantings of a mysterious caterwauler who was screaming, 'They got what they deserved. Justice has been done.' I said something of the order of 'What the f*** is she on about?' The solicitor assured me it was the disgruntled mother of a girl in the previous case to ours who had been battered by her boyfriend. 'Why then shout in the plural?' I asked, as the cameras were poked full-flash in our faces. The previ-ous case had been half an hour earlier. Unless the wife-batterer had been doing the Buddhist Temple Walk he'd have been long gone by the time we left. I had the distinct impression that the show was put on for us, though perhaps I'm becoming paranoid.

The case was adjourned to Bolton Crown Court for a first hear-ing in September and, again, we were allowed to get on with our lives as normal. The only problem with being on bail and awaiting trial or, as in our case, awaiting a hearing because we had entered a guilty plea, is that it seems impossible to plan anything or get on with life. I felt as if I was in some kind of suspended animation. Between July and September, the date of our first hearing at the Crown Court, there were several days spent going over case notes and preparing for the first meeting with the barrister. During those long and tedious afternoons spent down at the solicitor's office, going through reams of papers detailing the things I had done, I was taken aback by the sheer amount of stuff I'd made. If all my failures and recycled or destroyed work had been added to this list, I thought to myself, it might have taken another year to prepare for court.

I really couldn't see the point of all this paperwork and legal wrangling. As far as I was concerned, the procedure should have been simple. I had pleaded guilty as charged, so slam the door on me and let's get on with it. However, the slow-grinding wheels of justice don't work like that, do they?

September came around and the day of the hearing started in a now-familiar style – a taxi ride, followed by a crocodile of reporters in pursuit, as we legged it for the doors of the courthouse. Inside the building, all was quiet and calm, and quite a relief. Looking at the screen listing the day's hearings, I saw we were due to appear in Court Room Three. So into the lift we went and up to the waiting area for Court Three on the top floor.

Bolton Crown Court was built in the mid-seventies. It's right by the bus station on the site of the old Bessemer Steel Foundry, an ugly concrete block of a building, with no redeeming features. Definitely a product of its time. If it was a little taller, it might pass for one of Göring's flak towers in Berlin. The waiting area was buzzing with robed and bewigged lawyers, and it wasn't long before I had my first meeting with the barrister charged with representing me. I was ushered into a small room where he sat with the solicitor and his secretary.

True to nature, lawyers being lawyers, the barrister did all the talking. He explained that the case against me was overwhelming and that, if I was in agreement, he was consequently entering a guilty plea. In his learned opinion, that was the one and only option. Other long-winded meanderings followed, though my attention became ever more focused on his old horsehair wig sitting on the table in front, looking for all the world like a sleeping moggy. By now, the legalities were of little interest to me. My options were nil and I was resigned to my fate – a substantial period of custody.

In the late afternoon, we were called into court and as we walked in I saw that the interior was just as soulless as the exterior. Having watched occasional episodes of the telly series *Crown Court* as a kid in the seventies, I was expecting something akin to the Old Bailey – old oak panelling, an old crouchback of a judge with a face like a port wine decanter, and an eyrie-style dock, high up and railed in polished brass. I was to be disappointed on all counts, bar one. I'd best not say which.

We sat behind a glass partition, looking out over the bewigged heads of the lawyers, facing the judge's empty seat, complete with a large royal coat of arms above it – which, incidentally, I thought could have been better carved. There were various people in the gallery – journalists, reporters and others. Two of the investigating officers from Scotland Yard, toting a selection of my wares, displayed them for one and all to gawp at. A croak of 'All rise' and in came the judge. The pantomime was underway and, for the first time in a while, I could at last begin to see an end to it all.

The formalities completed, my learned counsel entered our guilty plea and he and the prosecutor began their verbal table tennis, pinging and ponging their way through the details. The prosecutor opened his address with something about this being a case of the 'Artist and the Princess', referring to an ancient Egyptian alabaster that had been sold to the Bolton Museum several years earlier, though neither I nor my dad ever named it the Amarna Princess. Perhaps he was hoping for a dramatic headline.

The hearing continued without any further attention from me. Another croak of 'All rise' and I awoke from my daydream. We left court to be informed that the hearing was suspended for sentencing and that this would happen in November. One step closer to the finish line.

There was one last meeting with the lawyers during which they made it clear that due to the seriousness of the case, a custodial sentence was inevitable. 'Tell me something I didn't know,' thought I. The barrister, who occasionally wore another professional wig as a judge, suggested I should expect a sentence of between three and five years in prison. Quite a sobering thought, but not really a surprise to me by that stage.

During this final discussion, my solicitor happened to mention a particular work, a drawing attributed to Leonardo da Vinci, identified by the Yardies as one of mine. I had done many copies of the Old Masters, particularly in my teens and twenties when I was learning, as most artists wishing to improve their drawing skills do. This one was a sketch that had apparently been sold to the nation some years earlier by an English aristocrat, in lieu of death duties. The drawing was supposed to have been in his family for centuries. But if, indeed, it was my handiwork, it couldn't have been more than 20 years old. Either the aristo had been telling porkies or he had been a little 'confused', shall we say. I'm not aware of any action being taken about it. As far as I can see, some of our fellow citizens have the amazing ability to bend the law without ever breaking it.

Our last day in court, the 16th of November, 2007, is not very well remembered, though the usual journalists' jamboree does come to mind. One long streak who was holding a large microphone in his hands – at least I hope it was a microphone – kept shoving it in my face and shouting 'How long did you think you would get away with it?' I just thought, 'Poor sod. What a way to earn a crust.'

Once again, we had to sit there in the waiting area all morning. Finally, at about 2.30, we were called into court – my mum, me, and my dad. The prosecution began rambling on, my barrister interjected occasionally to little effect and then, would you believe it, another adjournment. For reasons best known to himself, the judge wanted to delay the sentencing until after 5pm. When he finally addressed the court, I wasn't listening to what he had to say and just waited to hear the sentence. Mum was given one year suspended. My dad's was deferred for medical reports. I was to serve four years and eight months. And that, finally, was that.

I was handcuffed, quite a first experience, and taken out through the back of the court and downstairs into the cells. The court staff at Bolton Crown Court were all very nice people who showed the utmost courtesy and decency to me. It's something that stays in the mind. Before being sent off to prison, my barrister came in to congratulate himself on being 'spot on' as far as the sentence was concerned. He had expressed his opinion several times over the last weeks. Three to five years he said. It was the solicitor's assistant – as far as I could see the most switched-on of the legal eagles – who pointed out that the sentence had actually been set at seven years. The barrister looked puzzled by this, until he was reminded that for an early guilty plea, one third is deducted, and that four years and eight months is two thirds of seven years.

That sentence was longer than any comparable one for faking artwork in recent times. Myatt and Drewe, who nobbled the records of the Victoria and Albert Museum to a point where future researchers will find it virtually impossible to tell fact from fiction, got one year and six years respectively. At least my works will eventually be weeded out as the obvious flaws in most of them come to the notice of better-seeing eyes. The only other fakers to be 'caught in the act' that I'm aware of were Tom Keating, who was let off from his trial at the Old Bailey apparently on account of his ill health despite being only 59 at the time and going on to live another seven years – I think he received his own television series as a punishment – and the late Eric Hebborn, who, though exposed, was never charged. They say he had friends in high places, the traitor and Surveyor of the Queen's Pictures, Sir Anthony Blunt, being one of them.

Personally, I have never considered my sentence excessive. The law's the law and where would we be without it? Never being one to bleat, I've always been minded to get on with my lot without complaint and make a good job of it, something with which all those with whom I served my sentence would not, I think, take issue.

My first adventure as a convicted criminal was a ride in what one and all referred to as a 'bus'. This was actually a large white prison van. I'd seen them around and about the town over the years and had always imagined them with a bunk down each side in the manner of an army truck. They actually have a central corridor with individual cells so tiny they barely measure hip to knee. Very claustrophobic. Another curious thing is that the tinted glass makes everything outside look dark orange. This description is for all those who have ever wondered what they look like from the inside. Here's hoping it forever remains a second-hand experience.

The bus rumbled on in the dark, the radio playing loudly and the 6 o'clock news telling me what I already knew. The first stop was something called Risley – not Risley Park, but a Cheshire prison. One person was dropped off there and on we went, with me not having a clue where I was to be deposited. This eventually turned out to be Runcorn Custody Suite, a large police station with cells for 'prison overflow', whatever that is. The van stopped, turned off its engine and the door to my chemi-loo-style compartment was opened a few inches. I was instructed to put my hands through the opening and on went the handcuffs. I felt like a serial killer, who, given the slightest chance, would have throttled the guards.

I spent three nights in that place and on Monday morning was loaded back onto the bus and taken to Walton Gaol in Liverpool.

This was a prison that fulfilled my own image of what a prison would be – an unmistakably Victorian institution, complete with suicide nets and all. Thankfully, I only stayed there a short while, less than two weeks, before I was asked – which made a pleasant change – if I would agree to be sent to a place called HMP Kennet? Without considering where on earth it was, I immediately said yes. I imagined it must be somewhere in the West Country, as I'd only heard of Kennet in relation to the Kennet and Avon canal. It actually turned out to be a 20-minute drive away, just outside Liverpool, by the M58. So again, as at Walton, I was surrounded by Scousers, hundreds of the buggers!

I've noticed that in the British tabloid press Liverpool and its people always seem to get a bashing. All I can say is that the Scousers I met, both inmates and staff, barring a few dangerous ones, were amongst the most decent people anyone could wish to meet. Head and shoulders above the supposedly cultured and gentlemanly dealers and experts I have spent most of my time dealing with over the years. And they tell better jokes.

HMP Kennet was a new prison. When I arrived, in December 2007, it had only been open for four months, so it hadn't quite filled up. The time I spent there wasn't nearly as bad as I expected. The first four months were spent in the education classes taking a business studies course and, for the first time in my life, getting to grips with the computer. As all 50-somethings will know, computers weren't in the schools in our day. Well, not the ones I went to. And after that time, my line of work didn't feature the modern world much. Certainly not computers.

By late March, I was sick of the classroom and asked to be put into the gardens. Although the whole place was still something of a building site, they intended to landscape the rubble-strewn grounds and so, for the next few months, I was to be a gardener. It was an opportunity to be outside for a change and the nice weather was coming. Spending most of my days on the garden crew, rotavating, raking and laying turf, yard after yard of it, was a pleasant enough way to while away my sentence.

In late June, my categorisation was reduced from a category C prisoner to D. This meant it would now be possible to move me to an open prison. My solicitor thought it would happen two or three weeks after sentencing, but, as things turned out, it was to be over seven months. I arrived at HMP Kirkham in July, 2008, and was to spend the rest of my time there doing a variety of tasks – the last of which was painting. Walls not pictures, I might add. Kirkham was as unlike most people's idea of prison as I think it possible to get, though no bad thing for that. I just can't help thinking that most of my sentence was a waste of everyone's time and effort. The actual police investigation, court procedure and the first two months of prison were, I admit, unpleasant. The time after that was spent mostly at ease, and compared to my spell as a full-time carer over the previous years was considerably less effort and certainly of less use.

During my time in prison, both Channel 4 and the BBC broadcast drama documentaries that were supposed to be portrayals of my life and of events connected with the case as it had been reported in the press. Each of these broadcasters wrote to me in advance to ask if I or my parents would like to co-operate with the programme's content. With hindsight, it is something I should have considered.

In the chapters ahead I have written down my life and events as I see them. Anyone interested can perhaps have a more honest look at the story, for what it's worth.

IV.

In the beginning

I WAS BORN IN 1960 in Bolton, a large town to the north of Manchester formerly known for its cotton mills and heavy engineering. All that, as they say, has long gone and many readers will only be familiar with the place through fat northern comedians taking the piss out of it. Thankfully, this wasn't always the case. Some of the most important textile innovations of the past 200 years were down to Boltonians. And two of the most influential artists of nineteenth-century America, Thomas Cole and Thomas Moran, hailed from hereabouts. Even the captain of the ship who rescued the *Titanic* survivors came from the town. So, as you see, it's not a complete backwater.

My own arrival in Bolton was on a very warm day in June, 1960, at 4.05pm, at Bolton General Hospital, now called The Royal Bolton. I was the sixth child of seven; five boys and two girls. My eldest brother, Edward, was born in 1947, and the youngest, my sister Sharon, in 1962. Mum and Dad were also born in Bolton in the early 1920s, but none of my grandparents' families were originally from there. My maternal grandparents were Scottish and Welsh. On my dad's side, Gran was of Liverpool Irish origin and only Granddad was anywhere near local, coming from a long line at Summerseat, near Bury. He apparently had Flemish and French forebears, so I suppose I'm a candidate for Euro citizenship if anyone is.

Granddad was a spinner who worked the cotton mills of Bolton all of his life. He was a promising footballer until he was shot in the chest during the Great War and had his left lung removed at the age of 18, a rarely survived procedure at the time. In the 1930s, the government stopped his war pension because he refused an exploratory operation. They only reinstated it in the late 1950s after my dad and uncle asked the local MP to see into it.

My dad himself was shot in Italy at the end of World War Two while doing humanitarian work for a UN agency delivering medicine to a children's hospital in Al Capone's old hometown of Foggia. It's something for which he has had a war pension since his twenties, despite being labelled a 'deserter' on national TV – a particularly hurtful lie. Thankfully, I haven't yet been injured in Italy or anywhere else on my travels, though since my conviction I've been watching out for art dealers and experts with guns, trucks, steamrollers or fast cars, whether here or abroad!

Mum and Dad met in a town centre pub called The Millstone whilst he was on leave in 1945. 'Well might it be called The Millstone,' Mum would sometimes say, 'your dad's been one of those around my neck for years.' But I think it was love at first sight really. They were married in 1946 and my brother Edward was born in 1947 into a country where rationing was still on – something he still harps on about in Monty Python style when feeling sorry for himself. My parents went on to have four more children close together. My brother George, who died as an infant, my brother Arthur, then sister Samy, and my brother George Richard. For the next five years, the family was pretty much complete, until I came along. My youngest sister, Sharon, arrived 20 months after that. She was the only one I could boss about as a kid, something I took every opportunity to exercise, according to her, otherwise being mainly on the receiving end. Having said that, I was always made a fuss of and taken on endless rides in my pushchair by one and all. My sister Samy reckons that amongst the family members I was almost as popular as our dog Trigger. Not quite as loved, as she makes a point of saying, but nearly.

Trigger was a labrador–collie cross who liked to chase motorcycles, getting a broken leg once for his trouble. He had the reputation of never eating his own dog food, and as he lived in a house full of kids he made a living out of being fed unwanted dinners 20 times a day. I suppose officially he was my brother Edward's dog and we were only allowed to take him for a walk if we had been given the 'imperial' thumbs up, usually gained by polishing Edward's scooter, my brother being a sixties slave to fashion and DED MOD at the time.

I think those years had some bearing on my lifelong indifference to music. I'm imprinted with most of the vocals of the Rolling Stones' 'hits', having repeatedly absorbed them at ear-splitting volume and getting a clip around the ear if I shouted at Edward to turn it down. Other singers from the era indelibly marked on my innermost ear had such obscure names – to me at least – as Lead Belly, Woody Guthrie etc. These were written in some style in marker pens all over his red and white portable record player – another untouchable – along with my sister Samy's contributions such as the Walker Brothers, Small Faces, and so on. My early years were therefore lived at high decibels, the only musical relief being short bursts of classical music, the only thing I enjoyed listening to. But the youngest can't stand against the higher forces of big brother and sister. My own favourite sound is the wind in full-leaf trees, something unmatched by any composer. Nature, at full stretch, always surpasses art. With hindsight, I have sometimes wondered if my earliest artistic efforts were a kind of response to always having my own tastes overruled. At least in drawing and such, I had little competition!

Early on, I was always referred to as 'the little wizard'. This was on account of my being born on the Summer Solstice, the 21st of June, 1960. My sister had been doing a school project on Stonehenge and the Druids at the time. I presume her lessons had made some reference to the significance of the solstice to the builders of the place, though, as is now known, it actually had nothing to do with Druids. Stonehenge is almost as far in time from the Druids as the Druids are from us. A similarly tenuous stretch separates Druids from wizards. But the connection was made and a convoluted name-trail landed upon me from the beginning. I once asked my mum why I had been called Shaun, and pointed out to her that my brothers had all been named after our grandfathers and father. I was told that, originally, I was meant to have been called Robert, after my dad's uncle Bob. Years later, Mum showed me the wristband given to me in hospital when I was born. Instead of the plastic strap you get nowadays, it was made of blue and white beads, and spelled out 'Robert'. Shaun had been my dad's last-minute idea because of something that happened on the morning I was born.

My mum had always been in the habit of keeping active during her pregnancies. She stayed at work right up until a couple of weeks before her due date. Looking back, this was probably down to necessity rather than choice. She retired on her sixtieth birthday in 1984 and had never once in her life drawn either sickness or unemployment benefits. The morning of my arrival was a scorcher. She'd been doing the washing and had gone out into the garden to peg out the clothes. But before she could finish I must have decided it was time to put in my first appearance. My opening efforts made her lean on the clothes post and, looking down, she saw a four-leaf clover. She bent to pick it up and that, according to her, was my cue. My aunt went to call the doctor, and away went Mum to hospital. The four-leaf clover, I'm sorry to say, never did work its magic as I've never brought any good luck. But that's how I got stuck with my name.

One of my earliest memories is of flying through the air and crash-landing in a muddy puddle. My sister Samy had been running along pushing me in my pram and hit a kerb. Over went the pram and out I flew. I've been told that I was so fat I bounced really well and only got a few scratches. Years later I was knocked off my motorbike by a Datsun pickup truck and didn't bounce quite as well. My favourite toy was a big golliwog and a plastic sit-on locomotive bought from the Post Office to commemorate my no longer crapping my pants or, to put it more genteelly, when I grew out of nappies.

My first drawings were copies of my dad's drawings, ducks mostly. He'd draw all kinds of birds and animals on hardboard, then cut them out with a fretsaw for us when we were little. When I was about two or three, he grasped my hand and showed me how best to hold a pencil, with the thumb and index finger together, and the first finger much higher, sharply bent to act as a kind of shock absorber – a style I still automatically adopt and find best for sketching. Then he'd slowly follow an imaginary line and, lo and behold, a creature would appear magically before me. He would make us jigsaws of birds, animals and fish, all connected together with leaf shapes, which is how I learned to recognise many of the trees and plants in the countryside.

During my interviews with the Scotland Yard detectives they asked several times about where I thought my artistic talent had come from and if anyone else in my family had any artistic ability. I always replied that I was the only one with any artistic talent, if talent is what it was. I said this because, as I saw it, they might have tried to arrest the other members of my family as well. In truth, my dad can draw very well, mostly engineering drawings and such like, which he did at his job in Bolton Tech where he worked for many years. Mum can make fine lace, something she learned as a child from her Welsh granny. My sister Samy used to make her own fashions in the 1970s to a professional standard.

My brothers have all worked for the local council in one capacity or another since leaving school and haven't really had time for art and such. My eldest brother retired last year after 43 years and between them they have over 120 years' service to Bolton Council. They are all pretty handy, but not very arty. They can, however, tie trout and salmon flies as good as you'll see, and my brother Arthur knows history as well as any expert I've met. And I've met quite a few. My brother George Richard has had a lifelong interest in photography and has a good eye for it. He develops and prints his own work. The little I know of photography I've learnt from him.

My own photographic interest is mostly in connection with astronomy. As with most people, Patrick Moore's *The Sky at Night* was compulsory viewing. For Christmas one year I got a 4-inch mirror with the plans needed to build a telescope. I know it's not every child's idea of a Christmas present but I was well satisfied, though the building of the telescope would have been beyond me without my brother's help. It was through this telescope that I first got to see the rings of Saturn and Jupiter's moons. An added bonus was that it was a great excuse to stay up late.

Although I'm pretty low-tech – even texting is a labour – I've always found such things as gyroscopes, microscopes and all manner of scientific instruments a big draw. My first brush with colour was when I reflected the spectrum onto my hands from a prism I managed to get from a broken pair of binoculars. I had the idea once of inventing invisible paint by mixing all the elemental colours together to produce 'light paint' that would make things disappear. All I got was muddy sludge.

When I was five and about to start school, this obsession with colour almost proved fatal. I used to go to town on Saturday afternoons with my mum. My favourite shop was a toy stall in the old Market Hall. This was where I would buy the latest additions for my farm – plastic animals, hay ricks, pig sties, tractors. Hundreds of them were laid out on long shelves. I never knew which to buy next. This particular day my eyes lighted upon, of all things, a kaleidoscope. The stall holder, a big fat man in a white apron, not unlike my own reflection these days, handed it down to me. A twist of the wrist, seeing all those colours and shapes form, disperse and form again in endless designs, and it was a must-have. For the next few days the kaleidoscope became my eye. Walking along, looking like a Cyclops, I was oblivious to everything around me. This state of affairs came to an abrupt end one Sunday morning when I walked off the top stairs. That was it for the kaleidoscope. I later found out Dad had stood on it and into the bin it went.

I fell top to bottom and remember nothing of it, but, apparently, didn't get so much as a scratch. Our family doctor, a cranky Scotsman, reckoned I must have landed on my head thus avoiding any lasting damage. He was, and I don't think he would mind me saying this, a most unusual doctor. If any of us was unwell, he would arrive and shout through the letter box, 'Am I too late?' Then he'd come in and start playing with the dog, rolling around on the floor till he remembered what he'd come for. Dad used to say that he'd qualified in London during the Blitz by a unique method. When Harley Street was bombed, he found a blank doctor's certificate blowing along the street, filled in his name and hung it on his wall. Before that, said Dad, he'd been a butcher's boy on a bicycle.

My other calamities in pursuit of 'science' in pre-school days were a broken finger received when contemplating how best to stop a gyroscope, and almost setting myself on fire with a magnifying glass. Biology, meanwhile, proved nearly fatal for my mum when she slipped on a newt at the bottom of the stairs. I had lost it from my plastic fish tank two days earlier, but was frightened to admit to a rogue newt on the loose.

Still on the animal subject, some years later, when I was eight or nine, I happened to see an edition of a weekly paper called *Cage & Aviary Birds*. In those days, in the classified ads, they had Canadian timber wolves for sale and all manner of exotic creatures – all put paid to by the Dangerous Wild Animals Act of 1976. Somehow I got it into my head that a cormorant for fishing would be a good idea. Jacques Cousteau's Sunday evening programme, *The Undersea World of Jacques Cousteau*, was blamed for that one. I got my dad to ring a place listed in the classifieds to enquire, 'How much would a cormorant cost?' He reckoned the man wanted £1,000 and, by the way, did I know that cormorants were 6 feet tall and very angry birds. All bullshit, I thought. I'd seen cormorants on holiday. But £1,000 was too much. It didn't occur to me that the price was also bullshit.

A more successful animal exercise – I think it may have fallen into the 'creepy creature' bracket for some people – was my venture into beekeeping. I've always been interested in insects, mostly in relation to their seemingly effortless ability to hover. All flying creatures are a wonder, but I think insects particularly so. I used to collect butterfly eggs, mainly cabbage whites and tortoiseshells. I'd look after the caterpillars, feed them up to pupate, then watch them hatch and release a new generation. Butterflies led to bees. At such an early age, I wasn't allowed to 'have' any, so I'd resort to catching bumblebees in a pop bottle. To me, at seven, some of those bumblebees looked as big as a mouse.

I wasn't allowed a beehive till I was about nine. My brothers helped me build it from some plans I found in a library book. I bought a colony of bees from a local keeper after I had demonstrated that I wasn't afraid of them and knew the basics. They cost me an old 10 shillings, so it must have been just before decimalisation. My brother Ted knew the bee man. They were in the same fishing club at Eagley Mills where he had his first job after school. Eagley Mills was a 150-year-old cotton mill that was on its last legs when my brother went to work there. The mill buildings were all decayed and overgrown, so it was a fantastic place for kids to explore, with the added attraction of being a bit dangerous. It was also a wildlife haven, full of birds' nests, frogs, dragonflies and – my favourites –

big water beetles with iridescent blue borders. For some reason, the dark red and yellow banded dragonflies always reminded me of the choppers I'd see on the TV flying into Vietnam.

Beyond the overgrown banks and streams was an old ruin of a paper mill, complete with a chimney stack sprouting grass and willow saplings. One time, around Bonfire Night, I had the idea of standing inside the fire hole and setting off a rocket. The firework fizzed, the whole place filled up with smoke and up it shot inside the dark chimney. A massive flash and boom. And down came what must have been 100 years' worth of soot, leaving me ankle-deep in it, black as a crow.

The paper mill had been out of production since the end of the nineteenth century and had later been used as a dyeing place for the cotton mills at Eagley. It was neoclassical in design, rustic in the main working part, but with grand offices made of finely cut stone in good style, as picturesque as any castle or abbey, just as worthy of holding on to and far more relevant to our common history. Years later, when I was in the process of making a few Benin bronzes of circa seventeenth to eighteenth century, I needed some period wrought iron. Benin bronze casters would inlay certain parts of their works with iron, namely the eyes and the tribal marks. These would decay and, from my observations of actual pieces in the British Museum, which has by far the most comprehensive collection of Benin art – though the Museum of Liverpool also has a nice collection and, being more local, is the one I've seen more of – these iron inlays usually display the 'ropey' trademark of wrought as opposed to cast iron. I'd noticed that the old gates and railings around that old paper mill were all of this material, and more than once searched the grounds with a metal detector for pieces to use in my castings.

The Eagley Mills are now apartments. Its filled-in lodges and mill stores are a car park. Even the old school house is a 'conversion'. This was my first school. It had originally been built for the mill workers' kids by the first owner of Eagley, a man called Chadwick. He was a town benefactor and for his troubles is commemorated by a particularly glum monument in the 'piazza' in front of Bolton Town Hall – all frock coat, stovepipe hat and sideburns, on a heavily leaded bronze statue with a flaky black finish. Leading a bronze is accepted practice as it gives a better flow of metal through the mould, better detail pickup and less gas porosity. But the downside, if overdone, is a crappy surface. It doesn't lend itself to chasing for a high-class finish. So I suppose 'you pays your money and you takes your choice' in your monuments and your immortality.

Chadwick was a great Victorian collector of Egyptian artefacts. The core collection of Bolton Museum's Egyptology department is his old collection. It eventually became one of the best provincial Egyptian collections in the country and is well worth a visit. The whole collection – Egypt, the art gallery and the natural history collection, along with the aquarium – is all first-class and a royally good day's worth. I first remember going there on my first school trip. School, when you start, is a traumatic time for many children and I was no exception. My mum worked full-time and as nursery places weren't available I was looked after by my aunt during the week. I think she must have pampered me because Eagley Infants was somewhere I really didn't want to be. So much so, that after a few weeks of struggling to persuade me not to throw a wobbly every morning, it was arranged that one of the teachers, Mrs Hilton, who passed by on the way to school in her dark blue Ford Anglia, would pick me up. I didn't have much answer to this tactic and had to accept my fate. I can well remember climbing into the back of that car as it set off down the road, kneeling on the back seat and waving to my aunt, side by side with a nodding bulldog that always looked as if it was having a laugh at me. My daily wobbly thus backfired.

As a result of this lift to school, I was always the first to arrive. The rooms were single storey with high ceilings and huge timber

A-frames in the roof space, which I imagined would be similar to a ship. My time there is mostly unremembered, except for a spiteful old witch called Miss Petrie and a large sycamore – or as I preferred to know it, a 'spinning jenny tree' – at the top of the field that was our playground where we would gather to listen to a never seen cuckoo in the spring. The tree we named in Miss Petrie's honour. At playtime, we would pee on it, thus making our own version of a 'pee-tree'.

My only other memory of my time at Eagley Infants was of realising for the first time that my ability at drawing was different from most of the other children. I had taken a book to school on Friday, which was Designated Toy Day. I suppose this was a bit odd, for there I sat with my book amongst Action Men, toy cars and Sindy dolls. But as far as I was concerned this was no ordinary book. It was bought as a birthday gift for my brother Arthur, and he gave it to me. It was *The Book of the Horse*, full of photo illustrations of horses of all kinds, showing them at rest and in action. Inside the cover I always had a dozen or so sheets of cartridge paper and would sit and ingest the pictures, then set about copying them.

I could read before school, but I wasn't at that time much interested in what the texts had to say. The pictures spoke for themselves. Drawing away, copying the pictures as best I could, my teacher, the kindly Mrs Hilton, stood at my side and took an interest in these drawings. At home time, she mentioned them to my mum, but Mum was well aware already that I could do horses that looked like horses, instead of 'tables with a head' as she would say. By the age of 10 or 11, my drawing style was more or less as good as it was to get, and hasn't really improved since.

This has been a common thread in all my efforts. I seem to reach a certain level of competence pretty quickly, then lose interest and want to try something more challenging. This, I suppose, is why I've done almost every style and medium in art. But, as I told the detectives at my interviews, this has resulted in my efforts not being quite as good as they might have been if I had stuck at fewer things instead of being an example of the old saying: 'Jack of all trades and master of none.' This isn't false modesty. I don't believe I'm quite the Jack, nor the master, but probably something in between. The headmistress came to look at my horse pictures and pronounced them excellent. She had all the kids look at them, much to my embarrassment. She was what Benny Hill would probably have described as a 'big woman'. Mum told me years later that I had commented on her 'big muscles' when I first started school, something I can't say I recall. But they must have made quite an impression.

To get back to my artwork, I've always seemed to draw in more of an adult manner, not the usual childlike style. Even from my earliest efforts. It's been said many times that artists, and I'm thinking particularly of L. S. Lowry, whose efforts look childish to most people at first glance, only do such work because they 'can't draw'. This is a misconception. Lowry was an excellent draughtsman and this underpins all his work. But he chose to show his subject in a manner that he thought best conveyed the 'spirit' of his personal vision. Often this is much more difficult to achieve than merely producing a photo-like 'real picture'. Any art school can churn out students capable of such works. It's a case of almost mechanical production and had been perfected by the nineteenth century. Artists of the twentieth century had no interest in competing with photography, and this alternative way of seeing spanned what is now considered some of the greatest art, much of it childlike, but no worse for that.

My excuse for those early drawings in an accurate style was that I just drew what I saw before me. Most people say they are hopeless at drawing. I think the main reason for this is that when confronted with a subject and a blank page they try to see the whole page at once. What I like to do, instead, is to pick a point in the subject to be drawn – any point, preferably the lightest or darkest – and draw that bit, then another bit radiating out from it, always keeping in mind the comparative size, distance and angle from its neighbours. Never think of the whole or what it is you are trying to depict – just shapes and proportions. Then, when all the bits are done, stand back and there it is – or not. After that it's just a matter of practice. I would spend hours drawing and trying to model all manner of things, but the horse has always had a special place.

Contrary to most expert opinions, I have always thought sculpture more difficult to do well than painting. In my case, at least, a painting can capture a mood or emotion more easily than a sculpture. To get a feeling or a breath of life into sculpture – which is, after all, a monochrome experience, so it engages fewer of the senses – requires a greater effort. Well that's my way of explaining the case for sculpture, though I'm probably biased as sculpture is what I like most, and the horse in sculpture most of all. For me it encompasses the most dynamic structure, bone, flesh, tension and movement of all subjects, except the human form.

The first time I recall seeing a real horse was around the age of six. Until I was seven, Mum and Dad would take us on day trips to the coast during the school holidays. It's only an hour or so. They would pack our picnic in the morning and off we'd trundle like ducks and drakes with their brood in tow. This particular day found us in Southport, across the Ribble Estuary from the biggie resort of Blackpool, and not far away from the great port city of Liverpool. Dad got the deckchair man to put out a few chairs and a windbreak. I myself never managed to get to sit in a deckchair, but was plonked down in the sand on a towel with my sister Sharon and charged with making sure she didn't scuttle off. This was achieved by my inspired idea of tying her to the windbreak with my snake belt. The 'S'-shape fastener seemed to confound her attempts to undo it, her tiny fingers unable to contend with the powerful elastic of the dreaded snake belt – something I knew only too well as those things had been cutting me in half for ages. I managed to lose at least three of them only for some kind relative to buy me a new one, usually attached to horrible-looking short pants. Boys wore them until starting at the big school at 11, something that I believe is no longer so. The 'posh' kids of today wouldn't stand for it. I'm suddenly feeling a bit old!

Anyhow, there I sat, looking out to sea – or should that be looking out *for* sea. Anyone familiar with Southport will know what I mean. The sea goes so far out at low tide as to be almost beyond the horizon – well, to those under 3 feet tall, as I was then. All of a sudden a string of ants appeared in the distance. As I watched with interest, the ants grew larger and larger, until there in front of me were several huge horses complete with riders. The beasts were stamping and snorting with clouds of steam surrounding them. The most magnificent and largest of them was a grey whose name I was told was Samson. I didn't know the biblical Samson then, but the name suited him. I stood right up against him and looking up through the salty steam I could hear the great thing gasping like a pair of bellows. I can still clearly remember thinking at that moment that the nearest thing I'd seen to this was a Black Five steam loco on Bolton station. This horse made what I thought were similar sounds. The chomping, the heat, the steam, the definite sense of power, were all similar.

My dad was a self-professed expert horseman. He'd worked at Bradshaw Hall Farm as a kid when my gran and granddad worked at the Hall. He told us stories of an old horse there that lived into its thirties called Maggie. I have a picture of him with Maggie. She had been to France in World War One as a cavalry horse and was a rare survivor. It was my dad's job to ride the farm horses to the farrier before school, and then ride them back afterwards to the farm, bareback, with a switch out of a hedge. He had a word with the man who owned the horses on the beach and was renting them out for rides, an odd-looking fellow with a massive flat cap, hook nose and spindly little legs, tight pants, high boots and a baggy white shirt. With the order 'be careful you silly bugger' ringing in his ear from Mum, Dad mounted Samson and off he shot. In no time the giant Samson was ant-sized once more.

When they returned both of them were soaked and it was obvious they had been galloping through the surf. I stood there in awe of this great horse. Then, to my glee, the man with the big flat cap lifted me up and sat me in front of Dad. Holding onto the reins, I had Samson's mane looking forward between his twitching ears like gunsights. Then we started to move. I thought, 'Here we go.' But the horse just ambled along with his head swaying up and down. I'm sure he would have loved to get into top gear. Dad too. But with Mum being on watch, a walk was all I got. It was enough. I was hooked. Sitting there on Samson, I imagined I must look like the Duke of Wellington on his charger, Copenhagen, whom we always saw in Piccadilly Gardens in Manchester when getting the train to St Ives on holiday. Samson was that kind of horse.

After the holidays it was time to move schools and go up into the Juniors. School was no longer an intimidating place. In fact, it became more and more interesting. If only I'd had a bigger brain things might have come to something! My time at the Eagley Juniors lasted four years and was the most enjoyable time of my early life. The school was just two minutes from home. Even so, I was determined not to be the first to arrive each day, as had happened previously. More often than not, I was the last to run into the playground.

Just by the school was a defunct farmhouse with outbuildings, called Kay's Farm. We would always hurry past it as the year before the old farmer had met a sad and gruesome end. He had a little sawmill in the yard from which he supplied local shops with bundles of firewood. When I was a kid, most of the houses in and around Bolton still had coal fires and the wood chips would be used to light them. The saw was run by a pulley from a tractor flywheel, and my uncle, who was a qualified engineer, had already warned that the ratio between the flywheel and saw blade was too great, and that the blade might burst if put under pressure. For those who know such things, the noise it made was apparently much too loud. One Sunday afternoon, the blade burst and the farmer was killed. A piece of the blade knocked a chip out of the house around the corner from my mum and dad's – a quarter of a mile away! It's still there. So Kay's Farm had a scary reputation among the kids in Bromley Cross in the sixties. Today, all that is forgotten. The farm and its barn are now 'a des res in BX'.

Our headmaster was Mr Lee. His greatest concern was maintaining a scratch-free surface to the assembly hall's parquet floor onto which we would march and assemble every morning for prayers and a few of his pearls of wisdom, to the accompaniment of Holst's The Planets suite, or something from Mendelssohn, usually Fingal's bloody Cave, as our form tutor would call it. We got to know those tunes very well. I'm starting to hear them as I write.

My favourite lesson was the nature walk when the teacher would take us out into the countryside to collect specimens for the nature table. We would then paint the things we brought back and put them up on the classroom wall. I found this a relief from the mind-numbing arithmetic and English lessons. For me, maths and English were something you picked up as an aid to learning more important and interesting things. I've never really had a problem with maths, and know as much as I need, though anyone reading this book will know right away that I should have taken more notice of English at school.

I was most in my own element helping with the posters and making the labels for the nature table. I already knew the names of all the stuff we'd bring back – leaves, fungi, flowers and even the odd bird skull or owl pellet, along with last year's bird nests. These were the type of things I was most interested in. I wasn't alone in such interests and had quite a few mates who were equally keen. During the Easter holidays we would plan 'bird nesting' expeditions and set out early morning with our duffle bags stuffed with pop, packets of crisps and sandwiches, along with the obligatory binoculars and my bible, *The Observer's Book of Birds*. Somehow, our enthusiasm wavered as our food supply diminished, to the point where on the last bite of paste butty and swig of pop we unanimously voted for a suspension of our expedition until another day, and made our way home for tea.

I joined the RSPB at this time, aged seven, having read some stuff by Sir Peter Scott about his wildfowl endeavour at Slimbridge. At the time, I liked his paintings, though, later in life, I was less keen on his style. I still recall the address to which I sent off my postal order – The Lodge, Sandy, Beds. I don't know how much it cost but I remember that I had to redeem at least one savings book from the postmaster to afford it. I'd been a regular saver at the Post Office and would buy savings stamps to stick in my little red PO books whenever I had pocket money left over. Which was quite often compared to my little sister who burned her way through money like a thermal lance. I was never really materialistic, something I have continued not to be to this day. My letter to the RSPB was the kind of fawning letter you write if you're trying to get into a swish golf club. They replied and sent me my membership card entitling me to visit various reserves, the quarterly journal and my badge, which I still have – a hovering kestrel with the letters YOC beneath. The lady who had written to me pointed out that seven-year-olds weren't allowed to join the RSPB and that I was now in the Young Ornithologists' Club. So in it I was.

My brother Edward would occasionally concede to take me to lectures at the 'Bolton School' or the 'Tech' where such luminaries as Tony Soper and Chris Bonington would tell of their adventures and of natural history in general. I lapped it up. My brother was pretty inconsistent in these escorted trips and usually only took me when he was trying to get into 'the good books' at home.

Other treats from him – though I'm not sure that I've used the right word there – were when he took me fishing. The day would start at 4am when I would be grabbed by the ankles and dragged out of bed feet first to the order 'Get dressed, we're going fishing.' I'd put on my wellies and parka, then the fishing basket, folding net and a bundle of rods. I must have been robust as a kid because ahead of us was a two-mile walk to the Wayoh Reservoir, which in those days was a recommended brown trout water, though today it is all pikes and perch. We would walk through the lane in darkness, past Kay's Farm, as fast as my legs would carry me, then onto the road. The first bus to Edgworth was at 5.30am, so if we were later than usual I would hear it coming up the hill behind us. 'The bus is coming,' I'd squeak between panting steps, the fishing basket bumping the ground at each step. I always said this, and always got the same reply – 'We're walking it' – from the long legs in front, carrying only his Hardy bag and the best rod, which couldn't be trusted to me.

One painful memory of those times was when I managed to get a large treble hook stuck in my thumb. 'There's only one thing to do,' said brother Edward. I thought this meant a trip to casualty, a place I'd recently visited for stitches in my eyebrow from being hit with a golf club. Instead, out came a pair of pliers. 'Now this is going to hurt!' He proceeded to cut off the offending hook at its base, then pushed it through my thumb, and drew out the whole thing, barb first. To my amazement I didn't cry, though my bottom lip was almost chewed off. My bravery seemed to impress and my stock definitely rose after that. From then on, I got to go fishing much further afield and wasn't expected to be as much of a load carrier. More of a fisherman in my own right.

During all this fishing, looking for bird nests and the usual kids' stuff, along with school work, I was also pursuing my artistic efforts. It was at school that I made my first ceramic, under the strict supervision of the teacher. This first effort was a T-Rex and Godzilla hybrid, in black and red glaze. Over the time to come I was to produce a lot of ceramics. I eventually built up a fair knowledge of materials and techniques. Ceramic art is a fascinating subject, and so diverse. Surprisingly, much of it has developed along similar lines, even among divergent cultures and times, the Chinese contribution being the most outstanding and reaching what I think is the pinnacle of ceramic art, both in technique and design. Much of it has proved beyond me, though not for want of trying.

Pottery classes started out with what I thought of as 'Stone Age' thumb and coil pots, which, though a pleasant thing to do, held no interest for me. To which the teacher would comment, 'Shaun, remember that you had to crawl before you could walk.' At which point the Godzilla-Rex materialised from behind the jumper I had strategically placed on the table to hide my efforts. When it emerged from the kiln without exploding, as was forecast, I was allowed to do pretty much what I preferred. The Neolithic pottery was shelved.

My first copies of genuine pieces were done in ceramic a long time before I sold my first fake, or as I prefer to look on my work of this time, my first faithful copies in painting or sculpture. They were Victorian-style 'pot lids', usually white glaze earthenware, with an ill-fitting glaze and black lettering, mostly Gothic in style, used for such things as tooth powder and various creams of late nineteenth century date. The lids found a ready market for £5 –£10 each at the Sunday flea market at the Last Drop. No questions asked.

I'd been bought a small electric kiln for my twelfth birthday, along with a pottery crafts mail order catalogue. The materials to produce them were ridiculously cheap compared to what I could get for just one pot lid. I'd worked out how to make and colour them, along with the crackle glaze, so as to look authentic. Later on I would even go to the lengths of giving them a whirl in a gemstone tumbler I'd got to polish pebble and rock specimens from the Sloop Craft Market in St Ives, an old sail loft, full of hippies and craft workers. This gave a scratched and worn appearance, similar to those dug out of the cinders on the bottle tips, though the encrustations and iridescence you sometimes find was unachievable at that time. Years later, through trial and error – lots of error – I did manage to simulate such finishes for much older work. For the time being, my efforts were good enough and a good little earner. I eventually extended my 'bottle tip' range to the rarer clay pipe 'heads' – very quick and cheap to make. But for now, at eight or nine, I was getting to grips with the clay itself and learnt quite enough to be going on with.

My academic achievements weren't coming along as well. One or two of my classmates were steaming ahead of me. I didn't really have any trouble keeping up, I just couldn't be bothered and wished to do my own thing. Exams to me were merely a test of memory. My memory is fine, I thought, so let's do something else. This was obviously a silly outlook and something I've regretted. But, as my mum would always say to me, 'You'll please yourself, till you vex yourself.' So if you're reading this, and you're under 12, make sure you listen to your mum. If you're well over 12 and haven't quite hit your own mark, you'll know this already.

I've always been one to step out of the limelight, and always felt most at ease in the background at social events and such things. From the time of Mrs Rogers with the big muscles promoting my pictures at infant school to the journalists poking fun at me at the Crown Court, I've found exposure an ordeal. Another early example of my reticence was when we were doing a project at school about the Apollo moon landing of 1969. Somewhat convolutedly, this had led the teacher on to explorers, particularly Drake, who I think was something of a hero of his. Whatever project we would do, no matter how obscure or tenuous the connection, things would somehow end up in the sixteenth century and Francis Drake. This particular time we were to produce a large picture of Drake's ship, the *Revenge*, in action against the Armada, to be done on several stuck-together A1 sheets, about 7 feet by 5, by far the largest picture I'd seen outside a gallery, let alone had a hand in.

For the life of me, I couldn't see a connection between Drake bashing the Armada and one small step for mankind. But some of the teachers were a bit odd. The best part of the finished picture, though I say so myself, was the sky and sunset, complete with fire ships, all Turneresque and done by me. When the teacher came to look at our progress, I stood back and let my two friends take the compliments. One was my colour mixer, the other my brush holder, or so I saw them at the time as I'd been reading a book on Titian and his vast studio, and was of the mind that a painter should have his assistants, so I had mine.

Art books were something I would buy whenever money allowed, or ask for at birthdays and such. I didn't have a preference. Whatever I saw that took my interest. Sherratt & Hughes on St Anne's Square in Manchester had the best selection when I was a kid, although I can't recall how I knew this or who told me. This was where I bought one of my favourite books. It was a massive thing on the baroque artist Bernini, showing his great sculptures. I looked at them and thought 'I want to do such things', little realising the genius needed. To say nothing of a patron of the calibre of a Renaissance pope. I've always seen Bernini's work as the 'Gold Standard' in art, and he has remained my favourite artist. Seeing many of his things 'in the flesh', later in life, served only to confirm my belief that his body of work is the best.

The only artists I have actually met are two I have much respect for. The first was Barbara Hepworth and the other David Shepherd. With Hepworth, Mum and Dad had gone to St Ives when they were first married, and each and every year we would have our annual holiday there, the first two weeks in July, without fail. They would rent a house for us called Pelican Cottage, as close to the beach as it is possible to get – out the front door, 10 paces and onto the beach. The little harbour was full of fishing boats, some working and others decked in pennants for charter. Dad would take us all out tope fishing, which the advertising boards tied to the pier railings would describe as 'shark fishing', with a suitably toothy real-life shark 'smiling' at the tourists. Sometimes, it would be kept there for days and would go all wrinkly like a squashed beach ball.

At the start of the holiday, we would set off first thing in the morning for the train to Manchester, then across in a taxi to Piccadilly station, which was still dark and sooty from 100 years of steam, though by this time the steamers had gone for scrap and it was all diesel. We had two compartments in the old-style carriage; the ones with a corridor, 'Reserved' signs on the windows and pictures of locomotives framed above the seats. The journey would take all day, and was one of the best parts of the whole two weeks as far as I was concerned. The very best part was the change of engines at Bristol. One of my childhood heroes was Brunel and by the age of eight or so I knew this was the hub of his Great Western Railway. As soon as we stopped at Temple Meads, I'd jump out of the carriage and run up to the front of the train, hoping to get there in time to watch the engineer get down onto the track, uncouple the Deltic, then watch it rumble away. Minutes later in would roll its replacement. These were Western Class diesel locos, some in BR blue, others in burgundy and black, with nameplates such as 'Western Challenger' or 'Victory'. The power in them made my eyeballs shake as the vibration came up through the platform, and the driver in his oily hat, leaning his elbows on the open window, would peer down from on high, looking suitably imperial for such a job. Then the horn blast would blow me out of my trance, a guard's whistle and back I jumped in the carriage just as it clonked into motion. Dad and my older brothers, meanwhile, would give us anxiety attacks by playing 'last on' as the train gained speed. We'd arrive late in the evening. Something for supper. And off to bed.

The two weeks flew by – fishing, searching the rock pools, touring the town. St Ives, as almost everyone knows, had been an artists' colony for many years. We would visit the Sloop Craft Market, a large sail loft turned Arts and Crafts market in the sixties, with paintings, jewellery, all manner of arty stuff, and loads of Bob Dylan and Twiggy lookalikes smoking 'strange-looking cigars'. I could see them at night from the bedroom window, sat around a campfire on the beach. The 'St Ives Sioux', my dad called them. I would watch the artists at their easels, too, painting the boats and views for ages, and in my silent thoughts I'd be criticising their choice of colour.

Many of them didn't seem to follow the norm in this respect – cold against warm, complementary colour balances, tones, and such. Even as a kid I knew what was needed to get a 'proper look'. I decided to have a go myself and plonked myself down, sitting on a big iron anchor halfway down the granite breakwater. Feeling a bit self-conscious, I managed to get my mum to buy me a sailor's peak cap from the gift shop that was a bit too big, and hid under this whilst I painted the ships in the harbour and the wrinkly shark.

One day I noticed an 'old lady' stood over my shoulder, watching me, as I had watched others. She reminded me of my music teacher, Mrs Griffin, who was very much like her namesake. Once, she caught me eating in class and screeched, 'What are you up to boy?' To which I replied, 'I'm having a picnic, Miss.' This wasn't me being flippant. I really was eating a bar of chocolate called a 'Picnic'. Admittedly, I could have worded my reply better. I've never been very articulate, off the cuff. That encounter resulted in a whack, so I was now rather wary of the lady at my shoulder.

She was interested in my shark pictures and one in particular – the shark with a toothy grin, hanging tail up, its head resting on a lobster pot and some nets. Not wanting to upset another dragon, I said she could have it and off she went. I had hoped she might buy it, but no offer of cash came my way. 'She's famous you know,' someone said. 'It's Barbara Hepworth the artist.' I didn't know then who Barbara Hepworth was and have since wondered what she did with that picture. Thirty or so years later, I did a copy of one of her small sculptures, a goose, which was part of the Met's case against me. I hope she wouldn't have been too upset at my effort. I did try to do it justice.

I also did some copies once of an artist called Naum Gabo. He was Barbara Hepworth's friend in St Ives. The sale of one of these copies was a bit of a calamity. His works were mostly constructions of one kind or another, and for this particular one I'd managed to get hold of a collection of 1930s celluloid, with card, string and plywood, slotted together in the manner of a Gabo. I'd had an offer for it from a London dealer, but on the way it somehow broke, so I had to detour to a B&Q warehouse for a tube of glue, stick it back together and reapply some bits. These hung around for an hour or so until the glue set. The dealer took delivery, none the wiser, and my running repairs remained undetected. So, as they say, 'all's well that ends well'.

Cornwall also has some interesting prehistoric sites, standing stones and such like, to say nothing of its industrial and mining sites. All these would warrant a visit at some point during our stay. I've done quite a few Bronze Age artefacts over the years, with varying amounts of success, from early attempts at socket axes in bronze, which are about as simple as lost wax casting gets, to quite elaborate gold and electrum work. These were mostly things called 'dress fasteners', small croissant-shaped articles with a dished circular piece on each end, used as a fastening toggle for cloaks. I've seen them for sale at reputable dealers cast in solid gold. But those are almost always Victorian copies, or later cheap shots at such things. Making them properly required very skilled Bronze Age gold-smithing, and took every bit of effort from me, being only an amateur smith. They consist of several joined pieces, all hollow sheet gold, usually around 14 carat, alloyed with silver and very little copper, but with significant trace elements that are particular to this age.

Another much rarer piece characteristic of the Bronze Age in Britain, and even more so of the Iron Age, is the torc – a large neck ring made of metal. These I haven't had a go at, but I did once make an even rarer piece of ancient British goldwork, a ribbed beaker with a lost ring handle, pretty battered, as if it had come up under the plough – always a favourite look and one the dealers loved to see as this meant it must be genuine. The most difficult job there proved to be making the large sheet of gold from which to raise the said beaker. They have a very modern look to them, with a simple shape and a corrugated surface. The corrugations I rubbed in with a piece of deer antler, so the surface would look authentic under magnification.

Some of the most difficult goldwork to imitate is that of ancient Greece. It's almost impossibly minute and a real challenge. One of the last things I remember doing at junior school was a project about ancient Greece and its politics, which mostly went in one ear and out the other. But my ears and eyes pricked up at the slideshow. Our teacher had been to Athens and showed us slides of the Acropolis and its ruined monuments. I'd seen pictures of the Parthenon before, but these images, flashed large on the wall, were exciting.

The main feature of this school project was the story of the 'Elgin Marbles' as they were always referred to. I believe it's more correct nowadays to call them the Parthenon Sculptures. Whatever their proper title, I was impressed by these things. I already knew they were in London, not Athens – my ever-expanding collection of books had made sure of that. So I had the idea of asking my brothers if they would take me to the British Museum, they being old enough to be allowed to travel to London. I knew my brother Ted had already been there and, to my complete surprise, he agreed, with one proviso – that I got someone else to pay for both of us.

Just a week after starting the long summer school break, it was my eleventh birthday, and this was put forward by me as a good reason for everyone to contribute to my trip in place of cards or presents. The date was set for August and, come the day, off we went. Perhaps August wasn't such a good idea. The place was jam-packed with people, all intent, as I saw it, on preventing me getting a good look at anything. We went in, turned left and into the Egyptian gallery. It was like Aladdin's cave with too much to see at once. The granite and basalt sculptures were especially impressive. Even then, though I didn't know exactly how they were made, I knew they must have been really difficult to do in such hard stone. The head of Ramesses II looked even bigger to me as an 11-year-old than it does now, towering over everything.

Next it was a walk through the Assyrian Gallery. Wall tall reliefs, similar to cartoon strips, though much better, with massive winged bulls covered in script. All very mysterious. Little did I imagine then that my dealings in such things would lead me to where I am at present. Then, at last, the object of our trip – the Elgin Marbles – laid out before us in a huge, almost empty room. At the end of the room I noticed a horse's head and went to take a closer look. Though pretty battered, it was a fantastic thing, much more impressive, I thought, than the human bits. It reminded me of Samson at Southport and I had the immediate urge to make one of these, too. By the time I'd been through as much of the museum as time would allow I must have had at least 100 years' worth of work in my head. Needless to say, having the desire to produce such fantastic things as I saw that day, and actually being able to do so, required 20 years of patient trial and effort. Even then, there was more failure than success.

The return home was spent looking through the books and pamphlets I had bankrupted myself in buying. Still, it was one of the best days I could remember. Later, I found out that my brother Ted was already planning such a trip and that I had come up with the perfect excuse for him to get out of paying for it. His own plan was to see an exhibition of David Shepherd.

I only found out about this when we arrived at Euston station and the taxi driver was told to go not to the British Museum, but to this gallery. I was none too pleased. But when I got there I was glad to see these paintings, mostly of African animals, but also a large portrait of a steam loco in an old engine shed, all mist and sunlight streaming into shadows. Quite wonderful. My brother Ted bought a signed print of it, the real thing requiring much deeper pockets than we had. From there we raced to the British Museum.

V.

The wrong direction

As far as art was concerned, my interest so far had been mostly to do with ancient history, the stuff I'd seen in museums, mostly sculpture, the more dramatic the better. The only exception to this was Picasso. His new way of seeing was something that fascinated me. What I liked about Picasso was that his work seemed thoroughly new for its time, some might say crude or, as in Lowry's case, childlike, but in both artists' work, and especially in Picasso's, here was someone who was quite capable of painting and drawing in the best style and tradition, but who was trying something new. That takes time, combined with huge effort and continuous practice. First he built his foundation, then he placed his 'modern' work on it. It's something many of his contemporaries couldn't or, in most cases, wouldn't make the effort to do.

I see this everywhere in contemporary art, and this lack of 'beef' is what I think has put me off much of it. If an artist hasn't got great facility, that isn't cause to dismiss them – if the vision and idea is there. But many artists of the present aren't 'bothered' about acquiring better skills. In my opinion, they won't last. To my mind, great art combines vision and ability, and if either is lacking then that relegates it to the second division. Being a struggler in this division myself, not through any lack of artistic ability – I can make a reasonable effort and have some knowledge of most styles and techniques – the problem in my case is lack of new vision. This can probably be put down to my early habit of soaking up too much of what had already been, instead of just getting out the paints and having a go without those preconditioned images in my head of the work of the Egyptians, Greeks, Italians and so on.

Anyway, at the age of 11 I started at the big school – Turton Comp – in September with some relief. At last I was able to wear long trousers, instead of those bloody silly shorts combined with long stockings. If for no other reason, I was glad to be there. When the school year began, the builders were still hard at work giving the place a make-over, knocking out walls and painting everything purple, blue and orange, in honour of its promotion from secondary modern to a bold, new, one-size-fits-all comprehensive. All seventies and cool it must have been, because the headmaster, I'm sorry, headteacher, said so.

The school year started with us being divided into forms and allocated a classroom. By happy coincidence, my form classroom was the pottery room, complete with kiln, clay bins, a potter's wheel and all the necessaries. Our form tutor, Miss Pickles, was one of the art teachers, a young woman with big afro hair and a late flower power wardrobe who reminded me of the St Ives Sioux and would have fitted right in amongst them. Thanks to my brother Ted and sister Samy, I was pretty well up on fashion for a kid, although by the early seventies my brother was a bit old for dressing up, I thought, and definitely in the old codger bracket. He would only have been 21, but when you're 11, old is over 17, isn't it?

I have to admit that I too was becoming a bit of a clothes horse. At our first-year Christmas party I was the height of fashion with a Budgie shirt, tank top, two-tone pants, patent leather platforms and a Crombie jacket. I must have looked a right berk, but didn't think so at the time. Smoking and anything other than fizzy pop were definitely out, although some of the older lads in the sixth form flouted these rules heroically I thought – and the sixth form girls, according to our teacher, were 'showing a bit too much'. Admirably so, I also thought.

Most of the staff were very old-fashioned even for that time. In the weeks before the party, our PE teacher had us practising ballroom dancing. I've always hated dancing, having two left feet. I always think men, or boys, as I was then, look stupid, and girls, conversely, look so right and elegant. Well, most of them. I hope that doesn't sound patronising to anyone or, God forbid, sexist. At home, there would have been no chance of any thoughts of male superiority for me as a kid. I wouldn't have dared. My sister packed a fair wallop. So it's just as well I don't have any such hang-ups.

The dancing in PE class was, I think, an embarrassment to one and all. Its only saving grace was that most of us lads thought it was a chance for a squeeze, though the teacher appeared to be related to a hawk with his sharp eyes and even sharper tongue. Another thing causing me anxiety was my mum's insistence on providing a large slice of the catering. The teachers had instructed everyone to bring something for the class party and we were all to ask our parents to contribute something. Unknown to me, Mum, in her usual take-charge mode, had rung the school and volunteered to do a big spread. Miss Pickles drove out to see her at work and between them they set in motion Red Face Day for me.

Mum worked at a large mail order firm in Bolton. She was the Catering Manager, required to provide over 1,000 meals a day and to cook personally for the management who all dined in an oak-panelled room complete with several ugly mugs in gilt frames gazing down from the walls. The building was one of the last great cotton mills to be built in the town, going up in the late twenties, complete with a fine copper dome. I was well acquainted with it. When younger, I would go with Mum when she was required on Saturday mornings. The security man and woman would take me on a ride all over the place in one of the big wicker skips, so I knew its every corner.

On the day of the party, Miss Pickles collected a carful of trifles, flans, savouries and all manner of food – filling boot and back-seats, floor to roof lining – which I later saw being scoffed by some very unsavoury characters, namely half the teaching staff at the school. Whilst Miss Pickles was there, Mum piled on my agony by showing her a picture I had recently painted – an oil painting of a David Shepherdesque snow leopard in a mountain landscape, just about my first good effort. It was hanging in her office, frameless. I prefer frameless pictures. Frames just seem to me to enhance bad pictures and distract from those that don't need them. Miss Pickles commented on its excellence, something that wasn't easy to achieve as she was a good artist herself. At school that year, she made a terracotta of an old lady sitting on a rustic bench with a basket of apples, about 14 inches tall and a fine piece of work. On seeing the feast and hearing the compliments on my painting, I went my usual shade of vermilion, and thought to strangle my mum as soon as I got home.

Mum was always unimpressed by TV chefs. 'All in a flap over 30 covers,' she'd say. Her cooking is first-class and at work I think she was the most popular person in the building. At Christmas she would receive huge numbers of cards. One year I counted them – 734. I've never known anyone get more than that. I'm lucky to get six. When the owner drove over from his HQ in Sheffield, she would do something special. He was a little Mr Magoo figure in a Silver Cloud, with a liveried chauffeur more toffee-nosed than his boss. His daughter had a Lamborghini that sounded better to me than a symphony orchestra. I thought, 'What a waste on such an old biddy.' At the time, she would have been younger than I am now. It's funny how youth distorts your view.

As things turned out, I didn't end up strangling Mum. As a result of the praise from the teacher for my painting, and the good feed all round, my dance partner of these last weeks seemed rather impressed with me, despite my crushing her feet. She was easily the best-looking girl in the class, so I was satisfied with that.

Schoolwork was still going well. All interesting stuff – physics, chemistry and biology, French and German, though I would have preferred Greek, Latin and Hieroglyphs. My favourite teacher in those early days was definitely Mr Best, the maths teacher, who was kindly, white-haired and old. In his first maths lesson he instructed us how to relax, resting our tired heads on our desks for 20 minutes in silence, almost falling asleep in the process, a great introduction that got everyone on his side from the beginning. His classes were always fun and we learned without realising.

We had some interesting teachers. Mr Nuttal had been a desert rat and if one of us could slip in a reference to World War Two, the rest of the lesson could be spent gazing pleasantly out of the windows or passing messages while he wittered on about his and 'Monty's' part in winning the war. My dad was too young to be in the 8th Army Desert Rats, but was later in the 1st Army in North Africa. He once told me to ask Mr Nuttal what a 'desert rose' was. Mr Nuttal coughed and mumbled back something inaudible. 'My dad said it was an improvised crap house,' I blurted out. I got the whack for that. But a restrained one. I think it amused Mr Nuttal as much as the rest.

The two years of art classes I had at Turton Comp were the only formal lessons in the subject I have had. Art lessons in a classroom environment never really appealed to me. My own way of doing things was to find something that took my interest or, more often than not, that seemed to find me, then read all I could about it and study the way I thought it would have been done. The creative side of it was less important at this time. It was more the challenge of being able to get as close to the standard set by 'Great Art', or my perception of it, as my ability would allow. On completion, I would usually stand back and see a thousand things wrong with my effort. These failures only spurred me on, and I was determined to improve, match and one day, I hoped, surpass the masterpieces that held my fascination. In the years to come, I may occasionally have approached that level, but I can't honestly say I ever bettered it.

Most of our art classes involved copying pictures and drawings of one kind or another. 'Your own style can wait until you know what you're about,' was said more than once. I suppose there's something in that. I once incurred a teacher's wrath by copying one of his copies – a blue period Picasso of a beggar. He'd been slaving away at it for what seemed to me like ages. To my eye, the teacher just didn't get the flattened perspective and had tickled the paint to death with his incessant meddling. Whenever I start a copy of something I feel it best to run through the salient points of the piece in my head, get the stages prioritised, then blast away at it without much further thought. In this way, I hope to capture the spontaneity of the original. Many times it would go wrong and into the bin it would fly. Any attempt at correction only made things worse. A new attempt is always the best solution. Just write off the time to experience.

The 'Picasso' was our teacher's pride and joy. He hung it on the wall, framed up, complete with a museum-style label beside it, and it looked quite impressive. Some time later, I copied this picture in our lunchtime, quite a long break, 11.50–1.45. My version was a pastel, done from the same book used by 'Sir', but more quickly. Unlike him, I signed it 'Picasso' and left it there by the clay bins. These were used by one and all as an ashtray and were invariably full of fag ends. The next day, on returning to school after lunch – I usually went home for my lunch, as our house was just two minutes away across the footy pitch – someone had pinned up my picture next to the art teacher's. To make matters worse, they'd added a strip of paper with an arrow pointing to my picture with the words 'This is genuine' written on it in bold felt tip and another pointing to the teacher's saying 'This is crap.' It was nothing to do with me, and something I didn't agree with, but I got the blame for the prank. I even pointed out, Sherlock Holmes style, that the writing hand wasn't mine. All to no avail.

Shortly after, the art department decamped to the old Infant School, the one to which I'd been transported every morning in the back of Mrs Hilton's Ford Anglia. This new location, and the enduring spite of 'Sir', was as good an excuse as I needed to dump art classes. Some of what I'd learnt from Miss Pickles in pottery class must have stuck with me, though, because in the years ahead my ceramics were amongst the best sellers in my range of copies and fakes.

Over the years, I've tried most styles, from Chinese to post-war art pottery, with mixed results. When I was working on getting the clay body right for the Gauguin Faun, I remembered the clay bins in my old form room at school. At the time, I was trying to get an effect that I'd noticed was common to all Gauguin's ceramics – tiny pinhole blemishes, looking like oozing volcanoes, very small, but distinctive of his stuff. Years before, I'd seen similar effects on ware coming out of the kiln at school. Pinholing in ceramics is common enough, but these were very Gauguinesque and they were the result of cigarette ash in the clay. I knew this for sure because the 'fag ash kids', as we called the smokers, would always use our clay bins as ashtrays. There was a big dust extractor fan in the wall above and they used it to whisk away the telltale pong before the deputy head got wind of it. Every lunchtime, he would prowl the corridors like a bloodhound, sniffing as he went. So I used cigarette ash in the Gauguin Faun to help it on its way.

Around this time I was bought an electric pottery kiln. It was what most established potters would call a sampler kiln, only about 1 cubic foot in volume and top loading, so pretty basic. As its name suggests, it was usually used to fire quick test pieces for bigger projects. But I was thrilled at the possibility of making whatever I liked when the spirit moved me, instead of under the direction of others. This attitude wasn't anything to do with me being bolshy. It's just that, for me, the freedom to work to my own timetable is the only way I can produce work to a satisfactory standard. My top loader was put to good use, and with only two refits of new wire elements, lasted me 30 years. It even fired the Gauguin Faun as one of its last projects in 1993, at the grand old age of 31. It was also the knackered kiln in the garden shed into which Sergeant Tango delved, much to the detriment of his suit.

The first 'products' to come out of that kiln were the pot lids I mentioned earlier. These had suggested themselves during one of my short-lived hobbies. In the early seventies there was a craze for 'bottle digging' on disused tips of the Victorian age, easy to dig and mostly cinders. We would shovel away in these places looking for the said pot lids, along with stoneware bottles and broken clay pipes, all of which found a ready market at the town's junk shops and fairs. The pot lids especially brought more then than they do today, which, allowing for inflation, particularly 1970s inflation, is quite a lot. They are, though, hard to find intact, and I soon tired of wielding a shovel in hope. One time, the digging almost proved fatal to me, which was my cue to leave it alone.

One of the best sites around was dug commercially for fire cinders, which were then used in the building trade. A digger would scoop out bucketfuls of these cinders and dump them on a vibrating mesh. The fine cinder ash would fall through onto a conveyor belt and be whisked away to a waiting truck, while the waste, and all the 'treasures' in it, would bounce down the mesh and fall onto the waste heap. Standing there was like watching the tide going out to reveal a treasure gallery. Slowly, things would emerge, followed by a mad dash for whatever had come to light.

I was usually preoccupied with my thoughts and missed a lot in the mad dash. Instead, after the digger man had left, I would go back to the cliff face left by the excavator and deliberately collapse it, exposing the best stuff before the next day's work. To undermine the cliff, I dug away at the bottom, and the next second, I was frozen solid in ash, with just my arm sticking out. Otherwise, I was completely buried. If I'd been alone, I wouldn't be writing this now. No jest. You would imagine that in such a situation you would be able to wriggle about and loosen yourself to make an escape. I thought this, but the reality is very different. Several of us kids had the same experience, so we always went along in a group and whilst we each took turns to get buried alive, there were always others to dig us out. We had an agreement to free the head first, so we could breathe, and also to go carefully with the shovels. Getting a split ear wasn't unknown, so as you can see, bottle digging wasn't without its perils.

After experiencing my third buried alive event, I gave it up. Instead, out of a sale of one of the lids, a genuine article for once, I bought a 'price guide to finds' and scanned it for something I thought I could reproduce that was not too ambitious. I decided upon some Victorian tooth powder lids. The fish paste lids were the most valuable, at £100 each, a great deal of money to me in 1972, but I felt they were beyond me. In any case, they were transfer-printed in colour, though at the time I thought them done in overglaze enamels, not realising that unlike the hand-painted work of the eighteenth and early nineteenth centuries, the fish lids were the product of Victorian mass production. This was explained to me by a kind expert at the Last Drop. Fake colour transfer, I couldn't do. But fake black letter print might be possible.

I perused my mail order catalogue, which had come along with the kiln, and sent off my order for what was needed – white earthenware casting, slip, clean glaze, black enamel powder and medium, along with transfer paper of a type described as 'fine on'. The whole lot cost me a fair chunk of my savings, so it was a Wednesday trip to the Post Office to cash in some of my savings books, then a wait for delivery. After everything arrived, my impatience to become an expert potter overnight resulted in half of my new stock ending up in the bin through one imperfection or another. This potting game wasn't as simple as I thought.

My first mistake was buying the wrong type of plaster for the slip mould – the first stage in the production of pot lids. I'd left out the 'Potter's Plaster' from my order list and, instead, purchased a bag of 'Herculite' from the builder's merchants, being impressed by its name, I suppose. This was used commercially in the building trade for decorative casting and mouldings, on account of its hardness. The man at the trade counter assured me it was the 'best stuff' available and so, at extra expense, I went with the Herculite.

As it was too heavy to carry, and being too mean to pay for delivery, I placed it onto the handlebars of my new bicycle, a five-speed BSA Tour of Britain in gold and black, a proper racer and my pride and joy, and spent all that afternoon pushing it home, cursing my decision all the way. The bicycle had been my Christmas present for 1970 from Mum and Dad. Both my sister Sharon and I had been bought bikes, though to my glee, hers was a crappy 'girl's bike', low crossbar and all, with little wheels that folded up. She complained that she looked like my gerbil on its exercise wheel having to pedal furiously to keep up. I too thought she looked like my gerbil, on or off the bicycle, and took delight in telling her so.

After finally getting home, I set about the task of making the mould for this increasingly problematic project. Having carefully watched the process of piece moulding being done by my teacher, I now began my own effort. To get a realistic look, I took the short-cut of taking the cast from one of my genuine finds. This pot lid, in common with most of our finds, was badly chipped, so I filled in the chips with Araldite, then sanded down the resin for a smooth overall finish. Moulding completed, it was time to put into action all that I'd learnt in pottery class. I rolled out a suitably thick slab of clay, laid it into one half of the mould and brought the other down, squeezing with all my might. Making these bloody things was proving almost as much effort as digging them up! Not only that, every attempt stuck to the mould like glue. Later, after much effort and swearing, the guilty Herculite was binned, and success was finally had when I got the Potter's Plaster I'd failed to order in the first place. It's not called that for nothing. The Herculite had been too dense to absorb the surface moisture of the clay and so aid its release after pressing. Potter's Plaster, being softer and more absorbent, does what it says on the tin. I've remembered my lesson in this. In all my later projects, wherever possible, I've made sure to use the right materials.

The pot lids, six in all, as many as would fit in the kiln at once, were loaded in and the kiln fired up. This too was a first for me. At school, every time we wanted to use the kiln, 'Sir' or his deputies would take command, probably fearing that we'd burn the place down – they may have been right. Following the instructions that had come with the Potter's Plaster, I steadily increased the temperature until, looking through the spyhole, I could see the indicator cone start to bend and, with a burst of immodest self-praise, switched off the kiln. The kiln, however, continued to radiate like a nuclear reactor. I'd placed it too close to the wall of Dad's shed and it was now singeing the flimsy wood. Even the roofing felt on the shed was going floppy at the edges. After this near-disaster, I shifted it onto the concrete garage at the bottom of our garden.

I should also have left its first contents to cool until the following day, but just before bedtime, not being able to bear the wait any longer, I sneaked out to have a quick peek. Lifting the lid a fraction, courtesy of the fireproof gauntlet my dad had got me from work, I was met by a blast of hot air that almost removed my eyebrows. Shining a torch into the now unglowing kiln, there, within the shimmering heat, were the six gleaming white pots. Suddenly, I heard a loud 'ping'. Something had gone wrong. I slammed the lid. That ping had the sound of doom about it. Sure enough, unloading the pots the next day after school, every one of them had a hairline crack from stem to stern. When I picked them up, they just fell apart. I vowed never to show impatience again in my potting ventures, but I'm afraid that trait has cost me dear on a few occasions since.

After this initial setback, things went along just fine. My next attempt produced perfect results. So I glazed them, making sure to glaze the concave underside with the crackle glaze, as I had noticed that most originals were glazed that way due to incorrectly proportioned ingredients that made the glaze shrink more than the clay on cooling. This was exaggerated where the glazes had pooled. Small details such as this are always something to be noticed and followed. The final part, the black lettering on the glaze, was achieved by marking out the transfer paper with my dad's tech drawing set – compass and dividers – and drawing freehand letters similar in style to the originals, then painting them in with enamel, before laying the whole thing onto the fired and glazed lids. A low temp refiring, and out came six pots that were beyond my expectations.

Although these had taken me two weeks to make I was quite proud of my efforts. Apart from looking sparkling new, they were not at all unrealistic. So I set about putting a few years on them. I soaked them in a soup of soil and iron oxide, followed by a short whizz in the gemstone tumbler I'd bought from the St Ives market to dull the shine. After a bit of experimentation they became indistinguishable from the genuine article. At least that was my impression. Everyone I took them to never questioned them and made an immediate offer, always at rip-off prices. As they only cost a few pence to make, my percentage, as I saw it, was always bigger than theirs, so everyone was happy.

Over the next couple of years I sold a lot of my pot lids, varying the design every so often after consulting my bottle digging illustrators' 'book'. Eventually, my 'bottle tip' range also included figured clay pipe 'heads' of famous people, mostly eminent Victorians. These weren't as valuable as the lids, but the range and speed of production was better. I'd model the various heads from Plasticine, then take plaster moulds from them, cast them in clay and fire them unglazed. Very quick and cheap to make, and good sellers. Other higher value articles I made were bone china doll's heads, and also hands and feet. These always had impressed marks on the back and were usually German in origin. By the late 1980s, they were available commercially in kit form for potters, but I made them in 1972 and, back then, they passed for the real thing.

Once I had solved the teething troubles my potting didn't take up a great deal of time and was very intermittent. I know it had very little to do with art, but this was my first contact with the antiques trade and some of the many sharks that swim in its waters. I sold those ceramics 'as seen', and the dealers always paid much less than I knew was fair. It was still a good deal for me though, compared to the time and cost of their production.

I was quite industrious in my school years. In the long summer holidays we would go out into the countryside and collect reed mace, or what most people call bulrushes, along with ferns, irises and whatever else was in vogue amongst the rich ladies that lived in the 'big houses' up the road. These rich ladies were always in fanatical competition with each other at their 'flower arranging, boasting and boozing' afternoon get-togethers. To collect the reed mace, we'd use my rubber dinghy, a garish orange and blue thing with a slow puncture that I could never locate. At every outing, it was frantically pumped up on the lake bank, slung into the water and in we jumped, paddling furiously for the reed bed, slashing down as many as we dared in a race with the rapidly softening boat.

Afterwards, we toured the 'big houses'. These days, they're the homes of footy players and their managers. Back then, they were mostly owned by Manchester stockbrokers and lawyers, who, their wives told us, were always too busy and rarely at home. Many of these women seemed sad souls, rattling around in deserted houses with little to do. Some of them could drink for England and, although they looked decidedly middle-aged to us 14-year-olds, some were quite an eyeful. I think they looked forward to our arrival. We would usually arrive with just a few bulrushes and say, 'Mrs so-and-so has bought all our stock, but seeing as how you've been such a good customer, we've saved you a few, but the price will need to be higher.' It wasn't very gallant behaviour, I know, but when I was a lad, I was a bit ruthless and a worshipper of Mammon.

The lawyers' wives were the randiest and paid the best prices for the bulrushes. One of them in particular never wanted us to leave and would let us into the snooker room to play billiards, where we'd spend all afternoon potting balls, while she got plastered at the bar. On the wall was a portrait of her husband, decked out in all his finery; horsehair wig, robes and all. According to her, he was a famous lawyer in celebrated murder trials. His ugly mug looked down at us from above a very fine marble fireplace in *rosso antico*. I knew this stone was highly prized in ancient Rome and quite rare in such a large well-figured lump.

Many years later, I wanted to make a copy of a recumbent lion that had been found on the Palatine Hill in Rome in the early eighteenth century. It had been in the collection of Henry Blundell, the Liverpool merchant, but was now catalogued as lost. I had great difficulty sourcing a suitable piece of *rosso antico* from which to make my copy and thought then of that fireplace and wondered, if only for a second, what had become of the bewigged lawyer and his bulrush-mad wife.

The gardens of the 'big houses' were full of stone statuary. These caught my eye from the start and put me in mind to have a go at something similar. I was sure I could do something at least as good. Looking back, I think the inspiration may have been wholly commercial, with not a glimmer of art. It led me out of the 'bottle tip' range that I'd been making for a while, and into the cast stone business. Well, concrete really, but 'cast stone' sounded as if it would appeal more to the type of people who bought our bulrushes and filled their gardens with statues. As things turned out, by 15 or 16 I was selling as many of these things as I could or would produce.

My garden statues were mostly 2 or a maximum of 3 feet tall. At 15, that was just about at my limit in managing their bulk. Most were based on classical semi-clad Bacchanalian-type males and females, along with some Davids and Goliaths. The David was nicked off Buonarroti, but I've never liked the distortions in his version, so in mine, the proportions were more normal. The original was actually designed to be seen from below and Buonarroti, being the genius he was, was compensating for the distortions in the perspective. But I couldn't come to terms with his calculations, so I decided my copy would be a 'loose' interpretation, and fixed it up with an oversized head of Goliath on which to rest his foot.

I also nicked a river god from a certain Mr Bernini. It was one of my best sellers, although of a standard that would have had him cringing for sure. Some of these garden statues I also made in terracotta at a request from the people who – through a friend of my dad's – took most of my productions, a large stonemason's yard at Trafford Park near Manchester. The terracottas were done in a similar way to the pot lids. Same principle, only on a much larger scale. As my own kiln was only 14 inches tall, they had to be fired elsewhere, so I'd press mould them, sharpen up the detail with my modelling tools, then let them dry before being collected. The owner of the mason's yard was quite impressed by them, especially by the popular reclining river god I'd ripped off from Bernini. Over time, I became sick of the sight of that beardy old god.

My school work, in the meantime, was, for want of a better description, 'bumping along the bottom'. During the spring of 1973, I had to decide which subjects to carry forward to O level. That was when I dumped my art studies. I was doing quite enough in my own time by now and felt I'd rather use my school time on other subjects. My greatest desire as a schoolboy was to become an architect. But I knew from early on that I was most probably too thick, so that hope gradually faded, which was most likely for the best, as I'd now be working on loft conversions and kitchen extensions.

Being able to sell the things I made gave me the opportunity to have a few hobbies that most of my school friends couldn't afford. So I decided to try horse riding, but before going to the expense of kitting myself out, took the precaution of going over to the local riding centre – well, a crappy old farm in reality, called Simm's Farm. They had loads of horses and ponies, for beginners through to 'top hands', as Mr Simm called them. As part payment, most of the kids would do a few hours at weekends shovelling shit and such things, and, though never one to shy away from getting my hands dirty, shovelling shit was definitely out. I wanted to learn how to ride, not to shovel, and told Mr Simm so. To this he boomed, 'OK lad, so you're not a shoveller, neither am I. Let's see what you can do up top.'

The only time I'd been 'up top' was sitting in front of my dad as a six-year-old on Southport beach. Simm's horses all had numbers instead of names and on hearing that I hadn't actually ridden before, he looked skywards and called for Number Seven, an elderly chestnut gelding, described to me as 'bomb proof'. At first, I couldn't even mount the thing, but over the following weeks, steady progress was made, along with a few falls. From ground level a horse always looks fine, but from the saddle, I couldn't get over how high up it all seemed or how long or hard the fall was when airborne.

My other money-draining hobby was dinghy sailing on the Delph Reservoir, up on the moors. The place was ideal as the wind was constant and always changing direction. So if you weren't a quick learner you could have plenty of unplanned swimming lessons as well. I loved whizzing around under wind power at the helm of my fibreglass dinghy and always promised myself a boat. Somehow that never materialised. Maybe if I win the lottery.

Not all the things I got up to cost money. Another silly pastime was working out how to move the huge boulders that sat precariously on the clifftops of our local defunct quarry. Several of us would spend our summer evenings slowly edging a mighty boulder inch by inch towards its doom at the cliff edge, using nothing more sophisticated than a few iron bars we had 'borrowed' from the goal posts of the footy pitch, with some well-placed rocks acting as fulcrums. This gave us 9-stone weaklings the edge over our many-tonned opponent. Sometimes we would have to pack up and return the following evening, before finally getting the rock over the cliff, usually to a resounding cheer as it hurtled down into the flooded quarry below, where its huge splash caused a mini tsunami in which the frogs and other pond life were forced to enjoy a once in a lifetime Californian surfing experience.

One of those boulders reminded me of the colossal granite statue of Ramesses II that I'd seen in the British Museum. This boulder was of yellow sandstone and before it met its fate on the clifftop I once spent a Sunday afternoon on my own at the quarry marking it out for cutting into the head of an Egyptian pharaoh, which, I could see, would fit nicely into it. The problem was that at 13, being a bit of a stick insect of a lad, I just didn't have the wherewithal to knock the corners off it. So I had to imagine what it would look like as a finished sculpture.

Another of our oddball pastimes was even more dangerous. I'd seen a programme on TV about a chap called 'Blaster Bates'. As I remember it, he was a bit of a Fred Dibnah character who blew things up with dynamite instead of knocking them down, Dibnah fashion. An interesting bit of the programme showed him demonstrating how to blow up a septic tank. This put me in mind of the deep-water tanks at the defunct Dunscar bleach works. Those tanks were full of 100 years' worth of aniline dye slurry, layered with all the colours of the rainbow, like banded agate. After some discussions at school, we decided the next day to go into bomb-making, Blaster Bates style.

As we couldn't get hold of any real dynamite, we made do with our own version, made of weed killer bought from the 'wooden hut' local ironmongers, where all the kids of the village would get their air rifle pellets. This weed killer was mixed with sugar and packed into an old motorcar silencer. We'd hammer over the ends of the tube, then punch a hole in it with a screwdriver for the fuse, usually a petrol-soaked rag or, preferably, an unravelled Catherine wheel left over from Bonfire Night. Tying the 'bomb' to a 10-foot willow branch, the straightest we could find, we were ready for action at the deep-water tanks. We'd light the fuse, thrust the stick bomb as deep into the slurry as we could, then dash madly for the cover of the concrete pump station to await the boom. Sometimes, the bomb would sink without trace. Other times, there was a huge bang and down would fall a rainbow of mud. Thankfully, the pump house had a broad overhanging concrete roof under which we would cower until all was clear.

Despite increasing the size of the bombs in our mini arms race we noticed the craters were not getting bigger. Obviously the pressure needed to be ramped up. So we floated out a raft of old doors rescued from the bonfire and loaded it to sinking point with large stones. Then we rammed two stick bombs beneath it at an acute angle and ran for the safety of the 'bunker', as the pump house had come to be known. When it went off, the fragmented stones and doors shot up through the tree canopy, snapping and shredding branches as they went, before raining down again. The blast almost cleared the tank of mud and blew a hole right down to the brick bottom as if a meteor had hit Lancashire, leaving a crater stretching from edge to edge. Today, I suppose we'd all be arrested under the Terrorism Act. Back then, it was just harmless fun. Still, after the peppering with rock fragments we decided to call it a day. The bombing was getting out of hand.

That was when I took up metal detecting. This was a fairly new craze in the 1970s. In my quest to find a treasure I travelled quite widely. Over the years, a great many important things have been found by detectionists and, despite the bad press they get and the sometimes hostile attitude of academia, many museums would have poorer exhibits without them, that's for sure.

Something else I dumped at school was history, though I was soon to regret my decision. Instead, I took geography, mainly because there were more field trips, and, besides, the geography teacher was much easier on the eye. Not very academic reasons, I know, but having to sit through history lessons taught by a boring John Cleese lookalike or a 20-something in a short skirt talking about hot rocks and lava flows, which would you have chosen as a 14-year-old lad?

My favourite book on history was *Whittaker's History of Lancashire*, especially the parts dealing with the Roman period. My interest in things Roman had been fired by my granddad. One of my earliest memories is of walking with him by the river Irwell, downstream of the village where he was born, a place called Summerseat, to visit the site of a small Roman fort, mentioned in *Whittaker's Lancashire*, and well known to my grandfather. My own hope at school was to locate a lost Roman settlement called 'Coccium', a small fort or marching camp on the route from Manchester to Ribchester. Measuring the length of the Roman road between the two, I marked the halfway point and discovered that this would put it around the village of Ainsworth at a site known locally as Cockey Moor. Its position is about a day's march from Manchester, and only slightly more from Ribchester, plus it commands a view down into the valley that carries the Roman road between the two. Also, in Whittaker's book there is record of a large amount of urns being ploughed up on Castle Hill, just half a mile away.

I've detected in this area and looked for earthworks in the fields, but to no avail. So my little foray into amateur archaeology was a failure. One success I did have was to find a Roman altar that's mentioned in Whittaker. This had been dug up in Ribchester in the eighteenth century and removed to Sharples Hall, near Bolton. I knew this old house well. It was about 10 minutes from my home. As a seven- or eight-year-old I'd been all over its overgrown park looking for bird nests. By the late sixties, it was almost derelict, except for a few rooms let out as bedsits to students. The egg collection, by the way, ended its days rather tragically. I'd been put in charge of my little sister – why I can't recall – but on this particular day it led to a falling out, most probably caused by my overzealousness. The result was that she and her pal took revenge on me by hitting each and every one of my eggs – once my most prized possessions – with a spoon. There in the sawdust-filled shoe boxes they lay, broken. My sister's dolls paid the price by being dismembered – heads, arms and legs scattered about the lawn, a massacre. Actually, it was a bit of a relief to be rid of that egg collection. Being a member of the RSPB isn't really compatible with this out-of-date hobby. In my defence, all I would say is that I was pretty young and didn't know better.

Anyway, among the rhododendrons and briars of my egg-collecting days I eventually found the Roman altar. It was very weathered but otherwise undamaged, about 4 foot tall with an indecipherable inscription on it. I took a wax rubbing of it, but even that yielded little. All I could make out were the first and largest letters, 'IOM', which I knew invoked the great god, Jupiter, but that was all. The altar was too heavy to shift, otherwise I would have rescued it. After drawing and measuring it, I left it where I'd found it among the brambles. The next time I passed that place, sometime in the mid-eighties, the hall had been converted into apartments and the patch of briar was a car park. I haven't a clue what happened to the old altar. It isn't in the Bolton Museum, so I can only presume that it went unrecognised into a skip and then on to landfill.

One of my dad's angling friends who would take us out on fishing trips in his boat on Bassenthwaite in the Lake District lived in a big rambling house some miles south of Carlisle, a city with Roman beginnings. He had a collection of Roman altars dug up in the nineteenth century in the big fort at Maryport on the Cumbrian coast, a few miles from his home. That fort was the western end of Hadrian's Wall, he would tell us, and one of his relatives had owned the land on which it stood. He reckoned that the Romans dedicated one altar every year and buried the old ones after 20 years – 20 being the number of them found together at any one dig.

This friend of my dad's seemed to know what he was talking about and, as a kid, I was impressed by his knowledge. He was a scrap metal merchant and car dealer by trade, and his house was an Aladdin's cave of antiques of all kinds. The fishing trips to Bassenthwaite were always a red-letter day for me, more for the chance to wander through that house than for the hope of catching a big fish on the lake. We'd spend the day out in the boat, bobbing around like a cork, with me, being the smallest, always stationed on the bow. On windy wet days, I'd take the full force of the oncoming spray until I looked like a drowned rat. I always got the feeling that I was only brought along as a windbreak, not an angler, but I didn't mind. Despite ending most days soaked to the skin and freezing cold, I was glad not to miss out on the adventure.

After the day's fishing, the best bit was to come. I'd be squashed into the back of his car and we would whizz along at umpteen miles an hour in his Jensen Interceptor with me perched on the tiny rear seat with all the fishing tackle. Amongst the collection of art and antiques in his house were some things I recognised and many I did not. I had free rein to look at and handle all kinds of first-rate artefacts. Particular favourites that immediately caught my eye were two bronze plaques from the Benin Kingdom in West Africa, each bearing an image of the king, or oba to give him his proper title. These were hung on either side of the entrance hall. I was already familiar with the fantastic art of Benin. I'd seen the

British Museum's collection, which is the best in the world, but to me, these two pieces seemed even better, probably because I was allowed to lift them off the wall and hold them, looking closely at how they were made – something that interested me even more than the actual work. Then, as now, the first thing that comes into my mind when I see a work of art is not how beautiful or fine it is, but how was it put together? Could I do as good a job? If not, why not?

Other treasures in that museum of a house, because that's what it was, were dozens of terracotta and bronze sculptures of all periods and style. They must have cost a great deal of money and Mr Whitton, the owner, would tell us of his dealings with the London auctioneers and Bond Street dealers from whom he'd bought these things. This was the first I'd heard of such places, though, unfortunately, they were to become more familiar to me in the future. For now, I was all agog listening to Mr Whitton's stories of car and art dealing, and its many pitfalls. Some of his best pieces, at least to my amateur eye, were his terracottas, mostly French and eighteenth-century. These were probably right, but who knows? Through my dealings with the art trade I've developed a jaded eye in all matters of genuineness. So much so, that these days I'm wholly unimpressed by authorship or the supposed age or origin of a work of art. Only its quality really matters. It's always best to buy only what you like. Then you can't be disappointed, can you?

Even back then, I couldn't have cared less if all Whitton's pieces had been casts, although I'm pretty sure they weren't. The best were by the eighteenth-century French sculptor Clodion. They knocked the spots off that thing I was to make years later in the style of Gauguin. Clodion's figures and relief panels helped me a lot in the design and style of my concrete and clay statues, which, although well short of his work, couldn't have been totally without merit because they sold well for a while. One outstanding effect I saw in the Clodions was the way in which the merest of scratches could produce a big depth of field in a shallow relief, and how just six slashes of the stylus could suggest a cavalcade of figures. I'd noticed this also in the work of that master of early Renaissance reliefs, Ghiberti, and tried hard to follow this example in the stuff I did.

Mr Whitton had a good collection of ceramics, and especially Chelsea. I've always been fascinated by pottery, from the great works of China to the art potters such as Bernard Leach whose lesser works I saw in the Sloop Craft Market at St Ives where he had his studio. I would pore over Mr Whitton's collection of pots whenever I got the chance, which was far too infrequently as far as I was concerned. I learned or, more accurately, I was shown how to see the subtle difference in Ming to Ching porcelain or the 'moons' in Red Anchor Chelsea – all things that need to be seen first-hand and can't be learnt from books. Later on, I had a go at replicating the Red Anchor ware, complete with its distinctive 'moons', although I got my look in a wholly un-Chelsea way, as I'll be describing.

Most of the pictures in that house were dark, dull Victorian potboilers with nothing like the presence of the rest of his collection. All except a group of bird pictures that were amongst my favourite things to see there. The labels on the back of the frames showed that most of them had been bought from dealers in the West End, one of which was a gallery in Cork Street with which I was already familiar, and would become even more familiar in the future. I'd see this gallery exhibiting at the CLA Game Fair to which I would be dragged every July by my dad and brothers. It was an annual ritual. At the fair, the canvas tents in Gunmakers' Row were interspersed with the occasional art dealer selling all kinds of sporting art – paintings, prints, sculptures and books. These were a magnet for me and I would be left there whilst my dad and elder brothers retired to the beer tent for a booze-up. I think they left me there knowing full well that I could be relied upon not to wander off. There were pictures by Peter Scott, whose prints I'd seen in the

RSPB magazines that I got through the post, great hawk paintings by the likes of George Lodge and, best of all, the watercolours of my favourite bird painter, Archibald Thorburn. Those were the pictures that Mr Whitton had on his walls, shining out amongst his dingy Victorian oils.

Thorburn's work is first-rate. I've never seen a poor effort by him, which is probably down to his instruction. His father was miniaturist to Queen Victoria, so that speaks for itself, doesn't it? That, along with the Scots work ethic. He apparently put in eight-hour days in his shed at the bottom of his garden, making him a prolific pumper-out of pictures, all first-class work. He was hugely popular in his own time, deservedly so, and must have sold a zillion prints of his original watercolours, this being his usual medium. However, one of his best works I've seen is a large oil painting in Blackburn Museum and Art Gallery, a covey of red grouse in a heather landscape, an excellent picture and well worth a look.

Always observant of the finer details of the things I was interested in, I noticed that Thorburn didn't go in for the conventional papers favoured by most watercolourists. The vast majority of them used rag papers produced commercially in a rough finish. These suit the medium best and bounce the light about the surface. Thorburn, however, used plain cartridge paper which he lightly washed before laying in the colour. When I copied his technique, I also used cartridge paper. It proved to be the only way to get the same effects. On the heavy rag papers the fine detail of the bird's plumage seemed lost and just didn't ring true.

The visits to Mr Whitton's were all too infrequent. But holidays in the Lake District were a regular feature of my childhood. Every September, just before the start of the new school year, we'd go up to Keswick and spend the week exploring or fishing. Mum and Dad put a lot of effort into those holidays, to say nothing of the cost of them. Many of my friends, though, didn't get holidays away at all. It wasn't that their parents couldn't afford it, but they'd impoverished themselves with mortgages that were virtually beyond them as they tried to keep up with or, preferably, better the Joneses.

My parents had done fairly well, although, as the media constantly pointed out at the time of my arrest, to say nothing of the later TV programmes, they lived in a council house. The impression was given that because of this we were some kind of underclass. From my earliest days I've experienced this attitude amongst many people. Given the opportunity, my impoverished school friends would often try to imply my inferiority on account of this 'council house'. From then on it's been a recurring theme. My parents actually lived there out of choice, and had done so happily since first moving into it on Christmas Eve, 1954, when it was new. Most of us were born and grew up there. As my dad said, when they first moved in most of his friends were still living in the town's Victorian housing stock with no facilities and a bog in the backyard. Our earliest neighbours were mostly men, like my dad, who'd been hurt financially by their service to their ungrateful masters in World War Two. After getting on their feet as far as money was concerned, they were perfectly able to buy a new house down the road if they'd wished. But they liked this home, as did we all. A chipboard and plywood shack, with a new tin box in the drive, may be many people's ambition, but it wasn't my parents', and it's never been mine.

I think most of the 'council house' bashing element in the media are only one generation on themselves from the bog in the backyard brigade. But by bashing those they misguidedly believe to be beneath them perhaps they hope to distance themselves from their own humble roots. One thing the press did get right was that my own regard for money has never been the driving force behind the stuff I've done – although I've been able to provide myself with sufficient for my needs since I was in long trousers. When I was still at school, I could afford to buy such things as the first LCD calculator and wristwatch in the class from selling my own work.

I can't recall exactly how much my garden sculptures brought in, but one of my schoolmates had a dad who was a sergeant in the Greater Manchester Police and he was telling me how much his dad was on per month. In that same month, I'd made almost as much. I was 13 at the time.

With all these arty things buzzing around in my head, school was usually taking a back seat, but one or two things were still of interest. For my tech drawing and metalwork O level the practical part of the exam required us to build a working steam engine. It was to be run on compressed air and expected to function properly. I thought it all gloriously out of date, which may have been its attraction. Making it was one of the most enjoyable things I recall doing at that time. It's hard to imagine now that Victorian technology still held sway in education during the 1970s, but it did. Some years later, the metalwork room, along with all its machine tools, was consigned to the scrapheap, and the room was used instead for mime and dance classes. How we're all going to make a living out of mime and dance in place of engineering and design escapes me.

By the time I built the steam engine, I had more or less decided not to follow an academic path. Though I didn't have a clue what I was going to do. Quite often, I would bunk off school, either to go fishing or to jump the train which was just half a minute from the school gates. My usual destination on these away days was Manchester. I'd go there to look around the art gallery or the Central Library by the town hall. On my way from Victoria railway station, I'd pass by a place called Koopman's Silver Galleries. It closed its doors sometime in the 1980s, though I believe it's still trading in London.

I've always had a love of fine metalwork. The craft of the jeweller, silversmith, bronze caster and even works of engineering in iron and steel, are all of equal worth as far as I'm concerned. So eventually I summoned the bottle to go into Koopman's and look around. From the outside, the shop had always appeared a little intimidating – a bit posh. I fully expected to be booted out of the door. On the contrary. They expressed no desire to move me on, so I'd spend ages in there looking at the stuff for sale, knowing full well that the prices were a lot deeper than my pockets. The finest piece I got to see there was a silver 'salt' by my favourite silver-smith, Paul Storr, whose work spans the late eighteenth and early nineteenth centuries. It caught my eye initially because I'd seen something similar at Mr Whitton's house, although that was made in porcelain by Chelsea in the 1740s – at least Mr Whitton said it was. Who really knows? It looked brand new. That's the problem with porcelain, and all ceramics. They always look brand new, even when they're hundreds of years old. Of all the things a faker can do, ceramics are the easiest by a long way. They generally cost the least in time and money to reproduce, and are the things most readily accepted as the genuine article – so long as you make sure to use the correct materials and method of production.

The silver salt was a spectacular object with hallmarks of 1815, so made in the year of the Battle of Waterloo. Of all my fakes, I never resorted to making English silver due to the fact that the hallmark-ing is still going on. Some of the Roman plates I have had a go at did, however, carry imperial control stamps of the period which are similar to hallmarks. I would cut these out intaglio-fashion in a mild steel bar, case-harden them, then whack their impression into the silver plate. I reasoned that as the Roman Empire ceased trading long ago, they couldn't prosecute, could they?

Besides gawping at silver that was too expensive for my pocket, my other reason for bunking off school and going into Manchester was to visit the motorcycle shops that were in profusion in the early seventies. One in particular was something of a Mecca for me – Sports Motorcycles on Liverpool Road. Thanks to the sale of my concrete and clay statues and their predecessors, the pot lids and 'bottle tip' range, I was fairly affluent as a lad. Finding the money to buy my first motorbike wasn't a problem, so long as it was second-hand. The real difficulty was getting my parents to sanction it as I was still only 14 at the time. My dad had been in the Royal Signals during the war and was a DR or dispatch rider, so he had been in a lot of crashes. This, and my mum's total dislike of motorbikes, was a hefty obstacle to overcome and required a bit of stealthy persuasion. For several weeks, I put away my various hobbies and made a point of doing my homework, making sure I was seen doing it. After a few mind-numbing weeks of this, I asked my parents if I could have a motorbike and to my amazement they agreed – although with several stringent conditions. It had to be kept at the 'off road club' of which my brother was a member. And my new-found academic fervour had to be maintained. I agreed to all this. I'd have signed my own death warrant to get that bike.

The dealer at Sports Motorcycles had a racing team of Ducatis and sold all the top makes of Italian, Japanese and – in the days when British bikes were still a going concern – them too. There were rows of BMWs, Moto Guzzi, Ducatis and, my favourite of the day, Laverdas. Further back were the big Jap bikes and a selection of second-hand stuff, big and small. I could have found the type of bike I was looking for in Bolton, where there were a couple of bike shops as well, but I wanted one from what I thought of as a proper motorcycle dealer – one with its own racing team.

I'd already learnt to ride my brother's Yamaha trials bike up on the moors at a place called Haslingden. His club used an old packhorse trail that ran over the moors to West Yorkshire through some great open country, cutting through valleys and streams, over humpback bridges, all quite historic in its way. I took a few tumbles along this track, mostly on account of my brother's 350 being a bit too much for my spindly frame. It seemed to have been built for someone with the inside leg measurements of a giraffe. Every time I came to a standstill, one of GR's mates would shout 'timber' as I keeled over and fell off.

My own bike was to be a smaller affair for starters, also Japanese, as were most bikes in the seventies, also a Yamaha, a 125cc off-roader in yellow, black and white. The 'kamikaze wasp' as my dad called it. I'd spotted it amongst the rows of used machines some weeks before on one of my away days from school, and now, with everything OK'd, I handed over my hard-earned money to the man at the bike shop and he promised to deliver it the next day. Part of the deal with my mum and dad was that I couldn't keep it at home. So it went to 'stabling' at the farm where the club kept quite a few of its weekend bikes. After paying club fees, there was no extra charge for this 'stabling', so it was a much better deal than a horse. No feed bills, and no need for a shovel either.

Unfortunately, my first bike didn't last very long. Reneging on my promise to keep up with classes, I zoomed over the edge of an old stone bridge and plummeted down a ravine. The bridge was an interesting construction. My quick glance at it as I passed turned into too long a look and, before you can say 'Shaun the skidder', I was splashing down in the valley below. The chap who dragged me out smelt like a brewery. He rode a Maico 400 with a pannier full of Newcastle Brown Ale on board. Even pissed, he managed to keep it on the road better than me.

Along with various cuts and bruises, I'd broken my collarbone. When my dad came to see me at Blackburn Infirmary he threatened to 'wrap that bloody bike round the farmer's head', but he didn't, and, probably out of sympathy, he and Mum gave me a second chance. My dad understood my 'need for speed'. He'd had it himself. As he'd say to me now and then: 'Risking it makes you feel more alive.' It's true. It does.

Soon after, I managed to balls things up again by riding my bike under age and with no insurance over to Belmont to meet some of my school chums who were also dodging class that day. We were caught by the village bobby while attempting a particularly difficult circus stunt. We'd decided it would be a good idea to see how many of us could ride the thing at once so we piled on jointly, six of us in all. The 'midget' up front did the steering, I operated the gears and rear brake, the others sat in the middle, and the fat lad at the back was put on the mudguard for better traction. We were all eventually let off with a caution, but that was definitely it for the bike. I was left in no doubt that as far as motors were concerned I'd have to wait until I was old enough to do things legally. And that was that. I spent the money from the sale of my bike on a good set of brushes, some best quality watercolours, several dozen sheets of Whatman paper, and set about becoming proficient at painting in the style of my latest craze – English watercolourists of the eighteenth and nineteenth centuries.

My new interest had been fired by an exhibition I'd seen at one of the Manchester public galleries, though I was already aware of English watercolours. Bolton Museum has a good collection of them and I would often go there for a look. After some time my efforts at copying their style got better, but only after many cock-ups and much burning through my expensive paper stock. I took particular notice of the colours used by each individual artist, or 'palette' as it should properly be termed. His typical composition traits and paint application. This attention to detail is all-important in getting a convincing look to any picture and if you get it right even a fairly average dauber can produce something half-convincing that 'ticks the right boxes' in the expert's mind. Thus I added a new line to my product range – the 'English watercolour copy selection' – and took a few along to the off-and-on purchaser of my 'Thorburn range', a prosperous dealer with premises near King Street in Manchester.

I'd summoned up the courage to call in on them one day on my way to the City Library and asked if they would be interested in my watery landscapes. Not as fakes – I didn't really understand that concept back then. They were merely half-decent pictures signed by myself. They must have had some merit because I managed to

sell as many as I could paint at £7 each. I know this sounds a comical amount of money these days, but in the mid-seventies it wasn't
at all bad, not for me anyway. Sometimes, with just a few quickly
splashed daubs done over the weekend, I could make as much as
some adults got for a week's work. These dealers were never interested in my own pictures – mostly landscapes of the moorlands
around Bolton where I lived or craggy Lake District scenes. No,
they had to be copies of things done by others. The cheeky buggers
even asked me to sign them in pencil 'well out in the margin'. In my
naivety, I went along with their requests and only later imagined
what their real reasons might have been for such odd requests.

The £7 I got for each of these watercolours was earned much
more easily than the sums coming in for my concrete statues. Those
things were proper hard work and I'd already started to do fewer
of them before the demand for the pictures started to take off.
I really liked to do the modelling of the original sculpture, but the
repetitive casting of them became boring very quickly and only the
fact that they brought in regular cash kept me interested in them.
The offer to buy a substantial number of paintings from me was,
therefore, something to consider. I didn't consider it for long and
quickly went into full production.

The dealer who was buying my pictures was a large Toby jug of
a man who smoked huge cigars that filled his small gallery with
a blue smog as he followed his clients about the place nodding in
agreement with every word they uttered. He reckoned that for his
£7 he would want a picture at least 20 inches by 16 and that anything less was worth half that amount. I pointed out that Thorburn
and the old-time watercolourists usually worked on a small scale,
but if he wanted them in uncharacteristically large sizes, I would
oblige. This bluff worked. I didn't know for sure that those artists
only did small pictures. In fact, I was pretty sure they did all sorts
of sizes and fully expected Toby to contradict me. But he didn't.
Obviously he didn't know quite as much as I'd given him credit for.

So he told me to do them as I thought fit, to follow the size and style of the originals and that the price would be £7 irrespective of dimensions. At that price, almost the whole amount was profit.

My best sellers were usually dark, dramatic views of ruined abbeys in a landscape, filled with gothic arches, or big skied coastals in the manner of the Norwich School painters. My other line was bird pictures, which sold even better, but took longer as the detail was more laborious to do than the loose washes of the landscapes. They were mostly in the style of Archibald Thorburn, or as close to it as my limited ability would allow – falcons, game birds, water-fowl and songbirds. They all sold well.

During my time painting for Mr Toby Jug I tried my hand at doing some oil paintings in my own hand and put several into exhibitions that I'd see advertised in art magazines in the school library. These went down like a lead balloon. Despite being what I thought of as a good standard I hardly sold any. I also took them along to the buyers of my copycat watercolours, but they too weren't interested. My own pictures were painted on Daler canvases, obvi-ously modern, and couldn't be aged to appear to be something they were not. That was the reason I told myself that none of the dealers were interested in my work. They only wanted stuff in the hand of others. So that's what they got.

The first time I knew for sure that at least one of the pictures I sold them had been passed off as genuine was in the late seventies on one of my annual visits to the game fair. There on the wall of one of the West End art dealers' marquees was a Thorburn picture of a grey partridge framed up in a black and gold Hogarth frame. Looking closely at it I saw the telltale marks that I always put in my work to make it recognisable. This one, however, was signed 'A. Thorburn 1911', instead of 'S. G. 1975'. Who altered the author-ship I don't know. It was obviously too poor an effort ever to be taken for real yet its 'provenance card' pinned to the wall beside it for all to see gave it an impeccable history – 'The property of the honourable blah blah blah' and so on. I've made up such prove-nances myself, but I certainly wasn't the first to do so, nor will I be the last. People seem to be blinded by such things. Look at the quality and never mind where it supposedly came from. Well, that's my opinion.

The last pictures I painted for Mr Toby Jug were done in the winter of 1976, some months after I'd left school. I told him that these would be the last as I had applied to join the Royal Marines and was off to their training camp at Deal in Kent on the 4th of January. He reckoned that I must have gone soft in the head, but wished me luck and we parted on friendly terms. I never sold him another picture after that.

Whilst painting the 'Thorburns', and no longer labouring for myself casting the concrete statues, I had more time to look into other things artistic and decided to try my hand at metal casting. Initially, just small bronzes, 2 or 3 inches tall, gods and mortals of mythology of the type pumped out in Italy by the thousand. According to their sellers they had been 'dug up' in Pompeii or Rome 100 years ago. In reality they were made in a backyard in Turin last week.

I had a few near-disasters in my early bronze casts. Unlike pottery or painting, messing about with molten metal requires things to be done carefully. My introduction to this craft was quite fortuitous. Throughout my life I've always seemed to come across things accidentally just when I needed to. Around the time I finally shook myself free of academia I decided to have a clear-out of my dad's garage and shed. They were now piled high with plaster piece moulds from my defunct 'bottle tip' range, pots, reams of drawings, bags of clay and all manner of 'rubbish' as my brothers usually re-ferred to my artistic endeavours. The biggest heap of 'rubbish' was the range of large rubber and fibreglass moulds out of which I'd made the cast stone statues. Although these had sold really well, I decided to get rid of them all and instead of dumping them at the council tip, the usual destination for much of my stuff, I asked my brother to run me over to the stone yard that had been selling them. They never actually bought anything from me, but allowed me to display my stuff in the stone yard and charged a 10 per cent commission on any sales. In the beginning, though, the chap who ran the place charged me nothing, so I decided to ask if he would care to have the moulds. I told him of my plans to leave art alone and that I was off to Deal for a new adventure.

It turned out he already knew all this as he'd been out boozing with my dad the week before and was of the same opinion on the subject as Mr Toby – that I was soft in the head to change direction. But he took the moulds gladly. One of his lads could spend Saturday mornings casting them, he said. I was happy to be rid of them. My dad, it seems, had been blabbing about my interest in metal casting and between them they had come up with a plan they hoped might divert me away from my new career in the Marines. A couple of minutes down the road, I was told, was a foundry where they were casting something I might be interested in – that's if I had the time to go and have a look. I was, of course, immediately keen and pleaded with my brother to make time for us to go and see this place.

The only other foundry I'd been into was the one at Bolton Tech. My dad had taken me along to see it as it was run by one of his mates, 'cast-iron Joe'. It was mostly sand-casting for industrial applications – huge sand moulds and a gas furnace as big as me – miles beyond anything I could envisage being able to do, but really interesting all the same. So I was expecting something on that scale. But this foundry was something quite different, a proper bronze casting foundry that used the lost wax method, something I'd read about and the type of work I was interested in emulating on a smaller scale. It's a method of casting that reproduces the work of the artist minutely, down to the detail of the fingerprints on the original model. And after every cast, the mould has to be broken, producing an original work each time. Just the thing, I thought, to get a realistic job done.

They were working on a life-size group of American mustangs, which, if I remember correctly, were destined for the city of St Louis. The man in charge was an Italian from Turin who seemed keen to let us look around and showed us into a part of the workshop where the dismembered sections of the life-size horses were laid out on the floor. They were to be cast, he told us, in a lightweight aluminium bronze and the sections would then be welded together, polished and patinated. When complete, he assured us, the joins would be invisible. These days, he concluded, all large-scale sculptures were done in this way.

This was something of a disappointment to me. I'd read the accounts of Cellini's casting of his 'Perseus with the Head of Medusa', which can be seen in Florence in the Piazza della Signoria, along with other accounts of the making of monumental sculptures of the sixteenth and seventeenth centuries, so I was of the opinion that what was being done there in Trafford Park was, somehow, cheating. I mentioned the Cellini story to the foundry boss, and how I'd read of the huge bonfire lit around the mould for the casting of the statue and of the townspeople giving up their scrap metal to fill the mould. 'Boolshit,' was his response. He went on to explain that such difficult work could never have been accomplished in such an ad hoc manner. The great bronzes of the Renaissance, he insisted, were cast by craftsmen at the leading edge of the technology of the day. These craftsmen would be in the exclusive employ of the great princes of the Renaissance or the Pope in Rome. They would have needed access to the foundries owned by such men, used primarily for the casting of cannon and mortars for war. The arty stuff would have come a poor second.

He did seem to know what he was talking about. So I just shut my gob and listened. He went on to show us round the foundry and I tried to take in and remember all I could. The big kilns were something I recognised, but I wondered why they would be needed in a metal foundry? All the books I'd read on the subject suggested that a moderate oven was all that was needed to melt out the bees-wax model from the mould before the bronze that took its place was poured in. I quizzed the man from Turin on this point and he explained that the mould must reach at least 500°c to 'clean' the mould of all the waxy residue left in its deepest recesses and avoid any 'pitting' in the finished cast. In my own first attempts at bronze casting, I ignored this advice. As a result, I set my dad's garden shed ablaze, almost blinding myself in the process. I was following the instructions of writers who had obviously never actually done what they were writing about. This was a salutary lesson. There is no substitute for first-hand experience and your own trial and error.

Before leaving that foundry, I was given two books on bronze casting featuring two of my favourite artists of the Renaissance – Giovanni da Bologna, more often known as Giambologna, and the master of early Renaissance sculpture, Ghiberti. Their names were quite a mouthful and it occurred to me that all these great Italian sculptors had long, almost unpronounceable names. I did too, only I wasn't Italian. If only I had been and was born 500 years earlier.

A few weeks later, I returned to see the mustangs, now finished and mounted in a group of five, just before they were shipped off to America. Remembering how they had looked scattered in bits on the foundry floor, I bent over them again with a critical eye to see if any of the joins were visible. They weren't. Not a trace of any brazing. The whole thing was very impressive. The galloping mus-tangs reminded me, I thought, of a work I'd seen before – a bronze by the nineteenth-century Wild West artist Frederic Remington, called 'Coming Through the Rye'. Apart from being unbridled and riderless, the St Louis mustangs were almost a hoof for flying hoof copy of Remington's effort. I mentioned this to the boss, the man from Turin, and it seemed to impress him. Before leaving, he offered me a job in the moulding shop. If I'd taken it, things might have turned out differently. Maybe he had been put up to this by others. My dad was always opposed to me joining the forces. He and my grandfathers had fought in two world wars. All three of them were wounded and disadvantaged by their service – a reality I didn't comprehend at the time, but one that's crystal clear to me now. I declined the man from Turin's offer. And have always regretted it.

As far as Remington is concerned, I've done a few pictures in his style. The art of the American West has been one of my favourite subjects for many years, though I've steered clear of Remington's famous bronzes on account of them being closely catalogued and recorded, something that's always a problem in fakery. The only opportunity I've had to copy some of his sculptural work came as a result of my learning about a twice life-size version of the 'Coming Through the Rye' sculpture made for the St Louis Exposition, a 'Great Exhibition' type show staged in the first years of the twentieth century. Made in stucco, and overseen by Remington himself, this giant version was later taken down and lost. So I came up with the idea of recreating all the heads of the cowboys from the lost original, about 30 inches tall, mounted on plinths, with an accompanying label, suitably aged, describing their supposed origin. I had little difficulty getting rid of them. Most people want to believe, even if the evidence isn't conclusive, so long as the work fits and they like the look of it.

Although well impressed by the artists of the Old West I've always been more taken with the art of the ancient world and with Italian art of the Renaissance and baroque periods. My first opportunity to see some of this in the flesh came in the year I left school at the age of 15. My eldest brother was married that year, and although our family was nominally Church of England – I was christened at Holy Trinity in Bolton, a 'Waterloo church', one of those paid for by an act of parliament in celebration of the defeat of the Corsican corporal in 1815 – my brother married into the Catholic faith. The place they were married was the first Catholic church I'd been in and I remember its solemn silence being interrupted at the wedding by one of my nephews shouting out in a moment of quiet contemplation 'Hey, who's that man hung up there?' He was referring to the carved figure of Christ nailed onto the great cross in the chancel arch. The outburst caused some amusement and even wrung a smile from the priest conducting the service.

My sister brought her latest beau to the wedding party and as everyone became more and more tanked up the conversation moved on from the splendid wedding location to the great churches of Rome. At that point, being one of the few guests still sober, I was all ears. For as long as I can remember Rome has always held a fascination for me and I knew its history from the founders, Little and Large, to the age of the baroque, and most things in between. This new boyfriend of my sister's seemed to know quite a bit about the place, too, and spent part of the evening talking to my dad who was also familiar with it. At the end of the war, he'd been in the Rome District Signals and would often describe the sights, something I would never tire of, unlike my brothers who would always run for the hills whenever Dad was in reminiscence mode.

My sister mentioned that she would like to see Rome too and her beau, by now well plastered, offered to take her – with my dad's permission, of course. He worked for a travel agent and said he could easily arrange a trip. Quick as a shot, I spied my chance and asked if I could go. No doubt wanting to make a good impression on Mum and Dad he agreed to take me as well, though this brought a withering glance from my sis, first at me, then at him. Even in his inebriated state that glance cut right through the fog of booze and he tried in vain to wriggle out of his promise. But I was having none of it. 'We don't like people who break their promises, do we Dad?' I blurted.

My dad, as usual, was on my side. So my sis and her wriggling beau were done for. Rome it was to be.

VI.

Rome and beyond

THE TRIP TO Rome was the first time I had been abroad and the experience started badly. Our flight was delayed for several hours and even though it was a cheapo flight at the back end of the day all the waiting around spoiled the beginning of the trip. My moaning, meanwhile, resulted in an advisory tip to 'piss off home' from my sister. I arrived in Rome tired, bad-tempered and sitting in the back of a clapped-out minibus which disappeared in a cloud of blue smog every time it came to rest in the traffic. We eventually lurched to a halt at somewhere called the Campo de' Fiori, a place I knew was within the ancient walls of old Rome, but which, even in the dark, didn't quite live up to its name as the 'Field of Flowers'. All I could see was a rather dingy-looking square that reminded me of a derelict version of the open market in Bolton, with an ugly black statue in a cloak dominating the view. However, viewed later from my second-floor hotel window, after a few hours' sleep – the market now full of people and the sky bright blue over the tops of the ochre buildings – it all looked far more promising.

My sister Samy and her beau, Dave, were on the floor upstairs and over the next few days every time they passed to or fro they would come in to ask what I wanted to do. I had no intention of wasting time following in their wake. From past experience I knew my mum and sister's style of shopping – in and out of every shop in town, down one side of a road, then up the other side, looking at all manner of, for want of a better word, crap. So I made my excuses and told them there were certain things I wanted to look at and that I would prefer to go by myself. They didn't need persuading to leave me behind and always seemed happy to go on their way. I would look at Dave as he spun on his heels, his arm draped over Samy, and think: 'You're in for it when you get to those shops.'

The statue in the square wasn't of much interest, a Victorian monument to a heretic called Bruno burned in that square in the sixteenth century. One of my favourite painters, Caravaggio, whom I'd read a lot about, had a connection with this 'Field of Flowers'. The possessor of a fiery temperament to go with his seventeenth-century genius, Caravaggio had murdered his tennis opponent around here, so the place wasn't without interest.

My first trip had to be to St Peter's. I had a street map that Samy and Dave had given me that morning, along with a lecture on how they were supposed to make sure I didn't go off on my own, but, as I was 15, what Mum and Dad didn't know wouldn't hurt them. But for God's sake watch out, were their final orders. I thought I would be OK as I was off to see where God hung out, the Basilica of St Peter in Rome, no less.

I hadn't realised when we first chugged to a halt outside the lodgings in the Campo de' Fiori that I was living right in the centre of the ancient city, just a couple of hundred metres from the Tiber. So off I set on that first day to walk a mere kilometre of riverbank, up to the bend in the river, where I could look across at the Castel Sant'Angelo which I knew was originally the mausoleum of the Roman Emperor Hadrian. Years earlier, I'd already walked his wall on a visit to Housesteads Roman Fort, but this great lump of a Roman fortress, topped off with a grand figure of the Archangel Michael, was in an altogether different league. I crossed one of the bridges over the river in a bit of a trance, and headed in a beeline for the dome of St Peter's. The traffic was utter chaos and in the days ahead I had a few close shaves and my sister's words seemed very apt. I thought she meant for God's sake watch out for perverts and kiddyfiddlers, as they were known where I came from. But the pervs weren't the danger in Rome. It was the traffic that was lethal.

I eventually made it into St Peter's Square, which I knew had been laid out by Bernini, and stood there taking it all in. For once there was just too much to see. One curious thing during those all too short days was that everything seemed so familiar. Not just the buildings that I'd seen pictures of and read about – the Castel Sant'Angelo, the dome of St Peter's – but all these vistas I'd never seen before. Many of the buildings were, or seemed to be, already in my head. I knew what they were before finding out anything about them. It all sounds a bit silly, but that's how it was all week long. I must have read more about Rome than I remember and kept it stored.

The interior of St Peter's was stupendous, even more impressive than my two favourite churches in England – the Norman pile of Durham Cathedral and Wren's masterpiece, St Paul's in London. The only thing that didn't seem to fit was, to my eye, the Baldacchino, the bronze canopy over the papal altar, location of the grave of St Peter. This was made in the early seventeenth century by, of all people, my favourite artist, Bernini. Even so, I didn't like it. Bernini's body of work is, to my mind, unsurpassed, but on occasion even he made a crappy piece. Another of his failures, and there weren't many, is that bloody silly elephant with an ancient Egyptian needle on its back outside the front of the church of Santa Maria sopra Minerva. Its trunk looks like something off an old vacuum cleaner and its face, at that time anyway, reminded me of a politician I'd seen on the TV news called Jim Callaghan. But that's my imagination for you. If any cardinals are reading this, I wouldn't mind melting down Bernini's effort in the crossing at St Peter's and redoing it to my own design... Only kidding! The Basilica was the finest thing my eyes had ever seen and though I've been back since, that first impression was breathtaking.

What was a pain in Rome was the amount of tourists and the time taken to get a proper look at things. I didn't get to see even half of what I wanted to. But I did get a look at the frescoes in the Sistine Chapel. My favourite figures on the ceiling are the Sibyls: the Libyan and particularly the Delphic Sibyl, whose face I find mesmerising. I must have copied it a thousand times, but I've never been able to capture it to my satisfaction. Everyone in there spent the whole time with their heads craned back, looking up at Buonarroti's ceiling, but the frescoes on the walls by other great artists of the time – Botticelli, Perugino, Signorelli – are worthy companions to the master's ceiling, though virtually ignored by most people that day. Looking at such brilliance made me feel very inadequate and by the time it was time for me to return home, the realisation that I was only a third-rate dauber was forever set in my mind.

The only other Vatican must-see for me was Raphael's Stanzas, the grand suite of rooms that had been the private apartments of Pope Julius II, Raphael's patron, and Buonarroti's. This took up a whole day and left no time to see much else. Raphael died before the whole scheme was completed but it's something that will live forever in the history of art. If you haven't seen them, make time and go.

My days in the Eternal City were whizzing by, and I had to give in to the fact that there was just too much to see in the time I had. Ancient Rome has been one of my abiding interests, but, even so, I limited myself to just one day looking at the Forum, Trajan's Column and the arches of Septimius Severus and Constantine, who must have plundered loads of older bits to build his cobbled-together arch. A particularly poignant sight was the scene on the inner span of the Arch of Titus, or 'tight arse' as our history teacher referred to him. This famous relief shows the legions carrying off the contents of the Temple at Jerusalem. The whole arch commemorates the sack of the Jewish capital in AD 70 by the Emperor Vespasian. I was already aware of the long history of Jewish persecution, from the ancient Egyptians to the Romans, continuing into Medieval Europe and culminating in the Nazi barbarities of the Holocaust. Standing there, looking at those stone-cut legionnaires carrying away the great Menorah of the Temple of Jerusalem to Rome where it stayed for hundreds of years until it disappeared from history in the barbarian sack of the fifth century, it occurred to me that history changes, yet stays the same. Had they won the war, the Nazis would most probably have built their own 'glory arch' in Berlin, depicting their atrocities in stone-cut reliefs. Thankfully, they didn't get the chance.

The most important things for me to see on that first trip were the two paintings by Caravaggio in the church of Santa Maria del Popolo, about a mile and a half from our hotel, across the park from the Villa Borghese. The two large canvases, each about 8 foot by 6, and done in 1601, were hanging opposite each other in the Cerasi Chapel, on the left of the church. One depicted the Conversion of Saul on the Road to Damascus. The other, the Crucifixion of St Peter. I'd first seen them in a book on Caravaggio that my mum had bought me years before and, even then, was struck by the dramatic effect of light and shade, the realistic perspective and the expertly done foreshortening that you see in all of Caravaggio's paintings. I was very interested in how he might have achieved these effects. And seeing as how Caravaggio never left any preparatory drawings or sketches, I came to my own conclusion that he must have posed the models and roughed out their forms in brush on the canvas with the aid of a *camera obscura* or another device. To capture the very difficult and complicated compositions he's so famous for, I firmly believe this would have been the only way to go.

I'm not too bad a draughtsman myself, though obviously not in the same league as Master C, but to get such accurate lines from just the eye's observance and the hand's sweep doesn't seem credible. I also can't believe that the artists of the ages before Caravaggio were lesser draughtsman 'freehand' than those who came later. The sudden quantum leap made in accurate draughtsmanship from the fifteenth century onwards coincides with a time of perfecting optics. By Caravaggio's age, good mirrors and lenses would have been known for a long time. And surely used. This use of aids to get accurate images doesn't take away from the great painterly expertise needed to create such pictures. Caravaggio's are amongst the best you can see anywhere. But, after all, spectacles were already being made in Venice in the thirteenth century and fine quality larger lenses, suitable for projection, were in use around the time of that striking leap forward in realistic perspective in the second half of the fifteenth century. This 'realism' was such a dramatic improvement that projection, and the tracing of the resulting image, must surely have played its part in the optical wizardry of Caravaggio and his contemporaries.

As far as sculpture goes, one of the earliest big leaps forward in perspective can be seen in the famous bronze reliefs on the doors of the Baptistery of St John in Florence created in the early fifteenth century by the Florentine Lorenzo Ghiberti. These are a spectacular example of the bronze casters' craft at its best. I've had many goes at relief sculpture, from half-inch cameos and intaglio copies of Roman hardstone gems, through to large terracottas and marble reliefs in the style of Clodion. One of my inspirations and someone I've learnt a lot from by studying his technique is the English artist William Hackwood. He did most of the reliefs and 'cameos' that are so familiar on the ceramics of the potter Josiah Wedgwood. But he was a very fine artist, not credited as he should be.

During the eighties, I made and sold a number of hardstone gems in the style of the ancients, mostly intaglios cut with all kinds of deities and figures from mythology. The best sellers turned out to be carnelians and amethysts carved in a style that led their 'expert buyers' to conclude they weren't actually ancient, but done in the sixteenth or seventeenth centuries in imitation of the antique. Those dealers loved to prove their superior connoisseurship by pointing out the details the cutter had 'got wrong' and which had been 'done in the style of his own age'. It was all I could do to stop myself laughing. I usually resorted to that old trick used down the ages to diminish the impact of figures of authority – I tried to imagine the dealer naked! I've got a pretty vivid imagination, so that soon wiped the smile off my face.

During my last few days in Rome, I went to look at the sculptural fountains in the Piazza Navona, done by Bernini and very showy things. Years later, I learned of a model of one of these fountains, the one at the northern end of the Piazza, the Fountain of the Four Rivers. It had been cast in solid silver by Bernini, or at least his workshop, as a gift to a female relative of the reigning Pope to gain favour and help along the commission of the actual fountain. As this silver model was well-documented, I had the idea to replicate it. At almost 3 feet high and a weight I never fully calculated, the purchasing of enough metal to finish it would have been beyond my pocket. So I never got around to doing it. The furthest I got was the modelling of the four allegorical female nudes. I sold a few casts of them in terracotta, obviously not as the work of Bernini, but as decorative things without a pedigree. What their purchasers sold them on as, I have no idea.

The last thing I went to see in Rome, and my favourite building there, was the Pantheon. It dates in its present form from the first century and seems to defy its age. There are several tombs within its walls and the famous Portland Vase, which now resides in the British Museum, was supposedly found here hundreds of years ago. Personally, I reckon it to be a product of a Venetian glassworks of the seventeenth century. But what do I know.

The most important tomb in the Pantheon is that of Raphael, though some kings of Italy rest here too. To the Romans, it was the great temple of all the gods, dedicated by Agrippa before the time of Christ. The gilt bronze lettering of the dedicatory was nicked long ago, but the fastening holes in the stone still give it away. I think the original building must have been similar in style to the existing front portion with its great granite columns surely brought from Egypt. The Egyptian masons were the ones to go to for granite work in the ancient world. Even now, some of their efforts would give today's workshops a few problems. The granite columns are one-piece turnings, almost 50 feet high. Built onto them is the later drum and dome we see today. It's an outstanding piece of architecture. The dome, in gradated concrete and greater in circumference than that of St Peter's built one and a half millennia later, grows thinner towards the top and if extended into a sphere would balance perfectly on the floor of the temple! The architect is unknown, but was most likely a Greek mathematician. Whoever it was, they've left us a gem.

Looking into the geometry of buildings such as the Pantheon has always been of interest to me. The relative proportions of good architecture are a good exercise for the mind. Getting the right proportions in a work of art is crucial to achieving the right look. What is it in a sculpture that tells you it is Egyptian, Greek, Roman? Above all, it's the proportions used by the artists of the time. They are subtle, but definitive, and regularly overlooked by copyists and experts. I've always paid close attention to such details, not particularly to dupe people with my concoctions, but just out of interest. It's the thing in a work of art or architecture that I notice first, before seeing the detail, colour or anything else.

Whilst in Rome, I made sure to take along my sketch pad and draw what I saw. They weren't very good drawings. I didn't have the time. I also discovered a fascinating mini manufactory. It was situated in an alleyway off the Piazza Farnese. Just a bench and a canopy in a recessed doorway, with a small furnace blazing away on the pavement, powered by bottled gas. On the bench was arrayed a range of rough little bronzes in fake green and black patinas, the type sometimes offered by dodgy antiquity dealers with 'found on the Palatine Hill in 1745' types of provenances. The whole set-up was transported in a large wheelbarrow. I thought it the best thing I'd seen in ages.

Through my crap Italian, and the stallholders' even worse English, I learned that the displayed bronzes weren't actually for sale, but if I stumped up the cash I could return in the afternoon and collect my freshly made choice. However, looking closely at the operation, I noticed that the moulds were as unreal as the statues. The bronze would have poured straight through them and into the sand box below. Oops. I had outstayed my welcome! They told me to eff off in pretty good English. One of them had arms like legs, so I promptly did eff off. They most likely bought in their castings from Hong Kong or somewhere similar. They really were crappy things. Not long after returning home, I managed to cast far more believable works in Bolton than I'd seen outside the Palazzo Farnese in Rome.

Some years after this visit, I had some success as well selling fragmentary pieces in bronze and marble of supposedly old monuments from the demolition of the original St Peter's in the early 1500s. Also some pieces rescued from the burning of the Basilica of St Paul in Rome in 1823. From this same basilica I did some reproduction saints' heads in fresco that were taken to be by Pietro Cavallini – an artist of the late thirteenth century – and identified as such by prominent experts. They'd never been anywhere near Rome. I painted them in my shed in the twentieth century.

Time finally ran out on me and my first trip to Rome was over all too quickly. I hadn't managed to see half of what I'd wanted, but it was still a fantastic holiday. Arriving back in Manchester and climbing into the minibus for the drive home, it was welcome to reality and quite a depressing journey. Bolton looked worse than I remembered it. Although I'd only been away a short time, I'd felt more at home in Rome and hadn't thought once of my real home. The town seemed so small and plain. But, to be fair, compared to 'the glory of Rome' most places would come up short, wouldn't they?

My dull mood was down, also, to the realisation of how lacking I was in artistic ability. I'd felt this sense of inadequacy before, when I'd first seen the treasures of the British Museum. Amongst my friends and family, I hadn't met many people who could draw, paint and model as well as I could. Even though I'd seen great pictures and sculptures in books, they didn't really register as being out there. Now I knew they were. I wasn't just a tiddler in a small pond. As far as art was concerned, I was a bit of plankton in an ocean. I had to get better or give up. My expectations had gone way up. I owe that to my Rome trip.

Back at school, revision for exams was something in which I had little interest. My mind was elsewhere. I sat my six papers and as far as I was concerned that was that. The summer of 1976 was long and hot, and now that school was finally out of the way I looked around for something to do. My mum and dad were pretty despairing of me and would take every opportunity to remind me that I had no job and no prospects. And that if I didn't go to college I'd end up in the gutter. Well, I didn't fall quite that far, but prison's not too far off the gutter, is it? I should have listened. But 'should' never mended anything, did it?

My first job came about as a result of my friendship with a lad from Harwood, one of my school friends. His dad ran an architectural salvage firm and I was regularly round at his house – more on account of his sister than anything. I was terribly shy in my teens. I'm not much better now. So I would hang around whenever she was about, thinking of any excuse to stay and talk. This lad had started work in his dad's firm. I asked if there were any jobs going. And into work I went. Most of the stuff in the salvage yard came from the demolition of the mills and factories that were being torn down at the time. We usually got to them before any real destruction had begun and had the run of the place. It was quite eerie to walk through these massive buildings, completely empty. The scrap metal men had usually been in before us, breaking up the spinning frames to be carted away and recycled in Japan or Taiwan into heaven knows what. All that was left were acres of oily floorboards looking like the flight deck of an old aircraft carrier.

The firm was based in one of Bolton's oldest mills, known as the Royal George, part of 'Flash Street Mills' in the town centre, first opened to a grand fanfare in the early years of the nineteenth century by Beau Brummell's fat mate, the Prince Regent. There were several Royal-this and Royal-that mills on the site, all set around a fine cobbled quadrangle. The famous American landscape painter Thomas Moran, whose work I particularly admire and have copied on many occasions, was born in Bolton and went to America as a child. Apparently, his brothers worked at these mills when they were quite new. The salvage yard, set in a quiet corner between the George and Sovereign Mills, was packed with loads of fine hardwoods, doors, panelling, fittings in wood and brass, which we would take from the offices and boardrooms of the soon-to-be smashed buildings. Setting off early in the morning, we'd travel all over the North West, mainly around Oldham and Manchester. These were the kinds of places seen in the paintings of L. S. Lowry and, though Lowry's millscapes were almost always imaginary views, the mills and, their environs on the Oldham Road is where he sketched and drew his raw material.

One part of the firm's trade was removing and selling the stained-glass windows we would find in the stairwells and entrance porches. We would measure them, cut plywood stretchers to fit each individual window exactly, cut away the iron bracings and leading that held them in place, and lower the window, stretcher and all, as carefully as we could, so as not to crack any of the hundreds of delicate pieces of coloured glass that went into making what were, in many cases, true works of art. I preferred the later pieces found in some of the last cotton mills to be built in Lancashire in the 1920s. Their subjects tended to be lighter and brighter than the grim high-Victorian stuff found in earlier mills. The best of them were in Tiffany style, with iridescent glass and beautiful marbling, depicting verdant scenes in a nouveau manner. They contrasted starkly with the grim religious subjects of the Victorian mills and seemed to be saying, 'Bugger all that hard graft of yester year. Let's have a good time.'

One very fine and poignant set of stained glass that I particularly remember was something we took from a Regency mill in central Manchester. The place was quite small and finely built. It should really have been a listed building. When I think of some of the crappy edifices that have that protection because of a tenuous connection with some turned-to-dust king or other such wastrel, this industrial gem certainly warranted saving. The windows set into the main stairwell depicted scenes from the slavery triangle between Liverpool, West Africa and the Americas. A vertical panorama, 50 feet tall, in 15 perfectly preserved panels of the best quality stained glass, it showed ships leaving the port of Liverpool; chilling scenes of chained and bound human beings in Africa amongst elephants, leopards and crocodiles; a slave market in Charleston; and views of the cotton fields. Lastly, there was the Manchester Cotton Exchange, with brokers and mill owners in frock coats and stovepipe hats, in a dark and smoky landscape of mill chimneys. All very evocative and a major historical artefact, if ever I saw one. We removed it and the panels were quickly sold to a collector in the USA, where they must still reside. By rights, they should have gone to the Victoria and Albert Museum. At that time, no one cared.

We packed them up and off they went on their journey across the Atlantic, courtesy of one of the other businesses that had found a home in the mills where I worked, an antiques dealer and shipper by the name of Monks, who ran the business with his wife and owned several antiques shops all over the country. They would pack sea containers full of furniture and junk, and send them off across the waves to their destination – the North American market. I was to have more to do with them during the eighties, but at this time, I knew nothing about them.

This first taste of work wasn't as mundane as I'd imagined and was really quite interesting. The offices of many of the old cotton mills we would visit had the look of being freshly abandoned – as if the workforce had gone out for lunch and never returned. Filing cabinets still with all the documents in them; desks and chairs, some of them fine pieces of furniture; even large gilt-framed oil paintings of stern-faced capitalists sporting side whiskers looking down from the walls of their fallen empires. All quite a sad sight. My parents and eldest brother had worked in these cotton mills in their youth and they would talk of them as places full of laughter and noise. By the time I got there they were deathly silent with just the sound of the wind blowing in where we had recently removed the stained glass from the windows.

My first job didn't last long. My mate's sister was, after all, my boss's daughter and, although we had been going out for a while, I think he preferred someone for her with more of a future, and made sure I knew it. Some months later, when I went off to Deal to join the Royal Marines – yet another wrong direction as it turned out – she dumped me. In 1983, her brother contacted me to say he had started up on his own and wanted to know if I was interested in sharing costs on a brick-cleaning machine he was getting from Germany? Within a few years, he'd built a big business from re-cycling the old bricks from those mills we used to visit, palletting them and flogging them to fancy housing developments in the South East. As usual I missed out on a fine opportunity. If only I'd invested, I'd probably be living in Cheshire's Football Belt, as he does. Years later, his sister Catherine wrote to me in prison, whether out of sympathy or happy memories, I don't know. I prefer to imagine it was the latter.

Throughout the six or seven months I worked at the reclamation yard I had some spare time to knock out a few pictures and ceramics. None were in my own style. All mimicked the manner of others completely. I didn't really know what 'my style' was. For as long as I'd been able to hold a pencil, copies were what I did. Many artists down the ages have learnt from copying the work of their predecessors, but, for some reason, I had done almost nothing else. It was never a conscious decision. Just something that evolved over time. I therefore thought it might be time to see if I could do something original. After seeing what proper artists could do on my recent eye-opener of a visit to Rome, I took it into my head to have a go at stone carving. It's something I'd wanted to try for a while, but my dad's garden shed at home wasn't really suitable. The tap, tap, tap of the mallet would have gotten on everyone's tits, neighbours included. So I'd put it off and kept to the quiet world of painting and pottery. Now, though, I had the opportunity to use the reclamation yard at weekends, when there was no one around to annoy. And could hammer away at full steam.

I knew where to get the stone – Gerrards, the kindly sellers of my garden ornaments. I also knew that marble sculpture was still probably beyond my ability. So I asked them what they recommended and settled on a block of lovely white limestone of a medium hardness. I worked on it at weekends for about three weeks and could bang away at that rock without disturbing anyone. My dad had got me the tools – mallet, chisels, even some marble points, along with an antique pair of compasses for marking and measuring the stone. These were given to him by an old man whose father had worked on the Anglican cathedral built in Liverpool in the early years of the twentieth century. I used them for the next 30 years on my own stonework and they now reside with the Scotland Yard detectives who took them away in 2006.

My first attempt at stone cutting needed to be something relatively simple. I thought first to do a version of Bernini's head of

Medusa, the one in the Palazzo dei Conservatori on the Capitoline Hill. How's that for overconfidence! Sense prevailed and what finally grew out of my stone lump was something Egyptian. One of my favourite periods is the Old Kingdom. The limestone funerary heads of this great artistic era are amongst the finest things in portrait sculpture. I always see something very modern in them. In saying modern, I mean modern to me. The works of such artists as Brancusi, Modigliani, Epstein, Gill and Henry Moore are close to the cut-off point of my interest in art. My 'art history clock' seems to have stopped on the day I was born. I know nothing of contemporary art and have always had little interest in it.

My first effort in stone turned out to be similar to the Old Kingdom heads of ancient Egypt – a bald-headed, plump, middle-aged man, who I decided might be a priest or scribe. After knocking him about a bit and mounting him as I'd seen it done in museum exhibits, I flogged him to our neighbour in the Flash Street Mills, the antiques shipper, Frank Monks. He and his wife would stop their van outside the yard and watch as I hammered away. This always put me off. Being watched at work always makes me feel self-conscious. I'd usually stop work until they buggered off. Mrs Monks or Eileen, as I later came to know her, asked to buy the head, but her husband began talking it down saying it 'somehow didn't look right'. I was used to this 'good cop, bad cop' routine. Unknown to them, I had been selling pot lids and pictures for years to dealers who were just like them. It was always the same routine – there's this or that wrong with it, 'so I can't pay top money', followed by me feigning to put the thing back in its bag and leave. This usually had the desired effect. I played the same game on the Monkses and eventually got a good sum for my first sculpture. I don't know what happened to it after that. But they came back for more, so they must have done all right out of that first purchase.

Shortly after finishing the sculpture, I chucked my job as a wrecker and spent the last few weeks of the year working for the

Associated Dairies, courtesy of my mum. The guy who delivered the dairy produce to where she worked got me on and I spent a not unpleasant few weeks rumbling around the countryside in a milk tanker collecting the white stuff from various farms. I wouldn't have minded being a farmer. But all those tons of cow shit were a bit off-putting. The whole place seemed awash with the stuff. I'm sure a cow must give more muck than milk.

Around then, I also had a go at being a 'craft potter'. I was aware of such names in modern ceramics as Bernard Leach from St Ives – my parents had a few of his Japanese-inspired pots from our holidays there – and the transported German potter Hans Coper. Inspired by Coper's 'thistle vases', I made my own 'signature pots' – pyramid vases. These were little more than Coper rip-offs. The same T-material body and manganese dioxide slip decoration, but instead of being thistle-shaped, mine were pyramids, large and small, cut to a range of upright designs. When finished, they looked better than I had hoped, quite original in their way. I completed the look with a Coperesque seal stamp of my initials set vertically in an Egyptian-style cartouche, to go with the pyramid scheme. To my surprise, they sold very well. Even today there must be quite a few in existence out there somewhere.

The problem was, I didn't want to be a potter. Although I enjoyed potting very much, it was a sculptor-painter that I wanted to be, as I began fiercely regretting my decision not to follow art academically: not for the instruction, but for the doors it could open and the contacts. Still, it's too late now, I decided, so just get on with it, Shaun. The sad point is, looking back from my 50 years and more, it wasn't too late at 17, was it?

As far as sales were concerned, my watercolours, done as best I could in my own manner, weren't going too well. However, a couple of Lakeland views that went into an exhibition at the Octagon Theatre in Bolton did sell for a good price. The purchaser was a Bolton councillor who later left most of his art collection to Bolton

Museum, the purchasers of the Amarna Princess statue that was one of the main reasons for my conviction in 2007. This councillor wrote to me at my parents' home to ask if I would be interested in painting other works for him. It turned out that some of his pictures were to be put in store and he wanted copies of them. I did several watercolours for him of Alpine scenes by the critic John Ruskin. I think these were inspired by Ruskin's obsession with Turner and they were quite reminiscent of the Yellowstone series of pictures by Thomas Moran. I had no problem doing them, as my own style is similar to his. So I got on with it and, yet again, instead of pursuing my own path, almost without realising it, I was copying other work again. No matter how I tried, all the paths seemed to lead back to copies. Deeply despondent at not being able to make any headway in my chosen direction, I decided to set off at right angles to it.

During my trips to Manchester for materials, I would pass by the Royal Navy Recruiting Office situated in a black and white 1960s' high rise. It was on the ground floor and had large posters in the windows showing what a life-changing opportunity lay within. So in I went, and came out again shortly after with a handful of bumf about how great it all was and an appointment to attend a medical the following week. More out of curiosity than anything else, I did go, sat an exam, such as it was, and that was that. A fat man in a green hat and red sash said brusquely, 'If you're up to the mark, you'll get word through the post in a few weeks.' He looked like Porky the Pig and I'd have bet he himself couldn't run a mile. Shortly afterwards, I heard from the Royal Marines and received a travel warrant for the 4th of January. I was to go to the Royal Marines training establishment at Deal in Kent. All I knew of Deal was that it had a Tudor fort.

As there were still some months to go before the big change of direction, I plodded on with my unloved job on the cow-shit express, which was gradually starting to grow on me. Cattle are quite an interesting subject to sketch and paint, though limited in their appeal as far as sales go. The best sellers in animal art, as far as I could tell, were cats, then dogs, followed by owls for some curious reason. Ceramic owls never fail to find a ready market.

For a time, I got interested as well in trying to copy the porcelain that I had seen at Mr Whitton's house. Mostly Chelsea along with some early Worcester. At the time of my 'First Porcelain Period' I wasn't too aware of the chemistry of the individual makes which gave them their distinctive attributes, but my models were quite accurate copies, even down to an enlargement of about 10 per cent to allow for shrinkage. These efforts weren't meant to deceive anyone. They were decorative lookalikes and wouldn't have fooled any expert.

During those months leading up to Deal, I tried my hand at quite a few different things, amongst them, for the first time, etching. It was something I had wanted to try much earlier, but the stumbling block was the printing. I solved this by persuading my dad to borrow a small rolling press from the print shop at the Tech. Described as 'small', it was so big it needed transporting by van. By this time, the garden shed had filled to bursting point with my 'rubbish' as it was generally referred to. Forgetting the fact that I was soon to be off on my new career with Porky Pig, I decided there was need for expansion. Backing onto the rear garden at my parents' house was a row of garages owned by the council. Several of these were to let, so I persuaded Dad to get one, ideally one that backed onto ours. Mum and Dad seemed unusually co-operative with all this and ceded to my every request. I think it was their way of trying to dissuade me from going south. It wasn't that they were overprotective, just that what I had decided wasn't what they hoped for or had in mind for me.

My new workshop became my priority. Spending a small fortune on plywood and fittings, I built benches and shelves for all my things and when I'd moved everything in there was still masses of space for a bigger kiln. As it was all concrete, I could do my casting without fear of burning the place down. The only not doable thing was painting. For me, natural light is a must. So, disappointingly for everyone else, I wasn't completely out of sight and mind when doing my 'barmy arty stuff', as my little sister put it. That, I had to do in the house.

My new 'studio' was making me have second thoughts about leaving in January. I had enough money to fit it out with all manner of equipment, chuck my job and still afford to pay my way for the foreseeable future. But, for some reason, just when I could have had a proper go at things and was happy enough with my life in general, I buggered everything up with this Royal Marines escapade.

I hadn't told Catherine, my girlfriend of these last five months, about my latest brainwave and when I finally summoned up the courage she responded badly. A mega sulk, as I remember calling it at the time. But it became more than that and I was dumped before even getting to the year's end. I've always had an impetuous nature and tend to go off on tangents without thinking of the consequences. The loss of someone in my life who meant a great deal to me made quite a dent in my reasonably happy life. That was the point at which I chucked in my job, packed up those monotonous bird paintings I'd been slaving away at for years and scrapped, broke, smashed or buried all my ongoing projects. The weekend saw the massacre of every one of my pots, clay models, moulds, and all the pictures and drawings I could lay my hands on. The floor of my concrete studio looked as if the bull from the china shop had thrown a tantrum in it. Disconnecting the power cable, I locked the place up. But, not to lose tenancy of it, I gave my dad the next few months in rent for the garage. Something deep within me seemed to know that one day I would be in need again of what was left of my art stuff.

The 4th of January arrived and after saying my goodbyes to everyone and prising myself out of the clutches of my weepy mother, I set off for the station in Bromley Cross. My dad came with me. He travelled to work at the Tech every day on the 8.10 from Blackburn to Manchester and, by coincidence, this was the time I had to set off to reach Deal by 5pm. Dad did his best to persuade me that I was making a mistake. He even offered to go back home with me and 'ring those cabbage heads in Deal' to tell them I wouldn't be coming. He went on to say that if I wanted to be an artist, and do my own thing, that was fine by Mum and him. There would be no more talk of further education. But the thought of backing out of a commitment was something I didn't fancy. I'll just go down there and see what it's all about, I said, and if it isn't for me I'll junk it and be back before you miss me.

I knew from reading the bumf given to me earlier by Porky the Pig that I had at least three opportunities in my eight months' training to exercise the option to leave before committing to nine years' minimum service. So as far as I was concerned there wasn't anything to lose by having a go. Besides, as Porky had said, they might 'boot me out before my feet touch down'. As things turned out, I took my final option to leave at the end of June, just a few weeks before having to commit to the full nine years. By the time I left, the original 50 of our troop had been whittled down, through injury or being unsuitable or being booted out, just like Porky said, to just 17.

My dad left the train at Bolton looking dejected. He was probably thinking of the bollocking he'd get that evening from my mum for failing to talk me out of leaving. I arrived at Euston after lunch in two minds. Was it to be the British Museum for a good look round or Deal? Deal won, though only just.

It was gone 5 when I arrived in Kent. Stepping off the train I saw a man dressed similarly to Porky at the Recruiting Office, only this chap was much thinner. Standing sheepishly around him were several bewildered teenagers and he gestured to me to join this far from merry band. Remembering my manners, I made my first mistake by referring to him as 'sir', to which he growled, 'Get this straight, and that goes for all you tossers, you don't call me sir. I'm Sergeant!' I don't recall his name, so let's call him Sgt Dickhead. The depot was a soulless place, all squat brown-brick buildings and what I took at first to be an all-weather footy pitch. It was actually the parade ground, complete with flagpole and a brass ship's bell. I got to know the sound of that bell very well. It was just outside our barrack room windows and every morning it would clang into life at 6 am, accompanied by a berk blowing a bugle.

The first few days were pretty easy-going; a few lectures and some form-filling, with spare time to look around and play snooker or pool. Not too bad I thought, and easier than I expected. A few lads gave up in those opening days without giving anything the chance to sink in. A couple of weeks later, I wished I'd been one of them as it got progressively more physical, though not impossibly so. One of the things that used to amuse me no end was the long run and march in full kit. We'd be followed for miles by a truck onto which the odd 'blower' – as those who ran out of steam were called – would have to struggle. The Company Officer, who also travelled in the truck, would then jump out and run past us making out we were unfit while they were fresh, not surprising given they'd only run half a mile or so. However, the boozing of the night before soon got the better of them and back they'd go to the truck to be replaced by another cork-nosed corporal. Most of us were only 16 or 17. We could have run all day if needs be.

My favourite times were when we went to the range. I'd had air rifles for years. I'd fired shotguns and even tried a particularly interesting flintlock called a Brown Bess that belonged to my cousin. A modern remake of a muzzle-loader used in Napoleonic times, it was loaded from an antique copper powder flask. Then you primed the pan, closed the snap over the charge, cocked it 'all the way back', as per his bossy instruction, and kaboom, a huge cloud of smoke and a kick like a mule. I managed to miss everything I fired at. I think it was the prospect of a face full of sparks that put me off and I just hoped I wasn't expected to shoot a musket here.

The range was on a long shingle beach beneath the white chalk cliffs that stretched on to Dover. Half the troop took turns at shooting and running up the targets from the butts. As the bullets came whizzing over our heads and thudding into the backstop of sand, it brought my granddad back to mind, and those of his generation who had the courage to stand up in front of such things and do what was demanded of them.

The range days were OK, but never being very prim or tidy, I found the bullshit a bit over the top. Loads of polishing and ironing of clothes, that kind of thing. The room with the shiniest floor won a sponge cake for polishing! More interesting were the days spent at a place called Kingsdown some distance inland. Running around the Kent countryside, playing at soldiers, I'd noticed lots of ancient features in the landscape, mostly barrows of a kind I'd never seen before. I suppose this proliferation was down to the long and densely populated history of Kent. Not having the eye of an archaeologist, I found it difficult to distinguish the different periods. One thing I did know was that the earlier barrows were precisely aligned between a settlement area and the horizon at the Winter Solstice.

I had worked that out myself a few years earlier at Darwen, a few miles from Bolton where the M65 motorway now passes over the road to Blackburn. High up on the moors is a double barrow that was dug out in the nineteenth century and proved to be Middle Bronze Age. At a spot below, near a pub called The Golden Cup, is a group of springs welling up from fissures in the rock from the descending water running underground. This, combined with it being on a defendable spur above the river Darwen, made it a likely settlement. Through a few summers I worked out the exact setting point of the Winter Solstice. And the sun does indeed set over The Golden Cup on the 21st of December.

Back in Kent, I didn't get as much free time to study the ancient monuments as I would have liked and the next three months were mostly spent learning a soldier's trade. The most interesting field trip was to a place in the Scottish Highlands, Loch Ewe on the north-west coast, where our time was taken up in various Action Man pursuits. We travelled up to Inverness on the overnight sleeper, by coach past Loch Maree and then on to the naval base. Ewe, a sea loch, is where the battleship *HMS Nelson* was torpedoed at the beginning of World War Two. There's a marker buoy anchored over it. I'd been to the Highlands before on a couple of fishing trips – well, my dad and brother did most of the fishing while I searched for banded agates and carnelians. I built up a good collection of fine specimens and, years later, when I had the confidence to try them, I used most of my collection to cut cameos and intaglios out of them in imitation of antique and later gems. They sold quite well.

The best stone I ever found was a large cairngorm, a famous and valued gem of old Scotland. They were usually set into big silver brooches, the type you see pinned to full Highland dress in the fine painted portraits of clan chieftains by Ramsay and Raeburn. This one, which I virtually trod on, wasn't found at their usual find spot around the Cairngorm mountains in the eastern Highlands but at a place my dad and brother Ted had gone fishing. We'd taken the train from Fort William at the foot of Ben Nevis to Loch Shiel. There, on the shore of the loch, is a tall monument dedicated to Charles Edward Stuart – Bonnie Prince Charlie of Culloden fame. I found the big cairngorm on that shore. It hadn't been cut or set and was still in its natural glacial polish and scratch finish, quite unusual in that place and pretty rare anywhere. A while back, I believe there was a discovery by the lake of an old inscription carved onto a boulder alluding to the raising of the prince's standard. I wish I'd seen it.

By the time we finished our basic training in Deal our troop was down from its initial 50 to 27. My parents travelled down to watch the passing out parade and to see me standing to attention like a toy soldier. But the Marines hadn't done with me yet. After a couple of weeks' leave it was on to the Commando Training Centre at Lympstone in Devon. It's an area I knew already from our holidays down the road at Dawlish. As a kid, I'd been taken every year to Cornwall and a couple of times to Devon. In Dawlish, I'd painted the black Aussie swans for which it was famous and gone out with my dad late at night to poach the hundreds of trout that infested the river running through the town. According to Dad this wasn't a serious poaching expedition. 'Just a taste of the old days.' But it fairly put the wind up me.

At Lympstone, our days were spent doing drills and on the assault course, which I liked, with a few hours on the range as well. Every time we'd go out to Woodbury Common to practise fieldcraft or map orientation some corporal or other would start lobbing their thunder flashes and set fire to the gorse, which – it being early summer – was tinder dry. The rest of the day would then be spent firefighting. By the time I left in June, firefighting was what I was best at.

With just a few weeks to go before the final tests for the coveted 'green beret', our troop was now down to less than 20 men and it would soon be time to make a commitment to sign on for the nine years – or take the final opportunity to leave. I'd decided long ago that I was going. Nine years seemed such a long time when I'd only just turned 17, so I exercised the option. I had to go and see a Captain – the first and last one I'd spoken to in my time there – and he said I was passing up a fine opportunity and was doing something I'd regret. I told him my mind was made up. Packing my bags, I got a travel warrant and scarpered. I've never regretted it for a moment. Leaving Rambo HQ, with my short but interesting adventure over, I was now amongst the ranks of the unemployed, and my mind turned back to where it had always really been – the world of fine art and history.

My first priority, even before I started looking for a job, was to sort out the wrecked garage, refill Dad's shed with my rubbish and get cracking on refilling my bank account, too. I still worshipped money a bit in those days, and even God. The last seven months' pay, if you could call it that, had been abominable – £14 every fortnight – for which you had to queue up, sign and salute the pretty pay clerk, a constantly blushing Wren with a chest more like a frigate bird than a wren. I hope that's not offensive. She was the only plus in the whole deal. Unlocking the garage, I immediately regretted my brainstorm of destruction. Everything that had taken so much effort to do was now broken and scattered. Even the moulds for producing easily made money-spinners were beyond salvage. There was nothing to be done but to start again from scratch. I must have been in some mood when I trashed the place as even my salamander crucibles, usually treated with more care than a Ming vase, had been hurled at the concrete garage with enough force to leave little grey ghosts of them on the wall. My grumpy sergeant would have been impressed with the grouping of the shots. All five crucibles had hit the wall within a few inches of each other without once taking aim.

The bin into which my painterly stuff had gone was full of snapped and mangled canvases and stretchers, overflowing paperwork, expensive and now broken brushes. I'd even done a 'kung fu' on the oak painting easel and that, too, was almost beyond repair. Most of my early drawings had bitten the dust as well, along with everything else I'd ever made in all sorts of materials. It was a moment of destruction I've always regretted.

At a loss to know where to restart my artistic life, I cleared up the mess and spent the next few weeks repairing my few salvaged bits. The painting easel ended up with three bandaged legs. If it had been a horse, it would have needed shooting. My parents had by this time given up on my going into any kind of further education and suggested I get a job, preferably on the council, like my three brothers.

Dad knew several people in the different council departments during the sixties and seventies and, before long, I was wriggling my way out of various job interviews he'd 'kindly' set up. I'd no intention of letting my dad find me a job. And I was certainly not going to follow my brothers into council servitude. Not that I was a lazy bugger or anything like that. On the contrary, I've always put in maximum effort from an early age. Whatever else I've done, rightly or wrongly, being idle isn't one of them. It's just that my mum's mention of a 'secure job for life' on the council filled me with foreboding. Looking back, I should have listened to good advice, shouldn't I?

To get my parents off my back and put an end to their endless plotting, I found my own job, working for the Co-op. This, I thought, would satisfy my mum's yearning for security. My thinking was that the Co-op, being a bigger concern than Bolton Council, offered me the chance to have a job that would last two lifetimes, if only I could live that long.

The few weeks in between getting home from my misguided adventure in toy soldiery and securing a job for life, were spent casting about for a new direction in art. For 'inspiration' I'd been spending a bit of time in the Bolton Central Library, hoping to get some ideas. As I went into the old reference section, with its oak and glass bookcases, full of the best and most interesting volumes in the library, I noticed, up on the balcony, one of the female librarians struggling with some documents. As I passed her, there on the table were loads of large sheets of old paper. The archives, I could see, were being stripped from their Victorian binders and rebound in the latest acid-free covers. The black and tatty ribbon-tied binders were strewn across the floor, and the endpapers and flysheets were now piled on the table. Many of them were foxed, iron-spotted or water-stained.

Having a quick look through, I saw that many were water-marked in dates ranging from the 1850s to the 1880s. I asked the archivist what was to be done with this paper, fully expecting her to tell me to mind my own business. To my surprise, she said it was to be disposed of. 'Could I have some?' I asked. 'Help yourself,' she replied. I think she expected me to take a sheet or two. But I rolled up the whole bundle. And as she looked ready to say I was a greedy bugger and to put some back, I came up with the excuse that I was designing large posters for guide dogs for the blind and would easily put all those pieces of paper to good use. Wholly untrue. But it was all I could think up on the spur of the moment.

At the time, it wasn't clear to me what I would use all this old paper for. I hadn't, to date, ever attempted to do 'fake' pictures. My works, pot lids aside, had all been copies signed in my own name. Although I had my suspicions about the reasons I'd been asked to sign those bird pictures in the margins, and thought some of them were being sold on as something they were not, that wasn't anything to do with me. I was happy to get my £7 a time. Later on, this attitude was to change and some of those sheets did eventually make it through to the faking game. But for now, I innocently tucked that roll of old paper under my arm and carried it off home.

I started my new job at the Co-op that late July and ended up staying for a couple of years. My task was to make up the butchery orders for the stores around the North West and to help the old fella who ran the place keep stock. I think he'd strained a bollock lifting the sides of beef or something and I was to be his new assistant. The job was quite physical. But I was a strong lad in those days and, compared to the making and moving of the concrete gods and heroes I'd been doing, most of the chunks of flesh in the Co-op butchery department were lightweights. One thing it wasn't was demanding on the mind. So to keep the grey matter ticking over, and confuse the van drivers who delivered the orders, I'd sometimes write out the delivery orders in Leonardo's mirror writing. Some of the lads would start doing likewise, but usually made things even more illegible by writing backwards with the letters as normal. This even confused me and a truce was agreed. 'No more double bloody

Dutch,' said the boss. So I wrote him a note to '6, 21, 3, 11 off' in Roman numerals. Thankfully, he didn't twig.

As long as I had a regular 9–5 job – well, 6.30–4 – I had a quiet life and no hassle from my parents. Art-wise, my thoughts were still stifled. Around this time, I visited my former employer at the Flash Street Mills only to discover they had moved on to new premises across town. As I was passing the antiques shippers, the people who had bought that Egyptian stone 'scribe' some months before, I decided to go in and have a look around. I entered the workshop to the sound of whirring saws and woodworking machinery and there, at the far end of the building, half hidden in a cloud of sawdust, was old miser Monks. Well I say old. He couldn't have been more than the age I am now. But to me, at 17, he looked decidedly decrepit. Knocking off the machinery he made his way through the piles of old furniture, stacked yards high, to the fading whine of the saws.

He remembered that I was the one who had cut the 'uninspiring lump' as he put it and asked, 'What are you up to?' Thinking he was implying that I was out to rob the place, I replied, 'Just looking around,' but he was only enquiring into what I was doing for a living, not suspecting me of being a thief. Not that there was anything there to steal. I'd built bonfires with better stuff than was littering the floor of his 'antiques emporium' and, to retaliate for the 'uninspiring lump' slur, I told him so. In addition, but for his wife's intervention, I would probably have told him to FO, and that would have been that. But she looked much younger than him and was very easy on the eye, so I bit my tongue and explained that I was now working at the Co-op and doing nothing arty.

As we picked our way through the bonfire fodder to have a look, I asked what he was making in that dust cloud of a workshop. Puffing on a big cigar and wiping his hands with a rag that seemed to put on more dirt than it took off, soaked as it was in a strong-smelling and, most likely, highly flammable wood finish,

I half expected him to burst into flames at any moment. He said that his main business, after shipping antiques to Canada and the US, was furniture restoration. The only antique part of some of his restorations, he joked, was the old polish. Then he quickly added that he only ever sold genuine antiques as antiques.

As he rambled on, I noticed a large old book on the table in his ramshackle office – a plywood box in the corner, fitted with a few panes of glass. The book was a pattern book of Gothic-style oak furniture – chairs, tables, some ornate dressers – the type of stuff that my favourite architect of the Victorian age, Augustus Welby Pugin, used to design. Gothic isn't a style I generally prefer, in art or architecture, but the work of Pugin is outstanding. As most people know, the bulk of the Houses of Parliament – fixtures, fittings, finer points – is down to his vision. I remember as a kid going to see one of his finest masterpieces, St Giles Catholic Church in Cheadle, a small town in Staffordshire, only an hour or so from my home. It was wholly designed and fitted out in his High Gothic Revival style, and the standard of it, and of the craftsmen of the Victorian age who made its parts, is as fine as you will see anywhere. A real gem of a building.

The 'Victorians', especially when I was a lad, were rubbished at every opportunity and made out to be old-fashioned, dusty people by the 'moderns' of the sixties and seventies, an age that, in contrast, seemed to me to boast very few great engineering and scientific achievements, and to consist mostly of getting pissed or doped up and writing crap songs. I always thought picturing the Victorians as old-fashioned was a joke. The Britons of the nineteenth century were, in their own time, the most modern thinkers and doers in the history of civilisation. They made greater strides than any of the ancients, even the Egyptians, Chinese, Greeks or Romans. We live in a world wholly created by these people and, as far as I'm concerned, their achievement is so great that even now we are still in their shadow. Those outstanding people moved things on to a new age, that will, I'm sure, be seen one day as more significant than the great ages of Stone, Bronze and Iron that are so often trumpeted as the waymarkers of our civilisation. It was Victorian achievement that moved the world into a new, modern age. All ages and cultures have their deserved place in history. But credit where it's due.

Mr Monks had a thriving business in reproduction furniture, mostly of this Gothic Revival stuff, and he seemed to know a lot about the antiques trade. On the wall beside his office was a glass case holding a rather sad-looking stuffed pike. Thus our conversation turned to angling. He reckoned that one of the hot properties at that time was fishing trophies. He couldn't get hold of enough of them. My ears pricked up at this remark and I asked, 'You mean stuffed fish like that?' – pointing to the glass case. 'No, they're too Victorian for today's market' – this from a man who was making a living flogging sticks of Gothic Revival furniture!

The trophies he was referring to were those carved wooden game fish, painted and mounted on a framed board, with details of their capture and vital statistics printed along the bottom of the frame. 'The best prices at the moment are for salmon and specimen fish. You don't know anyone who has one do you, or any old fishing tackle?' he asked. I'd seen these trophies illustrated in some of my brother's large collection of fishing books when I was a kid, but imagined that they were the work of a taxidermist, not carved wood. I asked if angling pictures were in demand – after all, I was in the middle of an ideas famine. 'Anything old and to do with angling has a ready market,' he wittered on. 'I'll ask around, see what I can find,' was my reply. When he told me that he was paying £50 a time for salmon trophies, it was all I could do to stop myself from saying that I had at least a hundred of them and a whole warehouse full of fish pictures as well.

I came away from Monks Shippers with a new line in saleable products. The only problem was I'd never carved a wooden fish in my life. So the first stop was my brother's library to borrow some fish books. One of them was ideal. It listed all the big salmon caught in British rivers over the last 100 or so years, headed by the whopper of 70-something pounds caught by Miss Ballantyne. The book detailed dates, locations, everything I needed. Remembering Monks's American dealings, I borrowed another volume as well on American trout fishing in a place called the Adirondacks. Apparently, it was, and maybe still is, the favourite fishing wilderness of the New York millionaires, so by my reckoning they'd have commissioned loads of trophies.

My first setback came when I visited the timber merchants in search of a large lump of wood. For my first effort, I'd decided to carve a real whopper of a salmon in the hope of relieving Mr Monks of lots of his cash. Just like the concrete statues I'd done, these fish carvings had little or nothing to do with art, but I always had an eye open to do things for selling, and kept up my proper artwork, at that time at least, just for my own interest. The price the woodman quoted for a piece in the dimensions I needed, at least 40 by 16 by 8 inches, would have made the whole venture uneconomical. I solved the wood supply problems by returning to the reclamation yard where I'd worked. I knew they had a huge pile of old floorboards from the mills, so, for a peppercorn payment, I cut up as many as I wanted to 40 inches in length, and glued and clamped a bundle together.

Joined timber for carving isn't ever ideal. The glued joints cut awkwardly and these floorboards were of pine, just about the crappiest stuff you can get for detailed cutting. But needs must. In any case, after carving those trophies were gessoed and painted, and what the wood lacked I hoped to make up for with my hand and chisel. After doing some detailed projections of the book illustrations, and scrounging a free salmon head from a fishmonger's on Bolton market so as to get the most difficult bits anatomically correct – namely the eye surround and gill plates, which are quite subtle – I hammered away at my glued pile of floorboards over two weekends. After cutting the final detail into the gesso coating and finishing off with a wet sanding, I painted on the detail and mounted the wooden salmon onto a plywood panel which I'd taken from the back of a 1920s wardrobe, and then set the whole thing up into an old oak picture frame.

Up until the mid-eighties, it was easy to get hold of these old frames for very little money. They usually held Victorian prints and the junk dealers I got them from would rip off the original backings, usually breaking the glass in the process, in the hope of finding a lost masterpiece tucked in behind the worthless print. My final touch would be to add the details of the fish's capture, which I'd copy out from the book, not forgetting to dab the screws at the back with nitric acid which rusted them in hours to look all of their supposed 80 or so untouched years.

The last problem in my labour-intensive product was the glassy 'brand-new' look of the topcoat varnish. This was solved, after quite a lot of experimentation, with a concoction I made up from the stuff I used to colour up the small, Roman-style bronzes I'd been making since seeing them in Rome the year before. Applying the mix, having added a few other things to it, I'd let it take effect before arresting the 'ageing' process with a wipe from a milk-soaked rag. This took down the shine and got rid of any odours of newness to great effect. My potion was reused many times on all sorts of paintwork and, to my knowledge, was never once detected or suspected. Finally, there stood the 'antique' salmon trophy, ready for market, and quite some effort it had been.

The next attempts, now that all the teething troubles had been surmounted, came along much more quickly and easily. My weekly wage from the Co-op at this time was £37 a week for over 40 hours of hard graft, so even though the salmon trophies were a fair effort the 50 quid I got for them was well worth it to me. The next day, in slight trepidation, I went to see Monks and, plonking the newly made wooden fish down at the door of his ramshackle office, knocked on the door. He came out to examine it and seemed quite excited. Before he could say anything I chanced my arm and blurted out, 'I'll want at least £70 for it', more in the hope of distracting his attention from my fakery than any wish to overcharge. My ploy had no effect. He calmly propped it up on his desk and, saying nothing, closely examined it for some while. 'Where did you get this from?' he growled. At that moment I had intended to say I'd got it from one of the mill boardrooms I used to help dismantle in my old job, a job Monks knew I used to do so I thought that tale would sound plausible. For some unknown reason, probably because I was still essentially an honest person, or maybe just naive, I told him I'd made it.

He stood there saying nothing, puffing on a cigar and occasionally stepping forward then back several times to look at it closely. Finally taking the cigar from his mouth and pointing it at the fish, he turned to me and said, 'Do you know, I've been in the antiques business for over 30 years, and that bloody thing would have taken me in.' He was intrigued to know how the aged finish had been done, but seeing as how I'd sweated over its formulation I wasn't going to tell anyone. So I explained it away, much as I did to those Scotland Yard detectives decades later, as 'just old tea bags and dust'. To that, he gave me a sideways glance and shook his head. 'I could use that in my restorations.' I began to suspect Mr Monks was an antiques dealer in the mould of my bird paintings buyer in Manchester. And, as things turned out, he was. Many of them are. As I was later to discover.

My decision to make a clean breast of where the salmon trophy had come from turned out to be a good decision. Instead of only being able to sell one of them to Monks, and then having to go further afield to dispose of more, he gladly paid the £70 I'd asked and eventually bought every one of them. Over the next few months I made as many as I could spare the time for. But the fish trophy making didn't last very long. One of the brain-numbing things about them was the detailed paintwork on the scales. It almost sent me bananas. Though all that wood carving brought on my technique quite a lot, just as my mass-produced bird watercolours had done: practice, whatever the subject, has its effects.

Later on, I tried my hand at those Gothic Revival designs. All those disciplined architectural lines and tracery took some mastering. They needed to be tackled with confidence and ability to achieve the crispness of cut found in original work, but all of them were interesting projects. Another good line I tried whilst doing woodwork for Monks were ladder-back chairs with geometric inlay in the style of Charles Rennie Mackintosh. My paint distressing mixture came into very good use on those things. I'm sure many a dealer thought they had discovered a hidden treasure buried under layers of old paint.

During the time I was working at the Co-op and carving wooden fish for a living, I still found time to practise 'proper art' – drawing, painting and sculpture. My sculptures were my favourite things. At this point, they were mostly done in clay in pursuit of the great art I'd seen in Rome. These were the things that filled my thoughts, not my job or the daft wooden fish and the sticks of furniture. My drawings led me to make what was my first, and, for some time after, my only autograph fake. I practised drawing in all sorts of styles and periods, always using new paper, but experimenting with the inks and crayons to suit that particular era. This was something I'd done from an early age. By my late teens I must have done thousands of them. Part of the interest for me was to make up the inks and colours myself.

The most commonly used ink of earlier times was oak gall ink, which is very corrosive and attacks the paper over time. This corrosive effect is one of the things looked for on genuine Old Master drawings. The corrosive nature is down to the dilute sulphuric acid used in its make-up. Mixed with iron, it forms a sulphide which, when combined with the ground-up oak galls, produces a green-looking, watery ink. This ink, when drawn onto paper or parchment, oxidises and turns the familiar sepia tone so often seen in 'old drawings' and legal documents. Genuine sepia is encountered far less often. It comes from cuttlefish and, besides being far more expensive, displays a purple hue with middling pH.

Another often-encountered medium is red sanguine chalk. This is very easily made by heating cheap yellow iron oxide in vinegar to produce the distinctive red pigment so often encountered in everything from ancient Egyptian wall paintings to the colour schemes of Roman villas. Just grind the resulting heated iron and vinegar sludge, mix to a thick paste with gum arabic, roll it out into chalks, leave to air-dry and start scribbling away. There are other things such as silverpoint, a great favourite with the masters. It takes a very good and confident hand to get something convincing with it, so I'll skip that one to save my blushes. Most of my post-eighteenth-century copies were in charcoal or graphite. Unlike the earlier stuff, these could be bought from any artist materials shop, so I didn't need to make them myself.

At the time of doing my first proper fake, I had a passing interest in the Impressionists, something quite unusual for me. The Impressionists had been 'done to death' in the seventies, but, despite their overexposure, the work they produced is so original, so outstandingly beautiful to look at, that I don't think it will ever fall out of favour. My own favourite Impressionist painters are Degas and Renoir, both of whom tried their hand at sculpture. Their painting hand is first-class, but I'm not greatly impressed by their sculptural efforts. It's just a personal opinion. Who am I to judge? Some of their paintings have the delicacy of pastels in the way the paint seems to be laid on with the draught from a dragonfly's wing. Not an easy thing to achieve.

Of the painters of slightly later times, the ones I most like are Lautrec and, of course, Vincent. The first for his masterly draughtsmanship, the other for being a painterly genius. Genius is a word

I use sparingly, but for van Gogh there's no other way to describe him. Both were heavily influenced by the great Japanese print-makers of earlier times, both were one-off originals, too. Not being at all original myself, I have a high regard for those who are.

Having the idea of copying a Degas drawing and, just for the devilment, signing it in the artist's name and seeing how far it might go, I was now committed to doing the most 'lookalike' fake I could manage. The old foxed paper I'd picked up in the Bolton Library came to mind. I'd use some of this to scribble away on in the hope of doing something convincing but immediately ran into problems with the paper. I was attempting to draw on it with shellac ink and the damn stuff just bled right into the surface as if I was writing on bog paper. At that time I knew little of the art of the faker and didn't realise that the size in the paper – the stuff it's treated with during manufacture to stop it blotting, essentially an animal glue made by boiling hoof and horn from the abattoir – breaks down over time. This fact, along with the corrosive action of the ink I mentioned earlier, is quite a stumbling block to doing an old drawing. As with most fake attempts, doing the arty bit is the least problematical. It's the ageing that's difficult and time-consuming. Especially if it's worth a lot of money. The more it's worth, the greater the scrutiny.

At the time, I couldn't overcome this bleeding ink problem and didn't want to re-size the paper as I thought this might give the game away. So I decided to do a charcoal drawing instead, a small ballerina sketch. Cutting up half a sheet into small pieces, I set myself a limit of half a dozen attempts so as not to waste too much of the irreplaceable old paper – at least at that time I thought it was irreplaceable. Immersing myself in Degas' style, but having at that time seen very few of his works in the flesh, I got the picture of what I wanted clear in my mind and quickly whizzed off six similar sketches. Picking the one that looked most convincing, and adding the 'D' and the squiggle signature, I fixed the charcoal and to give 'a little bit of authenticity' made up a small seal in imitation of the atelier stamps you find on many genuine works on paper. To avoid the problem of bleeding in the paper, I printed its impression on the drawing using a very viscous, home-made printing ink that was thicker than my head. Just for good measure, to colour it, I used red lead – lead sulphide. Modern reds are all synthetic and even at this time I made sure to use nothing on my work that wasn't of its period. I set it up in a suitably elegant and period frame, papered in the back with reused old paper from the backs of those oak frames I'd used to mount my salmon trophies, and even went to the trouble of gluing on that paper with furniture makers' 'pearl glue' which I'd noticed all nineteenth-century framers used. After all, if a thing's going to be attempted, it may as well be done properly. The whole thing took less than a week to do, including framing. Much less effort than those silly salmon. I photographed it and sent off my letter of enquiry, photo included, to a reputable London auction house and awaited their response.

That wait got my faker's nerves jangling for the first time and I must admit I found the whole thing quite exciting. Some weeks later, back came a letter from London informing me that they never made attributions from a photo, but if I would like to take the picture to their North West office someone would be there to have a look at it. I duly made an appointment to see the picture expert and, come the day, off I went with picture in hand – well, in a black plastic bin liner.

I hadn't been inside an auction house before and stood outside for a few minutes on the pavement feeling slightly intimidated and a bit guilty. I knew full well that if I'd taken my drawing to any of the antiques dealers back home I'd have been lucky to get a fiver for it, even if it really had been a genuine Degas. So, more out of a need to know from an 'honest broker' – as I saw the auctioneers at that time – how close I could get to the standard of a top-rate artist, and not with the main intent to rip anyone off, in I went.

The office was a plush affair and reminded me of Mr Toby Jug's shop, or 'gallery' as he insisted I refer to it, where I'd sold most of my pictures up until then. The haughty looking lady at the desk looked over her specs at me and asked what I wanted. After explaining myself, I was told to sit and someone would be down soon. Sitting there with my bin liner on my lap I almost bottled it and fled. Too late. In came a gentleman who introduced himself as the picture expert. Unwrapping the picture from its bin bag and placing the framed doodle on a desk easel he stood back to take it in as if he'd just drawn it himself. Standing there for what seemed like ages to me, he suddenly picked up the picture and took out his eyeglass to examine it closely, still saying bugger all. I thought he was going to ring the coppers, so I started to size up the exits. The room was lit by a large Georgian sash window and I had visions of leaping from this window and legging it up the street with the bin liner over my head, complete with an 'Elephant Man' style eyehole in it to aid my getaway.

He suddenly asked where I had acquired the picture. This little question took me by surprise, although it shouldn't have. While concentrating on drawing and framing it, I hadn't thought of a 'provenance'. Nothing I had made before had ever needed one. Eventually, these provenances became all-important – more so than the quality of the work. My thoughts flew quickly to Monks and his house-clearing work. The picture had come from a big house in Manchester, I said, but added that I knew no more than that. To change the subject, I asked if it was a print or a drawing. 'Well,' he replied, 'if you are in agreement, I would like to remove it from the frame to be sure.' 'Yes,' I squeaked, in an increasingly nervous voice. How much longer was this ordeal going to last, I thought, as the picture expert wrestled with the frame.

In no time he'd whipped the back off and, with what I noticed were trembling hands – probably not in anticipation of finding a long-lost masterpiece, but a result, more likely, of too much vino the night before – he removed the piece of old library paper from the mount, and made the rather encouraging comment that it looked as if the frame was original and hadn't been opened in a century. So far so good. His eyes immediately flew to the red atelier stamp, then a glance at the tonal difference in the paper where it had supposedly been hidden behind the card mount. This is due to light-fading over time and easily imitated with a pale wash, though on that old bleedy paper I used for my Degas it needed to be applied with an almost dry brush and a light hand. Simple stuff. But enough to kill off the hopes of anything without it.

Suddenly, the expert excused himself and left the room with the drawing. Again, my thoughts turned to what might happen next. He returned a few minutes later to ask if it would be OK to send it to London for further research, to which I agreed. I was desperate to get out of there. Handing over a receipt which described it as nothing more than 'a 19th c. drawing on paper for further research', I left with a quiet 'thank f*** that's over'. I never expected anything to come of it. But several weeks passed and eventually, much to my surprise, it was sold in a London sale as a genuine work. I went to London for the auction and it's still a happy memory. After the sale, a quick sum in my head to deduct the commission and the cost of that overpriced photo in the glossy catalogue, a price that now seemed piddling, and I had more money than I'd ever had before – a great deal more.

It was some time before I got my hands on the actual cash and, true to form, it started to burn a hole in the pocket. I was now old enough to ride on the road legally and instead of a second-hand Yamaha I treated myself to a brand new 250cc Montesa trials bike: Spanish and the best you could get. I was almost tempted, too, by that 1,000cc Laverda in Italian racing red I'd seen before, but not having a full licence and not wanting to be any more of a lawbreaker than my fake-selling had already made me, I kept to plan and got the Montesa.

VII.

Not doing Degas

La Bella Principessa
I saw this drawing in Milan in 2015 and despite all the frenzy in the press,
it is my work of 1978. Although it looks to have been gone over or 'restored'
by a better hand than mine. But, like me, no Leonardo!

Jefferson, by Jean-Antoine Houdon
This bust of the third president, Thomas Jefferson, is by the great French sculptor Houdon. I based the 'Greenough' bust — the one allegedly sold to another American president — on it. I'm showing Houdon's work here because there is no available image of mine.

Yellowstone, in the style of Thomas Moran
This little sketch — watercolour and body colour on tan paper — was a 15 minute splash of colour and light. Later, much to my regret, sold to my favourite childhood place, the Bolton Museum.

Gauguin Faun
This image makes it look better than I remember it. Done in three parts and authenticated by the Wildenstein Institute of Paris.

Goose, in the style of Barbara Hepworth
Done in my best terracotta clay. About three days' work for both modelling and moulding.

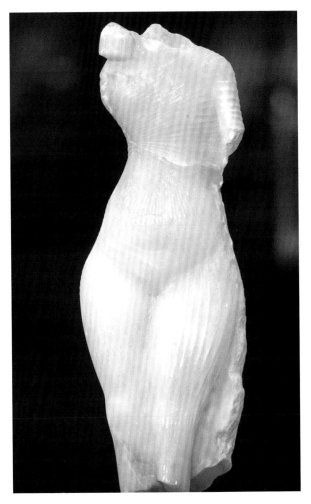

Amarna Princess
What more can I say!

Pot lids
These were the type of thing we dug up on the Victorian tips if we were lucky. My 'new' versions of them were my first fakes. This design was my best seller. Most lids are about 3 inches in diameter; this one was thought by its buyer in the 70s to be a 'Barbershop' piece. Anything American was at a premium, hence the design.
AUTHOR'S COLLECTION

Cross
A ' 12th century' silver gilt corpus, supposedly found in the tomb of King John at Worcester. Allegedly bought at auction by a senior member of the royal family.
A sketch because the image of its online catalogue description has been deleted.
AUTHOR'S COLLECTION

Risley Lanx
Sold to a dealer by my dad as a copy for £5000 in 1991. Then allegedly on
to the British Museum for a ten-fold increase.

Calcite head in Amarna style
Done in the early 1990s and never offered for sale.
A few days effort with wood chisel and rasp.

Assyrian priest
Looking worse than I remember it and the
one that brought my fakery to an end.

Before Kick Off
An oil loosely based on L.S Lowry's works from the 1920s and 1930s,
which I think his best period. Done in practice for my little stint
on the BBC series *Fake or Fortune* in 2015.

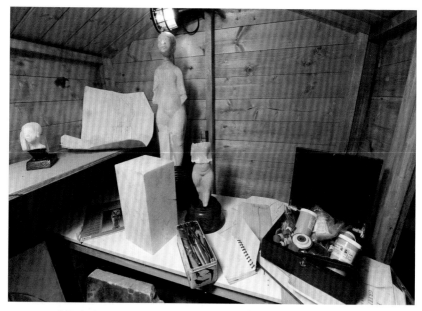

My shed — the 'northern annex of the British Museum' — as rebuilt by
the Victoria & Albert Museum for their *Fakes and Forgeries* exhibition in 2010.
Far too uncluttered to be authentic!

Me, my hawk, a 'Remington' and a gift
from my gran — the pullover!

AFTER THE UNEXPECTED success of that Degas sale, and the new-found money it brought, I had to be a bit careful of spending more than I could easily explain away. My parents were unaware of what I'd done, but they did know that I could make money out of my arty stuff. I'd been all right for money since the age of 13 or so, from when I had first started selling those pot lids. To 'camouflage' my spending, I started to put in long hours at work and in what spare time I did have kept busy doing legitimate projects, most of which were carving furniture details in oak for Mr Monks.

I still found time to enjoy the fruits of my ill-gotten gains. Every Sunday morning at the crack of dawn, even though it was the only day of the week I could have a lie-in, I'd be out and about on my new motorcycle. It was also the only day I didn't have to be at work, so for quite a while my bed took second place to my bike and I'd spend the day riding the trails up on the East Lancs Moors. But after a few weeks of this, the gilding seemed to wear off. Chugging away in the mud and muck of the moorland trails was fine, but on my way home I had to suffer the indignity of being burned off the road by every bike I encountered. A Montesa, despite being just about the best off-road bike you could get at the time, was no match for the Japanese road bikes that quite a few of my friends rode. They'd come whizzing by in a rerun of the tortoise and the hare parable, only in our version the tortoise never won. The 'slug' had to go. It was time to revisit that Aladdin's cave: Sports Motorcycles in Manchester.

Unfortunately, they didn't sell new Japanese bikes and, although I could now afford anything they had on show, several times over, my brother reminded me that my limit was a 250cc as I hadn't passed my test yet. In any case, he gleefully added, 'Everything here would be too much bike for you, kid,' referring to the Ducatis, Laverdas and Moto Guzzis that had caught my eye. Eventually, I got fixed up at a dealers much closer to home, a Japanese bike dealer in Bolton, where I bought one of the fastest 250s I could get – a storming race replica Kawasaki in lime green. It sounded like a giant wasp and was worth every penny it cost.

After buying that bike, I didn't get 'burned off' much. But I always treated it with a healthy respect. I was well aware that these things could be lethal in a moment of madness. Several of the lads I knew in my teens were to die in motorcycle accidents and I've had a few spills myself, including a 'big one' on my brother's monster bike, a Dunstall Norton. He'd bought it from a chap who raced in the Isle of Man TT. It was the fastest thing I'd ever been on. It ended its days embedded in the front of a Datsun pickup truck. That experience brought a pause to the speed need and the life-long, until then, motorbike fixation. If only it could have cured my other obsession – art – then the whole painful episode might have been worth putting up with. Unfortunately, my art bug survived the impact to grow ever larger. The only lasting cure for it would have been to squash me under the tracks of a battle tank.

Because of the six-day weeks I'd been putting in at the Co-op, and the carving away like a nutter I was doing in my dad's garage at all other times, no one batted an eyelid as to how I was funding my flash bikes. As the hedgerows and weeks sped by, the memory of the Degas drawing began to fade and my thoughts turned back to getting on with my artwork – though the temptation to do more fakery was definitely out. So I decided my art and craft equipment gathering dust and cobwebs in the garage needed an update. Some of it wouldn't have looked out of place in a medieval workshop.

The first thing to replace was the furnace I used for casting metal – a temporary affair modelled on the one I'd seen on that 'wheelbarrow foundry' in the back streets of Rome. It was soon superseded by a larger home-made thing that would have looked good in the backyard of the Beverly Hillbillies. Coke-fired and force-draughted, courtesy of a hairdryer I'd 'borrowed', it was finished off with an old iron downspout acting as a chimney. It looked awful, but worked amazingly well, melting a 20-pound weight of bronze in its crucible with ease and with enough draught to suck your socks off.

I had to choose my casting days with care. My mum and dad's house was in a smokeless zone so whenever they were going out for the day that would be my cue to fire up the 'Vulcan'. Getting it going usually filled the street with a huge cloud of smoke, but other people had barbecues that spewed out similar amounts of pollution so my attitude was 'bollocks to the neighbours', and I got on with casting. My parents never actually saw my 'Vulcan's barbecue' in action, but, thanks to my little sister, they heard rumours of it. Such was its bulk that when it was dismantled it filled three wheelbarrows with junk.

I really went to town on that refit, eventually buying a larger pottery kiln, a lapidary saw with some very expensive diamond blades, and some grinding wheels and burrs for the gem and hardstone work. The other side of the garage, meanwhile, was fitted out with new woodworking machinery for my latest venture. By then I was doing quite a few pieces for Monks – mostly carving details, Gothic tracery and finials, the more complicated the better as far as

I was concerned. I didn't mind doing these little jobs. The carving was quite sculptural and it wasn't as if they were mass-produced. I particularly liked the fact that there were no deadlines or delivery dates to work to. Monks left me to get on with things at my own pace and whenever I finished a few pieces, I'd take them in, and always got prompt payment and good prices.

One particular day, I took in my latest batch of finished pieces to his premises in the old mill where I used to work and Monks and his rather splendid-looking wife were overseeing the packing of loads of furniture into a big removal van. They said they were taking it down to their business partners' premises in a small market town in the Cotswolds and asked if I wanted to go. Monks had told me before of his trade with the London antiques dealers and also that his partners were involved in restoring pictures and suchlike. Needless to say, I jumped at their offer to have a look at the place.

I didn't know what I was expecting but at first glance the fine art restorers were something of a disappointment. It was a small set-up, a hive of activity, employing several 'restorers' working on all sorts of furniture. Some of them were fine-looking pieces, but others were being remade entirely from high quality wood recycled from what was described to me as 'undesirable nineteenth-century monstrosities' – High Victorian sideboards and tallboys, chopped up and combined to emerge as small sticks of eighteenth-century furniture. Since seeing those Cotswolds cabinetmakers at work, I've always been of the opinion that old Chippendale must have lived a thousand years to have made all the stuff that's been ascribed to him. Similarly with the vast number of paintings ascribed by 'experts' to the Impressionists. I once heard that there are several thousand 'authenticated' Renoirs in the USA alone. Obviously Renoir was as robust and long-lived as Chippendale, and just as prolific!

The furniture set-up was run by an elderly widow. She was assisted by her daughter and son-in-law. They, I was told, were picture restorers. I already knew Monks dabbled in picture 'restoration and alteration'. He mostly concerned himself with doing up potboilers and other people's treasured family portraits of great grandfather's ugly mug. Usually nineteenth or early twentieth century, and crap. Old Monks would praise the picture to excess in front of its soon-to-be fleeced owner, just so he could charge a suitably excessive fee for doing the thing up and, into the bargain, rob it of its frame. He'd persuade the gullible to have the painting reframed in a contemporary style, 'to improve its appearance', adding that he would dispose of the old frame free of charge. 'There isn't a market for fussy gilt frames anymore,' he'd sob, especially if it was a finely cut one and worth more than the daub that it surrounded.

The Cotswolds clients were of a different calibre. Many of them were involved in the top-end art trade in London, so they had good pictures and knew their stuff. Over the next few years, I visited this establishment many times and learnt a great deal about the art and craft of restoration and the technique of many fine artists of the past. The owner's daughter had learnt her trade at one of the premier London institutions. She was a top professional and always very kind to me. I think it's fair to say that I learnt most of what I know of the painterly methods used by proper artists from looking and listening to her expertise.

Another upshot of my new contacts was that it gave me another string to my bow in the form of a range of ceramics that sold as fast as I could make them. Like Mr Monks, the Cotswolds people did a lot of export business to the US. At the time there was a big demand for nineteenth-century English majolica pottery, so beloved of the Victorian middle classes, the type of stuff pumped out by the thousands in Stoke-on-Trent by such great potters as Minton's and the smaller concern of George Jones, along with a myriad of lesser-known firms. The widow who owned the place had a Minton garden seat in the form of a monkey holding a cushion on its head whilst fondling its nuts – monkey nuts, not its actual tatties. She reckoned it was going up in price so fast that it wouldn't be a wise thing to sell at the moment and Monks chipped in that he could get rid of anything in that style for good money. I decided there and then that I was now a producer of majolica-style pottery and that everything else would have to take a back seat until I'd mastered the craft.

Modelling the forms in clay and firing them wasn't a problem, but getting the right look to the glaze was a big challenge, especially the trademark turquoise-ground found on most Minton majolica. After some trial and error, I managed to get a passable effect. Before painting the colours onto the base glaze I mixed them with a low-temperature frit. When this was applied to the heavily leaded glaze, it brought up a rich sheen and colour, not a long way short of the Minton look. I didn't make these pots as fakes and never applied a repro factory mark. They were merely in the Minton tradition. But still went very well.

My best sellers were 'game pie' dishes and tureens modelled as wicker baskets with bits of animals and birds stuck onto them. Pheasants, partridge, pigeons, hares, even stags' heads. All pretty ghoulish to a modern eye, but the Victorians of the late nineteenth century apparently loved them and, going on the demand I had for them, so did the Americans of the late twentieth. I couldn't make enough. But, as usual for me, when I'd cracked the method of copying something it was time to move on to other things.

I also made some of those monkey garden seats. The large wares were only made possible because of the big kiln I'd recently bought. The original one that Mum and Dad had given me years before was now relegated to the garden shed. I used it for my experiments, firing small tiles covered in various mixtures and concoctions in pursuit of the finishes I would see on all kinds of pottery that interested me. The endless permutations in ceramics is something that has always fascinated me. I'd read of the trials and tribulations of the French potter Bernard Palissy, although I'm not sure how much truth there is to some of the tales of his efforts. I drew the line, for sure, at burning all the household furniture in pursuit of the perfect pot, as he apparently did when running short of fuel for his kiln. My mum would have skinned me alive for burning 'grandma's sideboard'.

Another off-putting aspect of those large Minton-style garden seats was the sheer physical effort of making them. They were damned hard work, similar in bollock-straining weight to the concrete work of earlier times. Tipping up the huge plaster piece moulds after I'd filled them with clay was just about at the limit of my strength. To ease the effort, and save straining my valuables, I constructed a Heath Robinson contraption that held the mould and tipped it with the lightest of touches during the manufacture of the big pieces of pottery. It was 'inspired' by something I'd seen on a day trip to a south Manchester slaughterhouse whilst on my day job at the Co-op butchery.

This particular day, we went off to the abattoir to see the whole process for ourselves, from the live beasts to the carcasses that would be delivered daily to our warehouse for dismemberment and packing. My mould-tipping device was based on the contraption in which the slaughtermen held the beasts when despatching them – a galvanised steel frame that would be clamped around the animal by pulling a lever and then, using a counterbalance, would roll it over onto its back for the dastardly deed to be performed. A quick slash across the throat with a big knife down to the spine and, hey presto, Sunday lunch.

While some of the party I'd come with were otherwise engaged in parting with their breakfasts, I went through to the section where they did the ritual slaughter for kosher. The rabbi who oversaw things showed us the knives they used and explained the ancient methods of ritual slaughter employed in the Jewish tradition, which I found very interesting. The sights and sounds weren't too pleasant, but I'm not at all squeamish. Blood and guts don't bother me. In fact, the structure of the body, animal or human, is something to learn from for anyone interested in art. It helps to know what goes where, if you hope to represent your subject accurately. Though cutting up cadavers by candlelight, as Leonardo used to do, might not be the most pleasant way to spend an evening alone.

When we got back to the Co-op, the old fellas in the party went into action cooking up an artery-clogging meal for all those who could stomach it. There weren't many takers. I always made a point of dodging these culinary delights with their archaic-sounding names: 'cowheel pie', sticky enough to paste paper; pigs' trotters or snouts; sweetbreads in soup, known to us as 'ram's bollock stew'; along with their signature dish, as the celebrity cooks put it these days, pig's dick and lettuce sandwiches. Yuck!

Most days, that job at the Co-op gave me a chance for an early finish and I used these extra hours to keep up with my own art. On days when I could get off early, I would usually zoom off on my bike to one of the Manchester libraries. They had the books that I couldn't buy in the shops, volumes that always seemed more interesting than my own. I'd mostly go to the art library at the Central and, more and more often as I got older, to the John Rylands Library at the university.

The original building on Deansgate in the city centre is a magnificent neo-Gothic effort built by Rylands's wife in her husband's memory and quite a monument, not only to him, but also to the talent of those who designed and made it. I'd been going there since school days. It wasn't actually open to school kids, but I was a big lad at 15. In the pre-internet days in which I grew up this was the best place to find out what I needed to know. There would always be long queues of gormless students making requests for books or other things, wasting more of my time than the reading up. Fortunately, one library assistant always let me jump the queue on one pretext or another. She was a humanities student and surely the prettiest thing I had ever seen, the wonders of Rome included.

Her name was Janey, and as I occasionally managed to squeeze out a few words of conversation – all the time hoping I wasn't turning my usual shade of shyness-induced scarlet – I discovered that she was at the university and hoped one day to become a teacher. On the days I went, I always wished she'd be there. Eventually, I picked up the courage to ask her out, only to receive an immediate knock-back. I felt my heart sink. However, her next words were, 'I'm meeting some of my friends in the pub later. You can come along if you wish.' It was all I could do to stop my big gob from shouting out an idiotic 'Oh yes please!' Instead, I just shrugged my shoulders and squeaked, 'Maybe, if I've time', and turned to leave. My nerve failed a few steps from the exit and I ran back to where she was standing to ask where and when. I was hooked.

Janey's friends seemed a weird bunch; male, female and a few batting for the other side. None of them were at all similar to the people I knew. Although fairly equal in age to me and my mates, they all seemed much older and more serious in nature, cleverer too. I suppose they'd had a better education or been better able to absorb a standard one, thus giving them a different outlook on life than me and my mates, most of whom, me included, were pretty thick by academic standards. All that evening, I felt like a fish out of water and but for Janey I'd most probably have ended the night by punching one of those self-important snobs right on the beak.

They were discussing an upcoming music thing they all intended going to, combined with a trip to Stonehenge, and as I know nothing of music I switched off my ears and just took in the sights. Suddenly, I was awoken from my non-musical interlude by a sharp jab in the ribs from my heart's desire. 'Are you listening or what?' I explained that I'd been put off music for life by all the crap issuing forth from my big brother's sacred record player. The noise kept interrupting my train of thought when I was a kid and led to lifelong musicophobia, or whatever it's called. So I made it clear that I wouldn't be going along on any musical adventures. It never occurred to me that I hadn't been invited.

This was music to the ears of a certain drip who was getting on my wick because of his obvious infatuation with Janey. I had already decided he was unsuitable for her. Besides setting his sights on my target and wearing his hair like a girl, his major sin was owning a Vespa scooter and a fishtail parka. As the evening wore drearily on and the students became more and more pissed, some of them seemed amused at the fact that I worked for a living, and in a manual job to boot. When I mentioned some of the things I made and sold in my spare time, they fell about laughing. I was in two minds about giving them a good kicking, but the piss-taking turned out to be a godsend. Janey came to my defence, fell out with the lot of them and stormed out with me following in her wake. She was only a slip of a thing, but had a temper to rival the gods of thunder.

As we walked through the streets back to her digs, I suggested she get rid of the drip and she laughed at my suggestion. To my great relief, he was nothing to her. In fact, at that time, no one was. I didn't know how to take that comment. Did she mean me too, or something else? As we walked, I found myself unable to shut my gob and went gabbling on about all sorts of things. Most un- usual for me back then. I wasn't normally as relaxed as this around girls. I've always been a quiet and shy type of person, though it's something I've tried not to be, to no avail. I suppose you can't be anything but yourself, can you?

By the time I'd finished my marathon rant we were at hers and, being the gentleman I have always been, I wished her good night and set off to find the place I'd parked my bike in the hope it hadn't been nicked. Our evening hadn't actually been a date as such, so what the bloody hell could I do next? Turning round, I rang the doorbell and was confronted by a buzzing girl wearing a green facepack and almost nothing else. 'Well, what is it?' I mumbled something beginning with J and she shouted out in an Amazonian voice, 'Jay, it's for you', and promptly waggled off down the hall showing quite a lot of cheek. Janey came to the door beaming a big smile, bright as a lightning bolt, and it made me forget what I wanted to say. My mind did a blank. Eventually, gathering my thoughts, I asked if she would like to come out with me on Sunday for a bike ride? It was all I could think of at the time. Then I started to gabble again, telling her of my motorbike and probably boring her rotten. I think she only agreed to go that Sunday to shut me up. I didn't mind what the reason was. I'd succeeded. She was now my bird. Officially.

When I picked her up on my bike that morning, her first words were to say that she wasn't going on the music thing with her former friends. That word 'former' was the best thing I'd ever heard. I fired up my bike and we whizzed off for a tour of the places I would go most weekends, the high moorland road and a place called Rivington Barn where hundreds of bike fans hung out. Once the home of the soap king and chemical baron Lord Leverhulme, it was where we would go to race our bikes.

Janey was a bit downcast at the thought of missing out on her now-cancelled trip. She'd wanted to visit Stonehenge, but didn't want to go alone. I jumped at the chance to be the white knight and offered to go with her, even pretending I'd wanted to see Stonehenge for ages, though I hadn't. We arranged to go that following week, but something unforeseen interrupted our plans and it was some time before I was walking amongst the stones of the henge with my favourite person.

By the time I'd taken Janey back to Manchester and got home that evening, I was knackered. But I then had to spend a couple of hours helping my brother with his temperamental monster Norton. That bike was more trouble than it was worth. The engine was oiling up and the timing kept slipping, so I suggested we leave it for the night and sort it out the next evening after work. With that, my long but happy Sunday came to an end.

The next day started badly and ended worse. It was a cold mid-February day, with snow on the ground first thing, so not really biking weather. I set off at 6 to walk the mile or so to work and promptly tripped over a bollard hidden in a snowdrift, creating a fine intaglio of me in the soft snow. I'd been half-asleep and hit the ground without even taking my hands out of my pockets, so the impression was perfect in every detail. You could even make out that my eyes were shut as I landed.

At work, the bad omens continued. First I trapped my hand in the freezer door. Then I almost impaled my foot with a razor-sharp boning knife. So I was glad to set off for home. My brother had taken the day off work and was already red-faced and angry when I took off my coat to lend a hand. We struggled with the bike for an hour or so, with the usual audience looking on – the founders of Rome, Romulus and Remus, better known as my dad and little sister. They would always turn up on such mechanical occasions to dispense wisdom. This got on our tits even more than the unco-operative junk from Birmingham.

I suggested we take the Norton for a test run, more to get away from the founders and to cool down my overwrought brother than any hope of getting it to run well. During the day, the snow had turned to rain and by evening had dried up altogether, though it was still bitterly cold. We managed to get the Norton into half-life, I jumped on and off we roared. About a mile from home it started to splutter. Only by putting it in a low gear with high revs could we keep it going. This thing did 65 in first, so you can imagine the difficulty we had staying within the speed limit, but, somehow, we did. On the way home, a Datsun pickup truck turned across our path as its driver did a right turn. He saw neither us nor the 10-inch halogen lamp set into the front of our fairing. I remember little of what happened next. But the result was a stay in hospital nursing a couple of broken bones and a punctured lung that seemed to be manufacturing fizzy red cola. Apparently, I'd also tried to knock down a concrete lamppost with my head and now had a skull fracture and fluid on the brain for my efforts, which kept me in and out of consciousness for two weeks.

There were no body scanners then, not in Bolton anyway. My examinations mostly consisted of a doctor moving a biro across the field of view of my heavy-as-lead eyes. Eventually, everything healed, though the jury's still out, probably, on the issue of water on the brain. One curious side effect I've had ever since, on and off, is that although I can generally hear perfectly well, the speech of others is sometimes completely garbled. In conversation, I'm sure people must think I'm nutty or something as I'm probably saying 'yes' when 'no' is called for. So if we ever meet you'll know why I'm nodding my head when I should be shaking it.

The smash allowed me several months off work and was the first time in my life, as far as I could remember, that I hadn't drawn a single picture in a whole week. Not even a scribble. I'd last seen Janey the night before booking the bed at the hospital and wasn't aware if she even knew of my accident. She did, of course, and although I couldn't remember, had been to visit me whilst I was still in dreamland nursing a swelled head. I also learnt the reason she hadn't wanted me to meet her parents. I had presumed they didn't approve of me, but it seems they had an aversion to motorcycles due to a family tragedy of years past. I could now see their point.

For some time after we only spoke on the telephone. Janey's finals were on the horizon and with all that entails, and my immobility, things just seemed to prevent it. Getting back to work in the summer even my thoughts about art began to fade. I still had most of that money from my fake drawing and wanted to move on from my job at the Co-op and become someone. Not that my job at the Co-op butchery was anything but respectable and honest work. My time there, and the people I worked with – nice people without exception – are a happy memory. It was just that I knew Janey and her parents were fairly well-to-do and someone who worked in a meat factory might not impress them. I could hardly tell them that I made a good living as a part-time manufacturer of crap, and that since my London sale I was now a wealthy crook. So for some unexplainable reason I had the idea of going into landscape gardening. It was probably that bump on the head.

For several months, I'd been putting in the odd weekend's work with my brother. He worked for Bolton Council maintaining the grounds of old folks' homes, and on his travels various requests had come his way to sort out gardens, trees and such things. So he had quite a few projects on the go that required extra hands. The trouble was, both my brother and myself were now creaking around like two old crocks because of that bloody motorbike. Always quick to act and long to lament, I rang the dealer who'd sold me the Kawasaki and flogged it back to him that afternoon taking a whopping loss into the bargain. Never mind. I was glad to be rid of the thing. I wasn't the only one. Mum, especially, gave me a tearful thanks. Unfortunately, that bike wasn't the last thing coming from my direction to give her grief.

My battleaxe sister, Samy, was at Mum's when the dealer came to collect the bike and sent him packing with a flea in his ear from her. Something to the tune of him being a dealer in destruction and selling death traps for a living. It didn't seem to occur to her that in all the time I had the Kawasaki, neither it nor I had a scratch to show. For now, though, bikes were out.

My next silly plan was to become the proprietor of a garden centre. If I couldn't go to my customers, I reasoned, they could come to me. In the late 1970s, garden centres were still thin on the ground. Unable to afford the outright purchase of a going concern, though a small one might have been within my budget at the time, I was determined, in the old Bernini tradition, to do everything myself from scratch, as I always did with my art and craft stuff. Most of it at least. True, I didn't build the kiln, grind the paint or – at that time at least – dig the metal ores and refine them for casting. But I could have done.

Surveying for a suitable site, preferably a bit rural, I settled on some disused railway sidings about a mile from my home. This was in the days of British Rail and, due to my dad's time in the scrap metal trade in the fifties, he knew that the BR land agent was based at Hunts Bank in Manchester. I was far more outgoing then than I am now, so I went to see this land agent to enquire about my chosen site and managed to get a preliminary lease agreement from him, conditional on my getting planning permission from Blackburn Council for a change of use. Dad suggested I needed professional assistance in submitting these plans, but, as usual, I ploughed on regardless. Having no intention of paying for a white elephant, I surveyed the site on my own.

For this, I plotted it in the traditional Egyptian manner, using a knotted rope arranged in the 3-4-5 Pythagorean triangle, pegged with my old tent pegs substituting for helping hands. All this wasn't really necessary, but it's a simple and really accurate way of getting a plan. The stumbling block was that the overgrown siding overlooking the Jumbles Country Park had become something of a wildlife haven. This was cited as the reason for the planning refusal that came through the post some weeks later.

Other plans that came unstuck in this busy year of disaster and enterprise included a first go at making paper – handmade rag paper for watercolours, at a few quid a sheet. That failed when the supplier of the cotton linters used in making rag paper, under pressure from his established customers, refused me any more supplies. Then there was a falconry centre, which failed because of my cold feet.

I'd been to see the estate manager of a stately home in Cheshire owned by the University of Manchester, a nice chap, ex-army, officer class, with two very old farting Labradors which he obviously adored. Those old mutts took an instant shine to me as I entered his office with my falconry plans and immediately came over to sit with me. This seemed to impress Colonel Blimp and, having heard my ideas, he offered me an old walled garden at a peppercorn rent for the site of the 'falconry centre', with the only proviso that I would do hawk flying demonstrations, once a day, out in the park. The rest was my own. As I said, I got cold feet and never took up his kind offer. I may be a passable art maker, but I'm surely no businessman.

By now the crash was starting to fade in both mind and body, and I swapped my two-wheel lifestyle for four in the shape of a Ford Fiesta in vomit green. It was cheap and cheerful and as I was becoming more of a miser I turned a blind eye to the colour. Come the summer, things were pretty much back to normal and, with Janey's exams out of the way and me still on sick leave, we finally got to go down to Wiltshire to see the pile of old stones. Before that I was invited over to her parents' house for a first visit. Janey was an only child, so her mum and dad were very protective. I spent the first meeting being stuffed with food and getting an education in the care of tropical fish, learning what a very safe hobby it was. I believe I made a good first impression and was soon calling round 'whenever I wanted'. They have always been kind to me, but God knows what they saw in me back then.

Janey and I spent that summer driving around. It was my happiest year. During her studies, she had done some fieldwork, 'proper archaeology' as she put it, at a section of Offa's Dyke in Shropshire where they had managed to find bugger all. I knew a little of this place. It was a defence ditch built across the English–Welsh border on the orders of the eighth-century Mercian king, Offa, stretching from the Severn Estuary to its terminal near a place in North Wales called Basingwerk Abbey. I once planned to do something in gold relating to King Offa. The idea was to cobble together an old provenance of its discovery in the eighteenth century in the vicinity of Basingwerk Abbey, and then let the experts make up the rest with their fertile imaginings. But I never got around to designing the thing. Standing now at Offa's unimpressive dyke, I mentioned to Janey that in my opinion his efforts were puny compared to the Roman earthworks further north. The comment earned me a swipe from her bulging rucksack. That rucksack was always three times heavier than anything I carried, despite the fact she was so waif-like. 'Strong in head, strong in arm' was her motto. When I pointed out that the saying was actually 'strong in arm, weak in head' it earned me another whack, along with a few sharp barbs about my total lack of formal qualifications. Academics are very touchy you know!

All day I nodded with feigned interest. But as far as I'm concerned, holes in the ground are for pissing in. So I suggested we spend a couple of days in London to visit the British Museum and the first-class galleries of the capital, then go on to Stonehenge, adding that I knew those museums and galleries like the back of my hand, which wasn't strictly true. We stayed with my aunt on the Edgware Road. Janey was well impressed with the British Museum, but when we went to look at the Elgin Marbles she, like me, wasn't too taken by them. I don't know what it is about them. They just don't live up to the hype. When I'd first seen them as a lad, they had looked immense. But compared to all I had since seen in Rome, even Belzoni's plundered granite colossus in the Egyptian gallery had somehow withered. Nevertheless, a wander though the galleries of the BM is always a red-letter day.

The next morning we said goodbye to my aunt and set off to see the pile of old rocks. It was the first time either of us had visited Stonehenge. It looked bigger than I had envisaged and older than its 5,000 years. The stones themselves look much more ancient than anything you might see in the Egyptian monuments that are contemporary with it, though that's probably down to the freeze-thaw winters we have in Britain. Still, for me at least, Stonehenge has an aura of very great age and is surely one of the greatest monuments that has come down to us from ancient times.

Our base was a pretty rough B&B in the village of Bulford about five miles away, so pretty handy. These were happy times for me. At last I felt free of my obsession with painting and all that rubbish. All year I hadn't done anything remotely arty and felt the better for it. Even our trips to the British Museum didn't fire me with enthusiasm. I was just a looker now, and not a doer.

When I got home, my dad told me he could help me find a new job if I wanted. He'd been showing some of my woodwork to one of his mates in the pub. This mate ran a large building company that held contracts to paint many of British Rail's stations and was now whizzing about in a Rolls-Royce. His 'speciality' was buying big Victorian houses, many of them former care homes decommissioned by the local authorities, all with equally big gardens. He'd bulldoze the lot and put up a small hamlet of 'select executive homes for the discerning', usually at equally select prices. I went to see him and was offered a job working for his master carpenter, a man from whom I learnt a lot.

I was already a fair hand with a chisel and lump of wood. It wasn't something I had ever been trained to do, but I can carve anything pretty well – wood, stone, whatever. My new boss, Mr Haslam, was obsessed with 'minstrel galleries'. They featured in all his constructions and he reckoned that this feature alone helped to shift the house in no time. My job was to carve the details. I'd been given it on the strength of an oak table I'd done. It was supposed to have been my last job for Monks. He'd supply the things cut and planed, then I'd carve the fancy bits and return it to him for assembly and finish. This one I'd kept and given to my brother for his new home. Monk could whistle for it. I could be quite bolshy when the mood took me.

The other aspect of my new job was doing illustrations of the developments as they would look in their new surroundings when they were finished. Usually in very large watercolour. These fanciful views were intended for the boss's office and I used a lot of imagination in doing them. Today, the trading standards commissariat might have a lot to say about them. But back then, the better I made them look, the better Mr H liked them. And he was my paymaster, so I danced to his tune.

The boss's office was also his home, a magnificent and wholly original neoclassical building that had once belonged to the Dukes of Bridgewater. It had been one of His Grace's lesser country retreats, but obviously built without regard to cost, as one does, I suppose, when one's a duke. It really was a beautiful place. Neoclassical art and architecture is one of my favourite periods in art history. But those illustrations I'd do for display on the grand walls of Mr H's HQ became a case of the tail wagging the dog when the landscape designs I made up, purely for artistic effect, started to be followed in the layouts of the real developments. It got to the point where the houses sat in landscapes that were more my vision than anyone else's.

As I wasn't doing any arty stuff at home, my evenings and weekends were my own and, for the first time, I seemed to have loads of spare time on my hands. Most nights, after work, I'd go over to Janey's at her digs in the city centre where several 'punks' had now appeared on the scene. Punks were some kind of musical type and quite something to behold. I'd got the rebel bug out of my own system early on, so this lot looked like right wallies to me. But I suppose I was similarly wallyish to them, only I wasn't held together with safety pins and snot.

My new job went down very well with Janey's parents, especially when I mentioned that my boss lived in the Duke of Bridgewater's house – as I did at every opportunity. Adding that I also intended to get myself a ducal pile one day. They laughed at that, rightly so, of course, as things turned out. But Janey never laughed. She believed in me.

About now, I did a quick swerve back into the field of painting. Not for money, but as a labour of love. Also to use as a prop in a small plan I had hatched. With Janey's recent graduation, I decided to paint her portrait in her graduation gown – minus the silly hat, which distracted from her fine features. For the painting, a half-length in oils, I pulled out all the stops. The stretcher I made myself from elm, cut with Janey's initials and hung with the best quality fine-woven canvas, tacked with tinned copper pins. I sized and primed it in the traditional manner and bought the colours, at some expense, from a supplier I'd found from my early dealings with the Cotswolds people. I intended that picture to last a good 500 years. The only iffy part was to come up with a style in which to paint it. This gave me the most trouble.

I did umpteen pastel scribbles of my intended masterpiece, something I always do on any big picture to work out the colour and tonal balance – what goes where and in what order. That way I get the scene clear in my mind. Then I can blaze away to capture an immediacy in the paint that is essential and gives the picture 'life'. After giving up on an original style, I decided to paint her in the deep chiaroscuro of my favourite painter, Caravaggio. It turned out better than I hoped. My best effort to date. Most importantly, Janey liked it – with certain reservations. Nose too big. Face too fat. Eyes not right. Other than that, it was 'very good'. That was enough for me. Eventually, my 'bird', as she hated to be called, withdrew her criticism for fear of hurting my feelings. But I don't mind criticism of my work. I never have. If something's crap, why not say so? My brothers and sisters always did, and over the years I took quite a verbal battering with regards to my artwork. I used it to spur me on and improve. Criticism works wonders.

When I took it over to Janey's home for her mum and dad to see, for some strange reason it made her mum cry. I had intended them to have that painting and said so, then moved the conversation on to how I'd based it on the style of Caravaggio, slipping in the opinion that 'the best place to see Caravaggio's work is in Florence'. I quickly added that it holds some of the finest works of art ever made and that we intended going to see it. A few weeks later, we were there.

Our hotel in Florence wasn't in the old city as my stay in Rome had been. It was a few minutes' walk from the railway station, but nice enough. It was run by a couple from Cardiff who were always pissed. They'd tell us how they had run businesses all over the place and finally settled in Florence. Their tales of entrepreneurial ineptitude reminded me of me.

First stop on our tour of the sights was Janey's choice. And she chose, of all things, in the number one city of the Renaissance, a Gothic pile! In the shape of Santa Maria Novella! Janey had a wicked sense of humour and always knew which buttons to press to wind me up. She knew full well that I wanted to go to the Duomo to look at the great bronze reliefs on the Baptistery by one of the Renaissance's best sculptors, Ghiberti. I'd been mesmerised by these things since the age of seven – if only in books. And although Santa Maria Novella is a fine edifice, I grabbed her by the hand and legged it over to the cathedral.

Still the tallest building in the city, the Duomo, or, more properly, Santa Maria del Fiore, with its glowing orange dome, was built by one of Ghiberti's contemporaries, the artist and architect Brunelleschi. When I first heard his name, I thought he was old Isambard's Polish granddad! Standing before the east doors of the Baptistery, looking at those gilt bronze reliefs – they are actually copies, but exact in every detail – I could see what the great Buonarroti meant when he described them as 'the gates of paradise'. And remember they were done in the first half of the fifteenth century. To my mind they are the first great achievement of the Renaissance.

During our stay, Janey and I visited most of the sights but, as in Rome, the crowds of sightseers got on my tits. The best thing was that I wasn't on my own this time and didn't have to talk to myself quite as much. Next stop was the Bargello, the sculpture museum of Florence, probably the best gallery I've ever been in, though all the galleries of Florence are first-class and need months to see properly.

I've always had this habit of saying things aloud and not realising it. Private thoughts usually best kept to myself. On this occasion, standing before the bronze of Donatello's 'David with the Head of Goliath', the first nude done in western art since antiquity, I blurted out, 'If that tackle wasn't out, you'd mistake it for a 13-year-old girl.' It came out without my lips consulting my brain and resulted in a few raised eyebrows from the gathered gawpers and the sharp dig of fingernails into my soft underarm. 'Shhh, you twit.'

For a long time, the Bargello was a prison and the HQ of the chief of police in whose name it is dubbed. Maybe these days I'd be uncomfortable walking its galleries. But although I'm now familiar with the insides of various prisons, the ones I've been in probably don't compare with the Bargello in its day. I should think that place was less than comfortable, wouldn't you?

We went on to see the Medici Chapels in San Lorenzo, with the sculptures by Buonarroti in their original positions. The thoughtful pose of Lorenzo's marble-cut figure reminded me of the Delphic Sibyl on the Sistine ceiling and is first-class in every way. But I was a bit surprised at the state of the unfinished facade of that church. I'm no scholar on those moneylenders, the Medici, who had it built, but I can only think that their money must have run out. When I got home, one of the things I did, just for my own interest, was to draw up a design for it. I don't know where that plan went. But it's still lodged in my mind in every detail.

We also went to see the frescoes of the very early and ground-breaking Fra Angelico, the Dominican friar whose work spans the end of Gothic and the beginning of Renaissance. These are at the Convent of San Marco, another Medici project, and very beautiful. Then on to the Uffizi, where there was just too much to see, and where I showed Janey what proper painting looked like. My portrait of her was more Beano than Bargello in quality. But I did the best I could.

One of the things I simply had to see was the great bronze of Perseus with the slain Medusa, by Cellini, which stands in the Loggia dei Lanzi, a kind of open-air sculpture gallery in front of the town hall. Cellini's bronze was one of the first things that fired my love of sculpture and I seemed to be aware of it since before I could remember anything else. I'd read the account of its making, something I'd recited to the man from Turin at the foundry on Trafford Park, to which he'd offered the expert opinion – 'boolshit'.

Our last art stop was the Basilica of Santa Croce, where our trip ended as it had begun with a Gothic pile, though it does have some redeeming features – a superb chapel by Brunelleschi and the tomb of Michelangelo by Vasari. The church is spoiled by a nineteenth-century facade which I would like to pull down and redo in honour of our greatest artist. Buonarroti's tomb is just inside to the right and across from him is Galileo. All around are frescoes by Giotto and sculpture by Donatello. Not a bad place to be, even dead. But this time I made sure to keep that thought to myself. Janey was holding my arm and her claws were as sharp as ever.

We managed to squeeze a couple of excursions into our trip. One to Carrara, taking in the house where it's said that Michelangelo stayed when choosing his stone. And then on to the marble quarries where I would have been happy to camp out for a year. They say Buonarroti would choose his blocks and could already see the figure in the stone. All pretty fanciful stuff. But it makes a good story.

For my own efforts in marble, I prefer Carrara as well. Parian and the other Greek marbles of further east seem too granular to me. But I suppose it's just a matter of what you get used to working first. I haven't done anything of note. Mostly fragments from larger works – heads, torsos and the like. Mainly purporting to be Roman, but also Greek – both classical and archaic – and some Persian. I've worked in other stones, too, from alabaster at the softer end, to granite for Egypt, and then on to some of the hardest stones to carve – cornelian and amethyst, garnet, jaspers, jades and all. The largest was a life-size fragmentary torso of a first- to second-century Roman general in a cuirass. The smallest were jasper and onyx intaglios from signet rings. With a wide range of ages, sizes and styles in between.

Stone is my favourite sculpture material and really the only material of proper sculpture. Bronze and terracotta is modelling rather than sculpture, though still a nice thing to do that takes great skill to do well. It's often said by painters that sculpture is easier than their efforts with the brush. To this I would say: you've obviously never stood before a stone block with chisel and mallet in hand. I've had a go at most things in art and for me, painting is only better than sculpture if it's a quiet life you're seeking!

For our final two days, on the recommendation of our hosts, we took a trip by coach to Pisa and then down the coast about 100 miles to Piombino, where we crossed by ferry to the island of Elba. It's only five miles or so and doesn't take long, but even on a dead calm day Janey was sour green to the gills and I spent most of the day feeling like an associate member of the Red Cross. I don't get seasick. I'd been to the Isle of Man in conditions that would have today's ferry from Fleetwood cancelled. Almost everyone on that boat was sick, but I was singled out for my iron gut by an old sea dog. Dad called him a 'golden rivet' – but not to his face. He was 7 foot 14 inches with arms like legs. I didn't know what a 'golden rivet' was until I joined the Royal Marines.

We were looking forward to Elba. But come the day, we couldn't really have cared less. An extra bottle of wine the night before – or was it two? – had a lot to answer for. It buggered up the trip. The only thing I knew of the island was that it was where Napoleon Bonaparte escaped from exile to meet his Waterloo, courtesy of Wellington. I've seen both Napoleon's Imperial Porphyry sarcophagus in Les Invalides at Paris and Wellington's Cornish porphyry one in St Paul's at London. And this last 'battle of the sarcophagi' surely goes to Boney.

Imperial Porphyry is something I've done a little of myself and it's damn hard work. Even with the help of modern diamond-cutting blades and burrs. It was the hardest rock in antiquity and the best lump of it you can see is a sarcophagus in the Vatican Museum that's said to have been the last resting place of Helena, mother of Constantine. Personally, I think it would have been made for the emperor himself and cut in Egypt where such hard-stone cutting had a long and glorious tradition. The sheer effort in the stonework of Egyptian masons and sculptors has always been a wonder to me. Things such as the colossal porphyry columns in Hagia Sophia in Constantinople – or Istanbul as it's presently known – are a testament to the iron will of Egypt's stone men. Not to mention the efforts of their forebears who worked in the service of the pharaohs. All great stuff.

Our holiday finally over, we landed back in Manchester to leaden skies and a feeling that we'd left most of our internals floating in the Med, courtesy of our boat trip and the projectile vomiting caused by the extra wine. By late September, Janey was back at university working towards a teaching qualification and I was back to my woodworking at Haslam's builders. Janey had a burning desire to be a teacher and I thought her eminently suited to that noble profession. Patient, kind, clever, with a sunny disposition and great sense of humour, she also carried a certain air of authority. Some might even call her very bossy. But not me. When I was a kid I would definitely have liked her as my teacher. If only all teachers could act and look like her. My own teachers, when I was at school, probably had to work with what sculptors call a flawed block. Flawed stones, no matter how carefully worked, never produce a good sculpture.

My job was trotting along well enough and no two days were the same. Oswald, the carpenter, did most of the fitting and we had two lads in the yard who cut most of the timber from the drawn plans. I did all of the detailed carving when it was called for. One strange and very theatrical project that sticks in the mind was the carving of a big post at the bottom of a sweeping staircase we'd built for a particularly eccentric client. What we had to carve was a life-size couple of entwined female nudes in mock art nouveau style, topped off with a unicorn's head. Very bizarre. Someone quipped the client must have been 'smoking his socks'.

The whole thing looked lethal when set up and I just hoped no one tripped on those stairs. They'd have been skewered for sure. The unicorn was just a nag's head with a broom handle sticking out of its forehead. But the two nudes were difficult to do. I was well paid, though, and money seemed of no concern to the chap who ordered it. For a moment, I wondered if he was in the market for rare works of art. But only for a moment. I didn't do such things any more, did I?

After carving that monstrosity I was kept busy doing all sorts and became a bit handy with the wood chisel. It wasn't art, but I couldn't have cared less. It paid well and my sights were set in another direction. During our trip to Florence, Janey and I had talked about getting a place together. Now that I was on better money in my new job and she was balancing two part-time jobs along with her continuing studies, we could afford it. The money from my fake drawing was still mostly intact and would have come in handy. But seeing as how I was now determined to get away from all that, it felt like dirty money and I didn't want Janey to be any part of it. We rented a small flat in Manchester, not far from the university, handy for both of us as far as work was concerned, although I couldn't have cared less if that flat had been on the moon. I was with my favourite person, just the two of us. And we'd finally shaken off those nutty housemates of hers, along with the out-of-date 'punk' boyfriends held together with safety pins and too-tight trousers.

I was doing well in my work and was being given more

responsibility for setting out the landscapes for new projects. We usually got to the site before the old house had been pulled down and would walk the unkempt gardens marking out the features Mr Haslam wanted to keep. He was especially keen on retaining any specimen trees. Haslam knew his market. He always insisted on building his houses in a mature landscape. It seemed to work, because pretty much every one of them was sold off-plan. He kindly said that my painterly impressions helped in that regard. So I hoped he might cough up a little more cash. But he didn't. Some 18 months later, when I walked away from that job, he did make me a great offer and even promised me an opportunity to 'follow in his footsteps'. But I wasn't interested.

This came about not because of any disillusion with my job – it was the best work I'd ever had – but on account of my own life going wrong in the worst way I could have imagined. It isn't very easy to put down in words. Not even after more than 30 years. Janey and I were settled in our life together and I was as happy as I'd ever been. Until she started to become unwell. The first thing was regular headaches, which the doctor put down to working long hours and studying too much. Later, she started to have problems with dizzy spells and balance. So our doc arranged for a hospital appointment. I could tell she was scared and tried to lighten her heart with reminiscences of our earlier times. The unforgettable 'Olympian' projectile vomiting from that ferry on our away day into exile on Elba, 18 or so months earlier. My run-ins with the 'snot and safety pin brigade' at her old digs, some of whom tried to lure my treasure away. How they always failed and sometimes got a fat lip for trying.

It wasn't of any real help. I just rambled on to keep my thoughts away from the present. We came away from that first visit to the hospital no wiser. This went on for several crushing weeks. Janey's mum and dad would sometimes take her to the hospital appointments and I junked my job at Haslam's so as to do more, but to no avail. Things gradually became more difficult and after Janey had a seizure it was decided she would go to stay with her parents. The flat, with its flights of stairs, wasn't at all suitable.

When she had that first seizure, I thought it was an epileptic fit. I was well used to dealing with those. One of my brothers suffers from the condition. Whenever he'd go into one, most of the family would go into a panic, but, for some reason, I'd always end up as the one to help out. Our old dog-loving doctor had shown us what to do and I would carry out his commands to the letter whenever it was needed. Clear the airway, check for breathing and, as the seizure subsided, place the person into the recovery position. I could hear the doc's squeaky tones ringing in my ear as I ran through the drill. It all sounded so matter of fact. When it's someone who means a great deal to you, though, as my brother certainly does, or who means everything, as Janey meant to me, seeing them in that hopeless state is quite something.

In a strange way, the seizure gave me some reassurance that things would be all right in the end. My brother lives with his epilepsy, held at bay with a cocktail of barbiturates, and I reasoned that Janey could do the same. I hoped that her illness was just that – the onset of epileptic fits. We could easily live with that, I thought.

She was eventually diagnosed with an inoperable brain tumour, deep-seated and aggressive. Within a very few months she was desperately ill and reached the surrendering point of going into a hospice. For a few days, she picked up. Looking back it was possibly an increase in pain relief, courtesy of those magnificent beings who cared for her in that place. She died several days later, in the early hours of the morning, when I wasn't there. What more can I say of her – she was the best thing.

The next couple of years were my unhappiest time. I left my job without explanation and stayed on at our flat for a while. I couldn't settle to anything and went on a number of trips to look at the things me and Janey had talked of – Egypt, Greece, Spain. Seven trips back to Rome, each one of them on my own. I spent what was left of my money on those trips and by 1983 I was somehow back at my dad's home. He and Mum had retired, and with all my brothers and sisters being busy with their own lives, and Mum not doing too well with her angina, I started to do more and more for them until I gradually became indispensable.

I believe most 'carers', as I became, fall into that way of life without realising and can't or won't go back on the commitment out of a sense of loyalty. Looking back, I think it suited my purpose. It gave me an excuse not to join in with things.

During my all-too-short time with Janey, I hadn't felt the need for art. I had kept to my work and the only arty things I'd done were her portrait and those illustrations for Haslam's. Art didn't seem important, or relevant. Janey knew about my 'Degas', and I'd told her of all the things I'd done before, but she would not have wanted me to do the dishonest things I have done since. If things had gone differently, I would never have gone back to my art and through it, into crime. But they didn't go differently.

VIII.

All that glitters

DURING THE MID-EIGHTIES, most of my time was spent back in my dad's garage, painting and working on all kinds of art and craft projects. Many of my efforts of those times were fairly substandard. For some reason, I seemed to have taken a step backwards as far as art was concerned. So a lot of them ended up being destroyed or, if they were in metal, recycled. I didn't consider them a waste of time. Everything I did helped me become better and more accomplished. I managed to finish enough things to bring in a basic amount of cash by selling the odd picture or whatever to dealers around the North West. I also did a bit of work for Monks again and through him tried my hand for a short time at picture cleaning and restoring.

As one of the many strings to their bow, Mr and Mrs Monks and their associates in the Cotswolds had a line in picture-restoring and framing, mostly for the trade in London, though they took in work from wherever they could find it. I remember quite a lot of pictures coming over from Ireland. The main studio was the Cotswolds one, but the big pictures would be brought up to Monks's place which had more space and less dust. I always thought it odd to have a picture-restoring set-up combined with woodworking. A dusty environment is the very last thing to have around pictures.

Cleaning and restoring 'potboilers' – mostly nineteenth-century oils – was something I didn't take well to. The whole affair was tiresome, boring and also smelly. Having made up my mind to have a go, I stuck to my task for as long as I could. Or at least until I learnt the basics. Then, as usual, it would be time to learn something else. During that time I picked up quite a lot from the Monkses. Both he and she weren't as barmy as I'd thought. But the most interesting stuff to do with old paintings was picked up from a woman called Carol.

She was a professional restorer and the daughter of the old widow who owned the Cotswolds business. She was married to a cabinetmaker who worked with Monks on cutting up the Victorian 'monstrosities' made of the best timber. They would then re-form the wood into 'repro' – small and elegant eighteenth-century pieces that sold for the best prices. I'm not sure where they got rid of it all. I suspect some of the nice things they made didn't go as 'repro'. But who knows.

From Carol I quickly learnt that the faking of oil paintings, which is usually imagined to be the stock in trade of the art forger, is just about the most difficult type of fake to do convincingly. The painting itself, the image painted in the style of a particular artist, isn't the problem. Where it becomes difficult is enabling that picture to pass expert or scientific examination. A host of details must pass under the trained eye of the expert. And for anything of great rarity and value that eye is usually situated at the end of a microscope in a laboratory.

The first thing, obviously, is that your hoped-for money-spinner looks like what it's supposed to be. In times past, not much more than that used to suffice. But, as in all cat-and-mouse games, an arms race of sorts invariably develops, and fakery and its detection are no exception. As detection is where the advances are usually made, the faker is left to play catch-up most of the time. My time spent on those old pictures taught me invaluable lessons on how things of age should appear. Learning the art of restoration and the cleaning of paintings was quite an eye-opener as well into the art trade. Most of what I worked on – always on the orders of a well-dressed dealer who came to collect the finished article – wasn't particularly valuable or of note. For the most part, my days were spent swab and acetone in hand taking off 100 years or more of dirt and discoloured varnish. As I said, quite a crappy thing to do. Repairing tears and holes, along with painting-in lost areas, was all in the day's work. And relining, even when it wasn't required, helped Monks to pad out the client's bill. Occasionally, older and better-quality pictures came in. But only Carol was allowed to work on those. She was the professional, a mine of information, and quite a good artist in her own right.

My problem has always been a lack of proper education in art. At that time, I was fairly ignorant of the exact methods and – more importantly for faking – the materials used by various schools of painting in the history of art. I knew a little – the stuff used on the Egyptian wall paintings found in the tombs; how to do fresco and oil painting from the ground up – but as far as knowing what pigments, oils, resins and varnishes were used by whom, and when, I was clueless. Thankfully, I'm a quick learner and before long I could see what Carol was about. She saw that I was keen to learn and was always willing to answer any questions I had. There were many. I must have been a pestering bugger.

Whenever I'd ask where she had learned her trade she would clam up. From others I discovered she was an authority on Dutch painting of the sixteenth and seventeenth centuries, that she knew all that was useful to know about Rembrandt and that she had once been an associate of a world-renowned Rembrandt scholar. I thought these tales were akin to the Cornish fishermen telling me that Barbara Hepworth had just walked off with one of my paintings when I was a kid in St Ives. But in this case it was true. Carol was the real thing.

After slogging away at nineteenth-century potboilers for some weeks I got a new line of work – still in picture restoration, but a little more than cleaning paintings. Monks usually brought his pictures up from the Cotswolds by car, the large ones tied to the sides of the blue Luton Van that was his workhorse. Anything smaller was wrapped in old army blankets for protection on the journey. This latest batch of 'canvases' was packed into a large black leather case in the boot of his BMW, which, looking back, I probably contributed to handsomely with my underpaid efforts. They were much older than the canvases I'd worked on previously. And some were on wood panel, heavily crazed and very gloomy. Setting them up on several easels dotted around the room he asked what I thought of them. Well, for a start, I said, I can hardly make them out under all that crap they're covered in. I thought I was being saddled with the worst job that no one else wanted to do. Monks assured me this wasn't the case. He actually wanted me to take off the whole surface of the pictures. Not just the discoloured varnish, but the paint as well, right down to the ground. A client of his, he explained, wanted several copies made of valuable pictures in his collection, and these were to be done on old canvases and panels. So as to look 'in period'.

He must have thought I was a right dickhead to believe that. Without making my thoughts plain, I just listened and went along with his cock and bull story. I was interested to see where it was leading and asked who would copy the pictures onto these blanks once I'd cleaned them off. Monks said that Carol would do that, as she was the only one good enough to be trusted with such a thing.

As far as I could tell, these were genuine early eighteenth-century pictures, or even earlier, so they had cost a fair sum and weren't to be ruined. I was to take off the paint, whilst leaving the ground and its maze of crackle, a simple job, he said, that won't take long. I asked him what I should do, therefore, to prevent the lique-fied paint – which is what you get when you apply remover – from filling the myriad of fine cracks all over the surface of the pictures, particularly on the wood panels which were by far the worst in this regard. His expression glazed over. I could see he had never done such a job before. 'What?' he mumbled. I repeated the question. Obviously, he didn't understand the processes involved at all. So I explained the problem, finally putting him in his place, something I must admit was a pleasure. Monks now knew that I knew that he didn't know quite as much about things as he pretended. No more bullshit then. Always up for a challenge, I suggested he leave me alone to sort it myself.

Having never done this type of thing before, I sat and thought up what was needed to solve the new problem. Filling the cracks while the paint was taken off required something that would be impervious to acetone stripper and alcohol, whilst being easily re-movable itself when the job was complete. After experimenting on a couple of small canvases I'd made up and coated with a hard resin – which I crazed over the back of a spoon pressed carefully onto the back of the canvas – I finally decided to use a water-soluble crystal wax solution. This had the effect of leaving the edges of the crazed segments sharp-edged and fresh-looking under the microscope.

Most fake oils painted over cleaned-off grounds – something that is fairly common in fakery – show a craquelure which looks softened and scrubbed. Under magnification, the individual chan-nels are clogged with paint or varnish, either from when the old paint was removed or from when the new masterpiece was painted. So that's certain death for any fake and its hoped-for sale. Crystal wax, though needing very careful application and removal, leaves no discernable trace. Well, none that I've ever heard of being detected, anyway.

Mr Monks was well pleased with the results. And despite his many requests to know what I had used, no answer was forthcoming from me. Most of the ways I've found to do things, through patient trial and error, are almost always the simplest solutions. A little logical thought usually suggests something to overcome the problem. This part of the game is something I've always enjoyed tackling.

Having taken the panels down to a suitable level for repainting, my plan was to remove the temporary filler I'd invented before Monks took them down to the Cotswolds where the new pictures were to be done, and where Carol would find out what I had used. In those days, I didn't want to give away any of my own ideas. Instead, my newly tamed employer asked me what I would want in the way of money to paint the pictures myself. I replied that to do the copies justice I'd need to see the originals, to which Monks and his wife almost swallowed their tongues. 'That's not going to be possible.' Apparently, their client was very careful in his choice of who could and could not view his treasures and I, it seemed, would fall into the 'could not' bracket.

It was all I could do to keep a straight face as they came out with all this. From the start, I'd suspected that these pictures were not what they said they were. But wishing to try my hand at producing a convincing copy on old supports and having no intention of putting a signature to any of them, I agreed to do them for the usual underprice, without even seeing what was to go on them.

Over the next week I was busy finishing the other pictures I was already cleaning or varnishing. Mrs Monks then brought me some colour reproductions of the four pictures to be copied – two small marine paintings and a still life, all in the seventeeth-century northern manner, with an early topographical view of, of all places, Washington. I was told it was a view of the Capitol building under construction. But could I not copy it as shown and, instead, paint a similar prospect from another viewpoint? I made it clear that without seeing examples of all these artists' work, first hand, the result would be wanting in technique. No matter, said Mrs Monks. Just do them as you think fit. She proceeded to open a small case filled with sets of colour and bottles of painting medium to be used for each picture. Supplied by Carol, I suppose.

The whole thing seemed to be turning into a serious case of possible fakery. If these pictures were just for decoration to hang in place of some originals why go to these lengths to use hand-prepared and hand-ground colours? But at that point I couldn't back out. So I just concentrated on the paintings in hand and off I went. I was now regretting having offered to do any of this, but I'd offered and that was that. I did them as best as I could. Then varnished them with the supplied concoction. After a suitable time, I removed the filler which had indeed remained free of paint and varnish. The finished articles looked a fair effort. Monks was pleased enough and paid up. Then he took them down to Carol, for I don't know what. Perhaps she added some restoration and signatures.

Due to the length of time that oil paint takes to harden, especially in impasto, I thought the new panels were unlikely to fool any serious examination. Some passages of oil paint, done thickly, can take 25–30 years to harden up. I said as much to Monks in a naive attempt to stop him trying something underhand and dropping me in it. 'The paint you used won't take that long,' was his matter of fact answer. Too true, as I later came to realise only too well. Carol knew her stuff. And if anyone says things like 'you can always tell a recent painting using this or that method of detection', I just smile and think of the days when I thought that too.

I find oil painting damn hard work, especially when trying to do a believable old one. I'll avoid using the overused 'Old Master' tag. It's misused on almost anything old these days, just like 'hero' is used for both sportsmen and the soldiers risking their necks in Iraq and Afghanistan. I think we all know who the real heroes are. One glance at a proper work of art tells you if the master's hand is behind it, or not, as the case may be.

Just about the last thing I ever did for others came as a request from Carol to paint her a copy of a Rembrandt. Before I go on,

I must point out that Master R could paint better with his big toe than I can with every facility. Those pictures I did for her were never meant to be an attempt at faking a Rembrandt. For one thing, all the Rembrandts are recorded, even the fake ones masquerading in some of the aristocratic collections of England and other places. Carol had taught me a great deal about the means and methods of painting, so I tried to paint her something worthy.

Rembrandt has always been one of my favourite artists and I think his etchings the best ever done. The light in them is superb. His 'Portrait of an Old Jew' in the State Hermitage Museum, an oil, is one of his best efforts, although portraiture is my least favourite painterly genre and only worth looking at when it's done by an exceptional hand. I think portraits of old people are always better and, although uncommercial – unless by an artist of Rembrandt's calibre – they are always more interesting. Old faces seem to tell the story of their journey.

For my own effort I chose a suitably Rembrandtian proportion for the canvas, something around the 70 by 60 centimetre mark. By this time, I was better versed in old Rembi's technique and thanks to Carol knew all the right ingredients. I asked her what she would like me to paint. Possibly a copy of that great picture in the Hermitage, only a thousand times less effectively done? Or did she have an idea of her own? On hearing my suggestions she requested something completely different – a small picture by Rembrandt standards, and could I do it on an old panel she had hanging about? Then, with another change of mind, she requested I do it on a copper panel. I started to wish I hadn't offered to do this painting. Besides, a suspicion had entered my mind that all this could be the start of something dodgy again. But remembering whose work I was to copy soon dispelled any thought of fakery.

I'm a reasonable hand with a brush and was at that time, too, but, as I said, not as good as Rembrandt's big toe. Eventually, I did three oils on copper, all using the right stuff, and with close direction from Carol. She took a real interest in my efforts and came to see them 'under construction' more than once, pointing out my inadequacies to the point where I almost bent them in half and told her to paint the bloody things herself. But I didn't. Carol wondered why I had three pictures lined up side by side. I told her this was how I always did things. From the time I was still at school and had to knock out those bird pictures in a hurry to get them done in between homework and study, I'd gotten into the habit of painting several pictures at once. It made better use of time and has always been common practice with artists involved in 'churning them out'.

I started as I meant to go on by making up the copper blanks on which the 'Rembrandts' were to be painted. I've seen a few oils on copper, some of which were claiming to be something they were not, and for the average daub that's OK. But as I was trying to do these pictures in a wholly authentic manner, I decided not to ruin the final effect by using an off-the-shelf copper sheet. These are supplied in standard metric gauges and mill-rolled perfection, with a very high purity – so obviously not seventeenth-century or anywhere near. On account of knowing a bit about early metalwork by that time, I made a good job of those panels. All kinds of metalwork has always been a fascination to me, not only the objects themselves, but what they are made of – how the metal was won from the ground, the methods used in its production. By my late teens, I knew off by heart the typical compositions of all kinds of metalwork from Bronze Age gold to eighteenth-century silver, and most things in between. Perhaps if I had paid more attention to my proper lessons back then, instead of cramming my mind full of 'all that silly rubbish', as it's been described on many occasions, maybe I would have done better. But 'that silly rubbish' was what interested me most. I just couldn't help myself.

The copper I used was left over from an earlier project. Something that had hung about in Dad's shed for over 20 years and was still there in its unfinished state when the Scotland Yardies came to see me in 2006 and took it away. It was the beginnings of a twelfth-century gilt and enamelled armilla, a kind of decorative shoulder patch, the type you see today embroidered in cloth on the shoulder of a US Marine, complete with screaming eagle or Star-spangled Banner. This armilla was in copper plate, cut with an image of the nativity and almost ready for the enamel inlay.

For my old-style enamels, I would always use recycled Roman glass, just as the medieval enamellers did – usually tessera, the little cubes of coloured glass used in Late Empire and Byzantine wall mosaics of the type you can see at their best in Ravenna. These are quite easy to get hold of if you know where to look. Many of the churches of the old Eastern Empire were razed at the fall of Constantinople and in some parts of south-eastern Europe these wall-mosaic tessera litter entire fields to this day.

These particular armillae had once been in the treasury of the Holy Roman Emperors at Nuremberg and disappeared in the time of Napoleon's looting tour of Europe, in the early years of the nineteenth century. I'd read about them and decided to make them reappear in the late twentieth, but only ever got around to finishing one of the pair. The other, as I said, was taken into custody and won't ever get finished now, will it?

The impure copper ingot that I had left over was cut and beaten into shape to form the three blanks for my paintings, which were done in an early Rembrandt style and technique of around 1630, a time when he would have been of a similar age to me when I myself attempted the master's work. After all, I had to give myself a fighting chance, didn't I? Rembrandt at 20 may be possible to run with. But that great artist at 50 would be uncatchable.

By the time I did these, I'd seen many of Rembrandt's works and, with Carol's guidance, painted three self-portraits, one in grisaille or monochrome – just black, white and ochre – and two closely following the master. One of them was a serious-looking youth in a gorget – a protective metal collar worn around the neck – similar to a work in the Hague. The other was jollier, in similar attire, but looking away, out of the picture. This was the best of the three and took the most effort. I modelled it as the deliberate opposite of a picture in the Ashmolean in Oxford, a beautifully done water-colour sketch of Rembrandt's elderly father. I tried to imagine this miserable old buffer as he would have been in his youth. Most likely slightly pissed and laughing at his own ugly big-nosed fizzog in a looking glass. That's how I painted him.

Carol finished off the effect of age on them, which was the first time I'd seen it done. Now I saw the reason for her wanting them done on copper. Oil paintings on copper are the easiest on which to simulate the effects of time. I've seen it written, especially about the fake Vermeers painted by the Dutchman van Meegeren, that he baked his pictures and used formaldehyde. None of that would stand up today. The formaldehyde may have been true in van Meegeren's time but these days it wouldn't pass the scrutiny of a 10-year-old armed with a shop-bought chemistry set. As for 'baking it' – those who blab such things have obviously never tried it. Heat, even modestly applied, destroys colour instantly, due to most of the pigments being minerals or metal salts that change chemically with heat application. All the great subtlety of a fine painting would be completely f***** up in no time.

The copper paintings greatly impressed Carol. She said they were the best efforts at copying Rembrandt's work she'd seen. Whether it was just flannel I don't know. I've no idea where they are today, but they were, in my own reckoning, the best paintings I've ever done. Certainly the most convincing. Carol took all three of them without paying me a penny. I never saw those paintings again.

During the years between doing those first pictures for Monks and the daubs on copper for Carol, I spent a few weeks at a time doing carving for Monks and the Cotswolds people, then going off to do stuff of my own – re-equipping my dad's garage with a new kiln and other things, and generally sinking back into a life of making, and hopefully selling, the things I produced. But without much thought as to where I was going. For some time I did quite a lot of copies of English watercolours of the early nineteenth century and earlier. These are the things I like to do most and are what I do best, at least in painterly terms.

I'd become familiar with the look and feel of the papers and the technique of painting them by being able to look closely – through some of Janey's friends, several of whom had part-time jobs in Manchester's public galleries – at some very fine works that had been donated by the great industrialists of the Victorian age. It's something I took full advantage of while it lasted. These pictures, by the leading lights and greatest talents of the age, were mostly amassed by Manchester businessmen and the cotton or engineering magnates of the first half of the nineteenth century. Men such as Joseph Whitworth and John Rylands, whose library I'd benefited from often. Looking through those pictures, most of them in store, I noticed that many were acquired from the famous fine art dealers Agnew's.

The founder of that business, Thomas Agnew, was a Salford lad himself, who'd made his fortune in the North before upping sticks and going to London. His shop in Market Street, established after the Napoleonic Wars, provided the newly wealthy of Manchester with the trappings of a cultured taste. The pictures he'd flogged to them, at top prices I'd imagine, eventually made their way into the public collections of the city as the wealthy industrialists became pillars of the establishment and fancied a bit of immortality as city fathers. Hence their generous benefaction to the humble plebs, most of whom, I suspect, would rather have had a living wage than a chance to gawp at scribbles, even exceptional ones.

Having a short time to see these things up close was a great help in seeing how they were done and, crucially, in getting the feel of the paper and even the smell of old pictures. It was something that a person outside of the art world, as I was, doesn't normally get the chance to do and, though I didn't know it then, I was later to use that experience in my dealings with the art trade. The watercolours I'd paint whilst not working for Monks or his associates were sold mostly at art fairs and to second-rank dealers up and down the country. I never signed any of them or claimed them to be anything other than what they were – watercolour drawings. They were, though, always done 'in period', right palette and paper and so on, and unmistakably in the style of my chosen artist.

Copying the hand of others has never really been the problem – finding my own style is the thing that has eluded me. Occasionally, the victim – I mean dealer – didn't recognise the work, but this was down more to their ignorance than my hand. Most art dealers are extremely knowledgeable and generally a well-informed bunch. But there are a few 'floaters' in amongst the good stuff. I'd usually end up selling my efforts for no great amount, certainly nothing approaching a 'real' price.

The most entertaining part was watching the spectre of greed take them over whenever they imagined they had recognised something of great worth being proffered to them by an ignoramus who didn't know its value. Most of the time, they could hardly contain themselves and went into a 'routine' I saw time and time again. Human nature is a curious thing, especially in all things related to greed and avarice. First, there was an expression of calm disregard. Then they made a few disparaging comments on the quality of the scribble and its battered frame.

I got these frames for next to nothing and if Monks hadn't nabbed them first in his quest for lost masterpieces I would dampen and carefully take off the paper backing, along with its board. Then I'd remove the usually crappy print from the card mount and, lastly, put things in reverse, substituting one of my equally crappy watercolours for the print and re-gumming the backing paper with new pearl glue to remain in period – just as I had first done with my 'Degas'. Then I'd set off to market with that week's 'productions'. For something special, I'd occasionally push the boat out and fit it up with an academy gilt frame, but that didn't happen very often. Most times something battered sufficed.

After the barrage of negativity from the hoped-for purchaser about the frame, etc., I would thank him for his trouble and attempt to prise the picture from his vice-like grip, reinforcing my intent by spouting, 'I've been offered so much for it, so I'll ask that fella for one last improved offer and let him have it for that.' My price and sales pitch was usually calculated on the day or even at the last minute. I never really had a master plan, usually setting my price on assessment of that dealer's depth of pocket, and that's no easy thing to do in the antiques trade. I've known some dealers who dress like wealthy City stockbrokers but haven't actually got a pot to piss in and others who tramp about in holed pullovers who I knew for certain were loaded. Their port wine faces and, of all things, their wristwatches were a good giveaway in deciding on how far I would go to 'wring them out'. My bluff of going elsewhere usually clinched the deal. And with a deep sigh brought on by having to open their wallets, they would always pay up.

Most of them had Monks's fixation with opening up the frame to have a proper look. I never minded that. In fact it only served to reinforce their belief that they had bought a 'right un'. This was the general run of things, with the odd variation. They had no compunction in ripping off an 'innocent', as they saw me, and buying for a relative pittance something they thought worth thousands, or even tens of thousands. And I would always encourage their suspicious minds. It added to the drama. I'd done my work well and had nothing to fear from their amateur sleuthing. It was a nice thing to stand back in feigned awe of this 'expert' at work with his penknife, surgically removing the picture from its old home of 'at least 100 years'. Or so they would keep saying on encountering every clue I'd laid for them, up to the point of an almost delirious squeaking greed when they read the barely legible squiggle on the back of the picture in faded pencil. That was it. They just had to have it. And they got it.

Most of the better (and richer) dealers were more familiar with the look, feel and smell of a genuine early watercolour than I was and it was sometimes difficult to get the better of them. Though once they had taken the thing out of its frame, this increased their desire to buy and they usually paid up pronto. At this point I would drop a hint into how I'd come by this 'find' – that's if they hadn't already asked. I usually used my spiel from when I'd sold that first 'Degas', telling them that I was in house clearance and regularly had paintings for sale, adding, 'Would you be interested in seeing other things when and if they came along?' To this they invariably replied, 'Yes, yes, here's my card. Give me a call anytime.' Then I knew I'd hooked them. Returning to draw more water from the same well was a rather risky thing to do, but I hadn't signed any of those pictures. The dealer had bought 'a watercolour', and a water-colour was what it was. So I felt no guilt in that.

Some of them bought off me repeatedly for years, though I was careful not to kill the golden goose and rationed myself to a few things now and then. They were always keen to buy more, so they must have found good homes for their purchases. I suspect some may even have added the odd moniker from time to time, but who knows? The pictures I flogged them were always good value for money and I did the best I could in painting them, always in original materials on original paper.

The need for paper on which to do my pictures was always an issue. I could sometimes get old papers courtesy of the well-known method used by fakers of times past of cutting the flyleaves out of old books. The only problem with this was that by the time I needed them, in the mid and late eighties, most old volumes for sale in antiquarian booksellers had already been raided for their spare blanks – probably by fakers of an earlier generation. This state of affairs led me to break out my old paper-making equipment from my days of naive enterprise. In any case, flyleaves taken from old books may have sufficed for second-rate 'Old Master' style drawings, but proper rag paper, the kind used for watercolour painting, was almost impossible to come by – especially bearing the watermarks I liked to use to send my dealer clientele into a frenzy of buying.

Reassembling the home-made 'adjustable' pulp tank, complete with pond liner innards – a must for being able to make a standard sheet or even a 'special' when required – I was ready to go in less than a week. Compared to the commercial stuff I'd intended to make legitimately years earlier, 'reproducing' old-style papers is a bit more involved. First, the wire mesh used on the deckle – the wood-framed panel covered in mesh that's dipped into the pulp to form the sheet needs to be of a pattern seen on old papers. Obviously, this isn't available these days so I had to make up my own deckles in stainless steel wire, a time-consuming and boring thing to do.

Always being a stickler for 'authenticity', I initially used copper wire, but ended up with sheets which looked as if they had a bad case of swamp fever – covered in green spots from the oxidised copper wire. So I went back to stainless steel. Who'd know anyway? I think the old-time paper makers would solve this problem by using something called 'white bronze' which was mostly tin with 15–20 per cent added copper for strength and workability. It's an alloy much used in Celtic metalwork as a substitute for silver. It's more resistant to discolouration and oxidation than silver, tin or copper, and you can see it used to spectacular effect in one of the finest works of ancient Celtic jewellery – the Tara Brooch, in the National Museum of Ireland at Dublin. Made by a master craftsman in the eighth century, it was re-found on Bettystown beach in 1850, more than 1,000 years after its creation.

I did quite a lot of experimenting with the various patterns found on old papers, and later used what I'd learned through trial and error to make up copies of very old papers to be used in my imitation 'Old Master' drawings. A surprising amount of those papers have distinctive watermarks in them and this seems to have as much influence on the expert's attribution as the actual work of art. Sometimes, an even greater influence. I've known works of terrible quality to be given the nod just because they're on the right paper. I suppose that's understandable, as finding a fitting sheet on which to draw your doodle is a one in a million chance, these days. But those experts never seemed to realise that making a small sheet of paper with an 'old' watermark is the easiest part of doing a drawing that's trying to be taken for the work of a great artist. Making paper is a craft. Drawing, in the manner of genius, is a rare skill. They should always remember that.

Looking at most old drawings, it's easy to imagine – as with looking at a Lowry – that it would be a simple enough thing to copy. In a way it is. However, especially for drawings that are 400 or 500 years old, there are many considerations to be taken into account – more than might be imagined. Simulating the natural degeneration in the paper, its sizing and the drawn image itself, took me a long time to get right. I would usually set about it by first making up a few sheets of paper with the relevant 'look' used by my chosen artist, or something available to him at that time. That's where the identifiable watermarks came in. To do this, I would buy up old and preferably damaged volumes of the seventeenth century – which used to be cheaper than you might imagine. Then I'd trim off all the unprinted margins and blank spaces for use in the pulp tank. It's surprising how much there is in a book. This is where the first hitch arises.

If you break down the paper into pulp by mechanical means, as is done with new fibre, the paper quality of the 'reformed sheet' is badly affected. So it's best to break down the old paper clippings over several weeks with a home-made chemical concoction – at least that's how I do it. After forming your sheet to a satisfactory thickness, or weight, to use the proper term, lay it onto a linen, or something else with the right texture to match the type of old paper you're trying to simulate, and cover with a felt for pressing. I used cut-up army blankets for my felts. They worked fine.

With several sheets being left to dry slowly, it's time to size the paper and encounter the biggest problem. As I briefly mentioned in my ramble about the 'Degas', the sizing in old paper breaks down over time, and if you try to draw on it with ink the whole thing bleeds as if you're writing on toilet tissue. It's a simple enough thing to re-size the paper with old animal glue boiled up from old vellum property deeds – another thing I've done in my time – but having a surface fit to draw on leaves you with the problem of how to get it past the expert who is looking for degradation in the sizing as part of his or her assessment of age. This was an early stumbling block in my efforts to do old drawings and the reason my Degas wasn't done in ink.

I eventually solved the problem by sizing in the normal way, drawing the picture, then applying a solution that I don't intend to divulge here – something made up from, amongst other things, a very toxic fungus and exposure to ultraviolet light. After the exposure to ultraviolet, this particular treatment leaves no detectable trace and a surface impression of un-bled ink on degraded paper which the boffins love to see. Their conclusion is, therefore, that the drawing must have been done on the sheet of paper when it was new and seeing as how the paper is now degraded, and of a type used hundreds of years ago, it must be authentic. Eureka! 'There you see, it's a genuine Michelangelo da Vinci van Gogh, and a very fine one.'

The only part of it that is a genuine artistic effort is the drawing. For that, just make up the ink – iron sulphide, gum arabic, boiled with crushed oak galls, sieved and left to cool. Then a quill, freshly plucked from a swan's bottom. And you're ready to go. I forgot to mention that the detrimental corrosive effects of the acidic ink must also be simulated, not forgetting that the paper gradually becomes more acid over time and that this, too, must be taken into account. But you get the general idea. Of all my old drawings, I never signed any of them. They weren't signed by the masters either. A great artist doesn't need to. His work is his signature and unrepeatable. At least it should be if he's called a master.

My 'Old Masters' were done in profusion, not all to the most exacting standards. Many would never have stood close scrutiny. But one or two may have. I just sold a few of them for what I could get. The most convincing of them were my earlier efforts when I'd first managed to overcome the difficulties and was busily proving to myself that it was possible to do such things realistically. These were sold at a soon-regretted low price. Over the years, I've seen one or two appear on the market as the real thing. Always described as genuine. Usually the property of some toff who's had them in the family since George Washington's grandpa was still a Geordie.

Having put a lot of effort into my drawings, I soon realised that most of the people I sold them to were a fairly unsophisticated bunch, so I started to churn them out with just enough 'height' in them for these dealers not to be able to see over. They paid crap prices, so they got crap drawings. After all, even in fakes, you get what you pay for, don't you think? Some of the best ones were sold to a gallery man in London, an acquaintance of Monks and Carol. I'll refer to him as Tom. It was my understanding that he had sold on my very first attempt at stone sculpture – the Egyptian 'scribe' in limestone – as the genuine article, though that had no involvement from me. I didn't find out its fate until many years after I cut it.

According to Tom, who was a bit of a boaster, he had been involved in the sale of a famous collection of genuine Old Master drawings, but I always took his claptrap with a pinch of salt. You can probably tell that I wasn't his greatest fan. When I'd first gone with Monks and his wife to see Tom's gallery in London – quite an impressive place – he'd asked if I could be trusted. Not realising what he was on about, I took it into my head that he thought I was a thief. So I told him he was a cockney knobhead and we got off on the wrong foot. As far as I was always concerned, that's where we stayed.

He did seem well-connected in the art game and had photos of himself with what he would describe as famous people dotted about his gallery. I didn't recognise any of them, but that's not to say they weren't famous. It's just that in those days if a person hadn't worked in Rome or Florence during the Renaissance, or helped in building the Parthenon or the Giza pyramids, I wasn't at all interested in who they were.

Tom was very interested in my old-style drawings and took quite a lot of them. I tried to get him to show his 'famous friends' my own landscape paintings, but, as with everyone else I dealt with, he wasn't interested in anything I did. Only the stuff that was in someone else's style. Those pictures of mine may not have been brilliant, but I always thought them reasonably good. I suppose they must have been dire – it was just me who couldn't see it. Neither Tom nor his friends ever bought a single one.

Through my involvement with Tom and his associates, I became more involved in working on the art of ancient times, which up to that point had consisted of just a couple of limestone heads and the seated scribe, all in the Egyptian style. Since I can first recall, the art of the ancient world has been one of my abiding interests, especially the monumental sculpture and stonework of Egypt.

Much of my knowledge of how those things were done has been learnt through little more than taking careful note of such things as the differing proportions, artistic styles and the methods of work employed in the artistic centres of the ancients. However, during the time I knew Carol and Tom, I also had the chance to visit a central London laboratory that did conservation work for some of the major museums of the capital, and Carol would often get scientific analysis papers from there for me to look through. These things were fascinating and unpublished. They detailed many of the points looked for in determining whether a particular object was what it claimed to be. This is where I learnt what things were made of – the stones, the alloys – and, crucially for fakery, what determined the minds of the experts in deciding on authenticity. To me, this was 'inside information' of great value, available nowhere else I could think of. Over the years it has stood me in good stead in my faking work, though that is now a thing of the past.

The lab was situated close to the centre of the London art trade, not a stone's throw away from such places as Bond Street and Cork Street. Tom's gallery wasn't a million miles from there either. Monks reckoned at least half his stock was dodgy, but at that time I couldn't tell the wheat from the chaff, though with hindsight, much of it did look second-rate. Tom always said that in his business it was a good idea to keep a low profile as far as antiquities were concerned and to deal in things that wouldn't come under too much scrutiny. Not rubbish or tourist tat, but mid-range antiques that were usually sold with unproved provenances.

One of his favourite 'provs', as he called them, was to pick the names of old colonials from the early twentieth-century obituaries in the old broadsheet London papers. The antiques and other stuff would then be sold as having once been in the collection of 'Colonel Blimp Esq.' or some Colonial Office civil servant who had spent time in India or wherever. Most of the things he sold were real, but I'm not sure how he came by them. His abiding concern was to legitimise his stock. These 'Colonel Blimp' provenances were yet another pointer for me as to how important a good story was in the sale of any work of art. What struck me back then was how easily his customers were taken in. I had little sympathy for them. If someone needs a piece of paper to tell them a work is a mini-masterpiece, then, in my opinion, they are unworthy of possessing such a thing. Not a genuine one at least.

As I moved on to pastures new I started to leave my painting behind and worked more on sculpture and metalwork, mostly in ancient style. One of the spurs for moving on to the art of the ancients, metalwork in particular, came about when Monks asked me to help out on one of his oft-taken trips to Ireland for furniture buying. Several times a year he would go over to Ireland to stock up on the stuff that he and his associates in the Cotswolds needed to convert into new-old furniture. He would also bring back the odd picture for 'restoration' and, although by this time I'd given up 'scrubbing' canvases, I agreed to go along.

I'd never been to Ireland before. Monks said we would be attending a couple of country house sales and staying in Dublin for a few days. I knew of the National Museum of Ireland's outstanding collection of Bronze Age gold and this was the main reason I agreed to go along. I'd wanted to see those things for a long time. Thankfully, Mr Monks had by this time bought himself a new van, and not before time. The old banger of a Luton Van he'd run till then, with its oil-burning engine, was probably a major contributor to today's global warming. It was a miracle of engineering how it went on as long as it did. Someone eventually put it to sleep by pouring a bag of sugar into the engine, which killed the old thing stone dead. As far as I was concerned, that person did the environment a great service, whoever 'that person' was.

The working trip to Ireland started early and we took the ferry to Dublin in similar conditions to the only other time I'd been on the Irish Sea, or 'the West English sea' as Monks referred to it. I don't think I've ever been out on the waves without them doing their best to part me from my breakfast, though, as I said, I'm pretty good with seasickness. When we arrived in the fair city, Monks and his wife stayed at a swanky hotel called the Shelbourne, while I opted for a modest B&B, though it was in a very fine Georgian terrace and a perfectly nice place. Anyway, I didn't intend spending much time indoors. I only had a few days and there were many things I needed to see.

First stop was the Treasury of the National Museum on Kildare Street which houses the finest collection of Bronze and Iron Age goldwork to be seen anywhere in the world. The great art of the Bronze Age goldsmiths was something I had already tried to imitate, without much success. But as I got older and wiser, my technique improved and eventually I managed to see and understand what they were about. Just as with my perseverance with painting, my efforts finally came closer to what I was trying to copy, although I can say for sure that none of my efforts ever matched the standard I saw in those glass cases in the National Museum of Ireland. Two of the finest things in there aren't Bronze Age at all. But both are either side of 1,000 years old and amongst my favourite things – the Ardagh Chalice and the Tara Brooch. If anyone thinks they are a good metalworker, go to see those things. If you can match them, I would like to shake the hand that does it.

For my own efforts in gold or silver, I would buy my metals from Johnson Matthey or Cookson Precious Metals, both on Vittoria Street in Birmingham's old jewellery quarter. When I first went there in the seventies many of the old workshops were still going, and some still are today, but over the years, many have gone the way of most of our once mighty manufacturing industry, along with the most valuable bit of it – the skill base.

The metals I bought from the bullion dealers of Birmingham were always in something called 'fine casting grain'. They sold all manner of sheet, bar and wire, in both gold and silver, but none of that was suitable for the old stuff I intended to make as it was all in modern alloys. The 'grain', however, was almost pure, so it was a simple thing to weigh out as much as would be required for the job in hand and add the alloying metals to match a typical mix of the period. Our present standards, as I'm sure most people know, are 9, 14, 18 and 22 carat for gold, and 925 parts per 1,000 for silver. At least, here in the UK. In ancient and even not so ancient times, gold was usually alloyed only with silver instead of the copper you get now. However, as the refining of those old times wasn't up to removing everything, many other elements can be found in old gold. All these are telltale signs that are looked for by the experts in ascertaining authenticity. So they mustn't be overlooked by the faker. For example, the gold trinkets of the Middle Ages and up to the seventeenth century – finger rings, hat jewels, pendants and such – the type of thing you read about being turned up by lucky metal detectorists – were in a 20.5 carat gold. And some late Roman goldwork is in almost pure gold. A marvellous metal to work, incidentally.

Once I'd made up the mix to its recipe and melted the whole thing in my small electric furnace – a digital Kerr Maxi Melt, controllable to the nth degree and superb for soldering fine pieces as well as melting metal – I would then cast the small pieces into the sheets or ingots I needed, using moulds made of cuttlefish bone, the type of thing you put in a budgie's cage for him to hone his beak on. Easy to shape and clamp together, set in the sand box and poured into, these cheap throwaway moulds produce excellently clean casts.

For the copies I did of the type of things they have in the Dublin museum, mostly Bronze Age gold, I would make up an alloy of around 80 per cent gold with 12 per cent silver and 1 per cent copper, plus some trace elements to point the examiners in the right direction. Gold of 87 per cent purity is fine stuff and pleasant to work. But Bronze Age gold did vary in its purity, being finest in the Early period, gradually debased in the Middle and finer again in the Late Bronze Age, although in all this time it never fell below 80 per cent pure.

My early attempts were always simple affairs – sheet gold

lunettes and cloak fasteners, plain or marked with geometrics, but always with the marks of modern tools carefully avoided. I'd go over them with microscopic care to be sure of that. The labs where my 'gold bits' might make an appearance had better optics than I did, but I recall a few of my efforts falling down on that score, at least in the early attempts when I was determined to get them right. There wasn't much in the way of soldering or wire and granulation work on Bronze Age gold. All that came later with my attempts at Etruscan, Greek and Roman stuff. The fine detail of Etruscan goldsmiths' work is about as good as it gets and I would always struggle to keep up with them – well, I never even came close really.

Tom took most of my products in this line and would then fit them up with the usual Colonel Blimp provenances. Even going as far as to provide them with an 'old' vellum note, written in a suitably eighteenth-century hand. If the piece was to have been 'found' during the canal diggings of the eighteenth century or 'unearthed' in the building of the railways in the nineteenth century, then a minor and suitably obscure aristocrat – though not too obscure – would replace Colonel Blimp as the first owner. Tom needed to be able to show that this bod had actually lived at one time and most of his customers were easily impressed by aristocratic name-dropping.

As I have already said, most of what I did later in faking my own 'old' provenances, I'd first seen done by others. Much of what remains of the Bronze Age really was dug up in the building of our rail and canal network. So Tom and the others who bought my work were on fairly solid ground in making up these stories. I sold them as what they were – gold ornaments. They may have been made in traditional ways and of the 'right stuff' as far as the alloys were concerned, but I never told anyone they were ancient. That was suggested by others with their false 'provenances'. Others still confirmed it through collusion, ignorance or stupidity. At least that's how I see it.

One of the best things I did around this time – a request from a London dealer – was a copy of a Middle Bronze Age beaker, something along the lines of the Rillaton gold cup which is now in the British Museum and once belonged to a King of England. It's said he kept his cufflinks in it and, in an act of great generosity – something all kings should exhibit – he gave the treasure to the nation.

These ribbed beakers are extremely rare and beautifully made – modern-looking to the eye, with clean and graceful lines. To make it, I cast a disc of gold of about 5 millimetres in thickness and 70 or so in diameter, in a cuttlefish mould – making sure it was in the right alloy, of course. Then I set about the difficult bit of raising it in the time-honoured way. First you hammer out the disc to less than half its original thickness, slowly and carefully to begin with, so as not to crack the metal at its edges. This requires some experience. I've buggered up loads of things through a lack of patience. Hammering metal to reduce its thickness, or change its shape, has the effect of hardening it to the point of fracture. So every so often it needs to be put into the flame until it's glowing a good cherry red. The heating realigns the molecular structure of the metal after its hammering, something I'm sure those ancient and expert smiths didn't realise, or even imagine. It must all have seemed quite a wonder to them. In fact, in ancient times, goldsmiths and all metalworkers were people of status, and still held respect until relatively recently. These days, unfortunately, the crafts have been well and truly downgraded in favour of warblers of catchy tunes and those who are able to do things with balls of one size or another.

When heat-treating metal – a process called annealing – most metalworkers, from blacksmiths to goldsmiths, prefer to work in low light as it makes the judgement of temperature by eye easier, or seems to. The right temperature and the time spent at that temperature is critical to good annealing and, through it, to a proper finished article. After dipping it in water – a process known as quenching – it's ready for its next beating, until the metal hardens again and the whole thing has to be repeated.

Having hammered the sheet of gold to the correct thickness, I could now shape it into the form of a small cup and at this point filled it with a blob of warmed and softened pitch. This was to reinforce the thin sheet gold while I impressed the ribbed detail of its decoration. The look I was attempting was akin to the corrugations you see on corrugated roofs these days. It's the best way to strengthen thin metal. We know it. The German armour makers of the Middle Ages knew it. And so did the goldsmiths of the Bronze Age.

To stay in period, I rubbed in this corrugated ribbing with a piece of deer antler borrowed from one of my dad's walking canes. When it looked right, it was time to warm the beaker in hot water to soften the pitch for removal. Not putting it back in the flame was important because the final distortions I'd put into the beaker while 'corrugating' it had hardened the metal and that, along with the now completed shape, meant it was now a rigid and robust construction. Just as a Bronze Age goldsmith would have made sure it was. The last two things to be done were to punch a couple of holes in it and then to tear them ragged, to simulate where the ring handle had once been. After all, I didn't want it looking too perfect after lying in the ground for the best part of 4,000 years.

Gold, especially of such fineness as used in those far-off times, is pretty much immortal as far as corrosion goes. But any object of such great age does show its wrinkles. In Bronze Age pieces, the age shows as a patina of random fine scratches and abrasions, worn down and succeeded by layer after layer of them, until the whole surface has a definite look to it – one easily recognised by anyone familiar with ancient metalwork. The faker also has to be aware of such things as tiny deposits left in the small nooks and crannies.

This is especially important for things supposedly found in the alkali chalk soils of the South Downs – which is where it had been decided this beaker had come from.

After I'd finished making it, Tom and Carol wove one of their tales around it. The customer for it, at least as far as I knew, was a regular buyer of antiquities in London and someone Tom knew quite well. He was a South African businessman who resided mostly in North America and a very rich man I'd heard. The finished beaker looked very convincing and all who saw it thought so too. Tom was pleased with his 'commission' and paid me what I thought a fair price for the effort. He'd bought the gold for it, I'd made it, kept the leftovers for my next project and been paid for something I would have done for nothing – though I didn't let Tom or anyone else know that while I was making things for others.

Tom had already sold several small items to this South African and his eagerness to acquire more, allied to Tom's ever-present greed, was what led to the 'Woodstock Cup', as it was christened, coming to light. I don't know the exact details of its sale, but it was certainly seen by experts and had an independent lab report done on it at the insistence of the buyer before he coughed up. As for its 'provenance', Tom was always boasting that he had access to the library and records of a learned and ancient society in London, one which held info on many early finds and excavations from all over the British Isles and beyond. So he probably based his provenance for the 'Woody Cup' on something he found there. I never saw that beaker again and I don't believe it has surfaced since, at least I haven't seen it. After this, I don't suppose I ever will. Not as the Woodstock Cup anyhow.

Over the years many of my works have been subjected to expert scrutiny and, in aesthetics, usually given the thumbs up. But, under lab tests, some have failed for various reasons. Many through my ignorance or lack of attention to detail – those experts aren't known by that title for nothing. Of course, they haven't been able to spot all of them. And the things I went on to make later were full of deliberate mistakes. Yet they still seemed to get through more often than not.

By this time, I'd tired of things and just wanted to see how 'wrong' I could do them and still get a pass. Without going into detail, you would be surprised by how many glaringly obvious mistakes weren't picked up on. I certainly was. Not all the things I made in those times were of such supposed importance or rarity as that gold beaker. Many were middling or minor works that wouldn't draw too many flies.

Among the more complex things I've done in gold was a copy of the found and re-lost Saxon brooch known as the St Mary-at-Hill Brooch. This thing gave me a lot of trouble due to the fact that I'm no jeweller. I'd first seen an engraving of it made at the time when it was discovered in the eighteenth century, along with its burial pot and some silver pennies of Bill the Bastard, as he's known up north. Or, if you prefer, William the Conqueror.

From its style I thought it late ninth or early tenth century, so it must already have been over a century old when it was hidden by someone who obviously never came back to collect it. Though it was described as English, it looked more continental to me, but what do I know? I made it to order for someone else in a typical alloy of the period, 20 or so carat, all done on pierced sheet gold with fine wirework and granulation, and set with a good sapphire, which I'd cut and polished in the old manner, as in the original. My only deviation from the engraving was to leave out the one remaining pearl of the four that were originally there. I just couldn't source a suitable pearl and neither could anyone I knew.

Some years later, I saw this jewel again, mounted in a black basalt Wedgwood frame – the type used to mount miniatures – complete with a description of it. It was surrounded by William I pennies and even a fragment of 'the pot in which they were found'. I can't say much about the authenticity of the silver pennies, or the pot fragment, but that Saxon jewel was less than 10 years old. I haven't a clue where it is now. I made it, but I never said it was old.

At the time of my arrest, the police took away a small Roman-style silver plate that had been hanging around for years. The original of that was found in the nineteenth century, recorded and then lost again. It was only a slight piece, about 7 inches in diameter, and depicting David fighting a lion in bas-relief. Early on in production, it went wrong, but I never got around to melting it down for recycling, so off it went to the storerooms of Scotland Yard, never to be completed.

In these busy times there were a lot of smaller things – Roman signet rings, one or two attempts at Etruscan and Greek jewellery – mostly beyond my ability. I did, however, manage to do a more convincing job on a gold and garnet eagle brooch of the one-time conquerors of Rome, the Visigoths. I set this with typical sulphur and scored foil backings, then put in the slices of garnet, which I cut from two very fine and large stones from India. Tom supplied them. Well three stones actually, but I told him I'd buggered up several cuttings and kept the last one for myself.

Among things in gold that weren't related to European history there were such things as a fifth-century copy of a Han dynasty imperial cosmetic container in the comical form of a goose laid on its back with its feet in the air. It was a small piece, about 3 inches long, all of raised sheet gold and quite an effort. The hollow twisting neck almost led to my screwing the job up and melting it for something else. I only made one of them and that was quite enough.

An easier job was a Japanese crown, all in crude sheet gold with a minimum of work, just a little soldering here and there. It was of a style seen in the eighth to ninth century, so not much earlier than the St Mary-at-Hill Brooch, only done on the other side of the world. It was actually Korean in style, from an era when Japan was ruled by emperors of Korean descent, similar, I suppose, to our own monarchs being of Norman and German descent. I made this long after my dealings with Tom and the others, and took it down to London to show it to an expert at one of London's premier museums – I won't say which. He examined it and snootily said it couldn't be from Japan as it wasn't stylistically Japanese. He didn't seem to know that at this time Japanese taste, at least amongst the ruling elite, was Korean. Whether he didn't know or had simply forgotten his history, I can't say, though I found his ignorance of the subject incredible for a well-paid public servant. I thanked him for his expert opinion and later took it round to one of the fine art auctioneers for another go.

The experts of the leading London auctioneers are first-class. If you can get past them, you can get past anyone. They really know their stuff. I suppose dealing in the real world of commerce sharpens their wits, at least it seems that way to me. Their Japanese expert made the Korean connection right away and was keen for me to leave it for further research. She seemed a skilled opponent and a proper lady, so I courteously declined the request and left. I didn't have the heart to deceive her, and she would most likely have rumbled my effort in no time and seen it for what it was – the product of an untrained and amateur artist, who, nevertheless, always tried his best.

My most ambitious project in gold was one that never actually came into being despite a great deal of time and effort expended on it. I first heard of this thing when I was still at school and had done some drawings based on surviving written accounts of how I imagined it to look. It was a large gold plate, made on the orders of Queen Elizabeth's minister Lord Burghley, and lost in the destructions of the Civil War. The Armada Gold Plate. I didn't work on it as part of any deception. It was just something that lodged in my imagination and had to be winkled out.

I drew and redrew the designs many times. As my knowledge of art history grew, I saw umpteen things wrong with the earlier envisionings, so into the bin they would fly, to be replaced by the 'latest' working drawing. I even got around to a final design and, after modelling the relief, cast a plaster version to be followed in gold. The final design was historically accurate and completely of its time – a strap and stipple work beaded border, set with classical roundels holding high-relief busts of the admirals of the English fleet, topped by the Queen herself, in a sunburst. The central roundel was divided in two, following a scant written description I'd read. In one half was Frobisher's ship, the *Triumph*, in three-quarter view from the stern, steering to port, with a minimal representation of the Armada on the horizon. The other half had an allegory of Astronomy, a naked young lady holding some compasses, her hand resting on a terrestrial globe supported by two putti. Overall, a nice thing.

I must admit to borrowing the main working style from the Elizabethan silver in the Kremlin, which I think was a diplomatic gift to the court of the Tsars, a quite remarkable survival. Considering the tumultuous political history of Russia, their treasures seem to have survived better than ours. Which is a bit silly, don't you think? Our Civil War must have been more of a squabble than we realise. The final bit of the design was a lunette at the bottom showing a sea monster kicking the crap out of the King of Spain and, for good measure, holding the Papal Triple Crown in its talons. I thought that touch might be something Burghley would suggest, being the religious bigot he was. Due to its cost, I abandoned the project years ago and binned the plaster along with its mould and the working drawings. Burghley's pockets were much deeper than mine have ever been. But, even though it was a 'Paul Storr' in terms of effort and skill, given a wealthy patron to fund my design I was confident then that I could have brought it into being. And still am. Though, I suppose I'll never know for sure, will I?

The only other goldwork I did was minor stuff: a small range of medieval posy and ecclesiastical rings, usually cut with Gothic script on the inside of the band. Quite a tricky thing to do well.

Many of my efforts had to go back into the melting pot on account of my buggering up the engraving. One slip and it's scrap. The best of them was a Bishop's Ring set with a bullet sapphire in a rubbed-over mount. I can't recall what happened to it. All these, like the Roman intaglio rings on which I did both the goldwork and the cutting and mounting of the hardstones, sold very well, although only for modest prices. This was just about the sum total of my efforts in the yellow stuff, though it was fairly typical of things I would do in all materials: wide-ranging in age, style and technique. I seem to have a low boredom threshold and don't like to limit myself to one thing for long.

As I stood there gawping at the great treasures in the National Museum of Ireland in Dublin on that first trip there, all those years ago, most of these things were still some way into the future. After a couple of days filling my head with these treasures, it was time to get on with what I was really there for.

Monks obviously knew a few dealers in Ireland and we spent the rest of the time visiting several of them. Most of the stuff he bought was furniture, the bigger the better. Some of it was in very fine wood and of dimensions that are commercially unavailable these days. I suppose those great trees of exotic hardwood were cut down to the last one standing by the end of the nineteenth century. The stodgy pieces of furniture were pitifully cheap considering the amount of material in them.

One of the places I recall best was a large antiques warehouse outside of the city on the road to Dunboyne, a large ramble of stone buildings which I understood to have once been a distillery. The business was run by two elderly brothers who looked rather comical. They would walk side by side, like Siamese twins, grumbling at one another. As one looked down, the other looked skywards. Two eccentrics, for sure, but nice people. Their father's sale of the distilling business was a sore point with them and probably the reason they seemed to hate each other, although they didn't seem to be doing too badly. Along with their antiques business they were also part-time farmers and horse dealers – not bloodstock, but nags for the continental meat trade. Although I love horses and think them nature's finest work, the thought of those fine horses and ponies in the yard awaiting their fate didn't really bother me. The meat trade is a harsh business whatever the animal that's for the chop, but short of us all going veggie, there's nothing to be done, is there?

Whilst Monks was negotiating with the Brothers Grim, I stood leaning on the rail of the paddock watching the ponies as they circled the yard with ears pricked, occasionally coming near to look me over. I was tempted to buy one and save it from the French plate, but reality prevented my good deed. I had nowhere to put a horse. Monks did. His wife had several of them. But he was a flinty-hearted old bugger. We loaded the van with large lumps of furniture and drove off down the lane, leaving the horses to whatever was to befall them. As we left, I could see the brothers in the wing mirror, still arguing hammer and tongs, one still looking up and the other down.

During the next few days we met many more eccentrics. The antiques trade does seem to have more than its fair share of these marvellous people. I could have spent hours rummaging through the antiques stores we went to, but, for reasons unknown to me, Monks was always in a mad rush. As a last call, we were going to a country house sale, but seeing as we had collected everything on the list and the sale wasn't for another two days, I made the most of my spare time and legged it for the museums.

I also managed to fit in a trip to the Chester Beatty Library to see their fine collection of Islamic scrolls and the many ancient examples of the Koran that I knew to be the finest collection of such things in the world, or at least one of them. I couldn't properly read the text but the superb decorative script of Islamic calligraphy is mesmerising in its rhythmic strokes and has always been of much interest to me. I think it amongst the best of things.

At that time I was working on a copy – not an exact reproduction of something already existing, but more of an imagined original – of a small Persian silver bowl of AD 1200 or so, to be inlaid with nielloed geometric design and some gold calligraphy. So I wanted to look at this fine calligraphy to see how it was done, first-hand. That evening, I resisted the draw of the Dublin pubs – just – and spent the night in my B&B scribbling away on the designs for the silver bowl, putting to good effect the memorised visions of those texts I'd soaked up during my visit to the Chester Beatty Library.

Although the Islamic world of times past didn't have the engineering traditions which bred the Industrial Revolution here in Britain, their great skill in ornamental metalwork, dedicated to the glory of God, must surely rank among the finest ever done. It's generally of exquisite quality and very hard to follow for anyone hoping to emulate it. I was no exception to this and struggled to keep up. The inlays of thin sheet gold were cut to a slightly larger than required size and punched into the undercut edges of the engraved areas, then polished flush. The remaining design was filled with ground niello, in the manner of enamelling, and the whole thing rubbed to a smooth finish, before having its age applied 'on top'.

There are two distinct types of niello used in old metalwork. The oldest, commonly seen on Roman 'picture plates' – silver figures in a landscape, with a background of black – are done in a simple silver sulphide. This is a bugger to work with due to its high temperature and intractability. It's similar to chewy toffee, only very hot, and needs to be done quickly, which takes a lot of practice. For my attempt at that Persian bowl, the inlay was done in the other kind, the heavily leaded niello, typical of the time. This can be made in a lump, smashed and pulverised to the consistency of sugar, and used just like enamel. Newly done, it gives a beautiful graphite-like sheen. This stuff was used in the Middle Ages throughout Europe, the Middle East and beyond, and had a tradition in German and

Russian workshops until relatively recently. The Persian bowl, similarly inlaid, was sold as a copy to a London dealer in Islamic works of art for not much more than its cost. I haven't seen it since.

The day after my interesting day spent at the Chester Beatty Library, I met up with Monks again and we set off for that country house sale at a place outside the town of Navan. It was a rundown eighteenth-century manor house set in overgrown landscapes, and when I saw it I immediately thought how perfect it would have been for my kindly old employer to demolish and fill with 'executive dwellings', complete with minstrel galleries.

Out in front was a broken-down water feature that was now little more than a few rocks in a bog. At its centre was the basin and pedestal of a lost artwork, which, judging by the bits left behind when the thing was torn from its mounting, was something that spouted water, cast in lead. They're usually boys or beasts, but who knows what this one had been. In those days, I was always on the lookout for interesting or rare lumps of stone, particularly marbles. It's ridiculously expensive now, and was then. Many of the types of stone used in ancient work just aren't available any more, not without deep pockets. I'd noticed that the pedestal of the missing sculpture was of a type favoured in Rome – a beautifully marbled piece of *rosso antico*, a red marble, veined in ochre and white. Scanning the auction catalogue, I couldn't find a mention of it anywhere. Knowing it must be worth a few quid, I said nothing and just kept my eye on it.

Monks was in his usual state of high anxiety. Dragging his wife along in his wake, he waded through the house looking for bargains to be had in the afternoon sale. Its entire contents were up for disposal, but there was no sign of the original furniture that must once have filled the place in elegant style. Most of the stuff for sale was relatively modern, though on this occasion, Monks wasn't after timber. His target for the day was two whopping elephant tusks which, I later found out, had been his real reason for the whole trip. I thought he'd finally gone off his rocker. By the early eighties, ivory was fast going out of fashion. The CITES agreement on endangered species in 1975 saw to that – rightly so, in my opinion. To kill such a majestic beast, just for its tusks, is madness, though I suppose those giant tusks from what must have been a colossus of an elephant had been collected back when elephants roamed Africa in their millions.

The things that took my eye in the sale were the pieces of Dublin silver, mostly early nineteenth century, all with estimates that were beyond me and which proved to be well off what the pieces actually fetched that afternoon. Monks got his tusks and I came away with a stuffed and sorry-looking snarling leopard's head, just about the stupidest thing I've ever bought. Something else I bought that day, which turned out to be a better deal, were two small obelisks in green onyx that had been catalogued as bookends. Nobody wanted them, so they were dirt cheap. They were actually of the finest green nephrite and almost without inclusions.

I knew this material was used in Ming period carvings and, some time later, put them to use on my diamond saw. First, I cut a couple of animal figures, one on a gilt bronze base with a period seal mark of the early Ming emperors. I'm not sure it was ever taken seriously. The remaining pieces became part of the green uniform on a 'hardstone' figure of a Russian imperial officer, a kind of stone 'toy soldier' in the Fabergé style, which I have since seen in a fine art magazine sporting 'Fabergé marks', something I definitely did not put on it.

After the sale, the auctioneer also sold us that block of fine marble after Monks told him we were looking for a cheap base for a sundial. To my delight, the block came home with me, along with the nephrite and the crazy leopard's head, all for very little money. The best thing I got out of the block of *rosso antico* was a copy of a Roman recumbent lion, about 16 inches long. Although there's no visual record of the original, at least as far as I'm aware, it's recorded as having been in the collection of an eminent eighteenth-century collector of ancient sculpture, Henry Blundell. Most of his fine collection is now in the Liverpool museums. To my eye, Blundell seems to have bought one or two turkeys, but I'd best not say more on that.

The 'lion in *rosso antico*' was catalogued in Blundell's collection as 'found on the Palatine Hill at Rome', but, along with many fine marbles bought by the English gentry in those times, it had probably been knocked up in an Italian workshop not long before he got his mitts on it. The reduced-scale Pantheon he built to house his sculpture collection in the grounds of his home at Ince Blundell Hall, near Liverpool, is a mini marvel and must have cost as much as the ancient and not so ancient sculptures. Several pieces of Blundell's collection are recorded as 'missing', but as far as I'm concerned, they'll stay that way now.

Before we left Ireland with our 'loot' we went over to see a couple of the ancient sights of that wonderful country. The Hill of Tara, a very ancient and famous location, is nothing more now than a grassy hill. But quite a few treasures have been unearthed there over the years. One or two of my Bronze Age gold articles have been given provenances obliquely referring to locations such as Tara. Not by me, I hasten to add. I sold such things 'as seen', for nowhere near the price of genuine stuff. They would disappear into the trade, only to resurface years later with new and imaginative pedigrees attached.

Those steeped in the art business taught me most of what I know about fakes and fakery. And as long as I was putting it into good use for their benefit that was OK. It was only when I started to do things for my own benefit that it seemed to get noticed.

The last stop of our trip was at the great mound of Newgrange set in a long bend of the river Boyne in an area massed with barrows and earthworks, some of them looking as if they have never been dug. The first large concentration of old burial mounds I'd seen were those inland from Deal during my brief falling-in with the Royal Marines. All the ones I saw then bore the telltale crater on top where earlier treasure seekers had dug them out or cut a trench straight through the middle with that good old Victorian 'can-do' attitude. A very interesting pastime, no doubt, but much more damaging to the archaeological and art historical record than my fakes.

Our visit to see the Newgrange barrow reminded me that some things are immortal, or at least appear to be, and this ancient sight is a good contender for that title. It was mesmerising. Sparkling in the sun with its white quartzite walls and its grassy dome sand-wiched between the pea green earth and the bright blue sky. At the winter solstice, the rising sun lights the long passageway down to its terminus – the presumed last resting place of its first occupier – as if to mark the passing of the year and the start of a new one. Surely that was its builder's intention?

The understanding of mathematics, geometry and so on of the ancients seems to amaze the modern mind. But I would imag-ine the builders of Newgrange to be down-to-earth and practical people, well aware of the cycles of nature, and skilled observers of the night sky. I can see the 'architect' sitting on a bench in the middle of a marked-out circle, accompanied by two hefty assistants carrying a rough wooden door frame, waiting there in the half-light of dawn on a cold winter solstice morning just before sunrise. As the sun peeped over the horizon, the assistants would rush out to the marked circumference and position the rough doorjamb to frame the rising sun from the perspective of their boss sitting on his fat arse at the centre. This done, the whole mound would be thrown up around the two points, the door frame and the bench, connecting them for all time with the rays of the sun. All that was done over 5,000 years ago. Quite a thought.

The trip over, we set off for home, though I did return to Dublin years later to see the 'lost and refound' Caravaggio, 'The Taking of Christ', which was rediscovered in a Jesuit house in Dublin in around 1992. It's a very fine painting from the hand of the master and well worth going to see. One of my favourite Irish artists is Roderic O'Conor, one-time associate of Paul Gauguin. I must admit to using him later when building the provenance of that crappy Gauguin Faun that came into existence in the early nineties. So I'd like to take this opportunity to apologise to the late Mr O'Conor. If we ever meet in another life, I'll buy you a barrel of Guinness.

I soon discovered the reason for Monks getting those huge elephant tusks at the old house sale in Navan and it was to send me off in a new direction. He asked me if I would be prepared to do some carving on them. Up to that time, I'd never done any ivories. And although wary of Monks's many daft ideas, I always wanted to try new things, so – before even knowing what the job would be – I agreed. I expected to have to cut up the tusks and carve the pieces into something figurative. But it turned out he wanted the whole thing to be done in carved relief along the lines of African art and, in particular, in the style of seventeenth-century Benin court art. I was already familiar with the bronzes of the West African Benin kingdom. I'd seen many of them in the British Museum, along with the even earlier bronze heads of Ife. There are also a few fine examples in the Museum of Liverpool where I'd go whenever I could as a kid. To me, they are some of the finest things ever done in metal.

Although I was more familiar with the Benin bronzes, I knew of the carved ivories too – the ceremonial masks, the two great leopards complete with their bronze spots and the huge relief-carved tusks that were used to flank the doorways of the oba's palace, usually set into the tops of hollow cast bronze heads. It now became clear to me why Monks had been so keen to acquire such large lumps of ivory. The idea must have been buzzing away in the old rip-off merchant's head for some time.

After a few weeks refamiliarising myself with the finer details of Benin art I set about cutting the ivory. Those tusks were of some age and, looked at closely, covered in cracks and fissures. Carving anything that already has cracks is difficult. Making it look as if the carving was done when the thing was new is particularly hard. That's because, just like the crackle in an old painting, reworking the surface softens the edges of the crack and advertises the fact that the worked surface postdates the one on which it's laid. For obvious reasons, I had to avoid any suggestion that the carving was done recently.

The court of the oba of Benin would have had plentiful supplies of new ivory from the great herds of elephant that must have roamed in those faraway centuries of the 1600s and 1700s. This was the period – the rarest and most desirable period to collectors of Benin art – that I was hoping to have ascribed to my ivory efforts when they were finished. The only way to cut those old and brittle tusks was to draw the design onto them, remove most of the material with a router, then carefully cut the finer details by hand. After applying the oxidised surface finish, and a little 'Victorian restoration' for good measure, the finished article looked quite convincing.

Monks wanted a couple of bronze heads to finish them off and to fill his pockets even further. I refused to do them. For one thing, only the late period heads would have been big enough to accommodate the huge diameter of those tusks. Also, at that time, my 'foundry' wasn't up to such big casts. I told him that if he had put me in the picture earlier and not been such a greedy bastard in wanting such large pieces of ivory, it might have been possible. And that was the end of that.

The carved tusks were supposed to be a joint venture between myself, Tom and Monks, but several weeks after I'd finished them and left them with Monks, they 'disappeared'. He reckoned they had been stolen. I couldn't prove otherwise. So I simply refused to do any more work for him or any of those arseholes I'd spent some of my best years working for. That ivory was to be the last thing I made for others. From then on, I only did stuff for myself.

Shortly after, Monks retired and went to live in Portugal with his wife and daughter, probably on the proceeds of those Benin-style tusks. As far as I know, he passed away in the late nineties. In my future projects, I dealt with most of the things I made myself. Occasionally, my dad fronted some of them. Nobody knew him in London. Not then at least. As the eighties came to an end, no longer involved with Monks, Tom, Carol or any of them, I didn't paint just for the pleasure of it any more and spent my time trying to concoct those oh-so-valuable 'provenances' that I'd seen so many times when my own work was being passed off by others.

This had been the busiest period in my life. And the time when I learnt most about the art world – both in how to construct things properly and, even more so, how infected it is with deceit and dishonesty. Some may say that I am part of that deceit and dishonesty, and maybe so. But I wasn't born that way. It was more a reaction to conditions that were ingrained in the market long before I came along.

IX.

Seeing is believing

F ROM THE LATE seventies and on through the eighties, until I stopped making what I thought of as copies, I'd tried my hand at most types and periods of artwork. Along with what most people would describe as craft – pottery, smithing, woodwork. I see all those things in the same light and as being of equal merit. Most of my efforts had seen a gradual improvement, as anything does over a long period of continual practice, and by 1990 I was just about as good at any of them as was possible for my ability. From this time onwards, the things I made were almost exclusively fakes in the proper sense. And no one could be more surprised than I was at the acceptance of such rubbish and at how things made with such obvious faults were taken to be the work of major artists by experts and the trade. The experience led gradually to my disillusionment with the world of art and, in the end, the amount of work I did fell off to a trickle. Though it was probably just a lack of inspiration that descended on me, as I suppose it does on all artists from time to time.

I always responded to this in the same manner – by destroying everything I was making, locking up the workshop and doing something else for as long as it took for the 'inspiration' to return.

261

This something else was usually several weeks spent out and about in the countryside, fishing, hawking or just walking the moors around Bolton. My boots, which I had just kicked through that painting, were put on and out I'd go.

For some time after giving up on Monks and his cronies, I spent my days training my new hawk. Falconry has always been one of my favourite interests. Ever since I got my first kestrel in my teens, followed quickly by a sparrow hawk, I've flown a few hawks and falcons. Sparrow hawks, incidentally, aren't the best hawks to cut your teeth on, but as usual, having read that they are difficult birds to get to know and highly strung, it just had to be the 'difficult pupil' for me to start on.

Done properly, falconry is very demanding of your time. The hawks need to be flown most days, weather permitting, if they are to become fit enough to keep up with their wild and wily prey. The best falcon I had was something called a 'tiercel' – in hawk-speak, a male peregrine falcon. The female, about a third bigger than the male, is the one known as a 'falcon' to falconers. With all hawks and falcons, dominant females are more aggressive than the male birds, so in that way they're a bit human, I suppose.

This tiercel was on the small side, even for his kind, but a brave little bugger in attack mode, regularly knocking over birds twice his size. I bought him in the mid-eighties as a captive bred from the Welsh Hawking Centre at Barry in South Wales for £500. He was a very intelligent chap, but most of them exhibit a remarkable understanding of things, and all from a brain not much bigger than a bean. If only the people charged with the running of our country could do as much with as little grey matter we'd all be in clover. After an unsuccessful flight he would alight on a nearby fence post or tree stump and look at me as if to say 'that was your fault, you berk'. Then he'd whizz off for a few minutes, refusing to co-operate. Peregrines are at least as smart as a good dog and cleverer than a horse – or even a few members of the art establishment I have met.

I would usually fly them locally. A particular memory is of a place where I've had some spectacular flights and chases – a knot of old beech trees set high on the moors in an unusual enclosure that looked as if it had once been cared for. These old beeches had been battered by the prevailing westerlies racing in over the moors from the Irish Sea. On a clear day, you could see the water sparkling in the winter sun out past Liverpool and the mountains of Snowdonia. The windswept beeches were the usual hang-out for the local rook gang, and on this particular day, I was out with my hawk when the windbags in the trees began making a great din: something they always did when they spotted the peregrine approaching, sitting contentedly on the fist of the berk carrying him. Suddenly, the tiercel shot off my hand and raced for the trees. As the rooks squawked out to meet it, there was nothing for it but to stand and watch the fight. Peregrines don't usually put the wind up rooks or carrion crows – they're a big tough bird with beaks like pickaxes – but this one hadn't read the script and went straight for them.

The usual objects of our attention were the game birds – partridge and the few grouse – that still live on the sparse unmanaged moors around the town. Until the 1940s, most of these moorlands were the preserve of the wealthy mill owners and closed to public access, but I'll refrain here from a rant about the unworthy and over-mighty landowners who still populate our land, and get back to the chase. If I was lucky enough to spot a small covey of grouse before they saw me, I'd cast off the hawk into the wind and wait as he flew off upwind so as to gain height as quickly as possible. He would then turn downwind and use the backdraught to pick up speed before turning sharply into the wind again, ringing up higher with each circuit, until he was nothing more than a tiny speck on high. Then he would range slowly to and fro, letting me – his subordinate assistant – know it was time for action.

Not wanting to bugger things up, I'd wait until the hawk was high overhead and, for best effect, slightly upwind of the sitting game birds. At that moment, I'd run in on the sitting grouse who had no doubt been watching their age-old nemesis climb and take station high above. With a clatter of wings and grumbling calls, they'd break cover and scatter in all directions. The old birds usually turned downwind and would come by me at a rapid rate, just skimming to left and right, a couple of feet above the heather. They knew through experience this was the best defence from a stooping falcon. And their tactics always paid off. The younger birds, the birds of that season, only a few months old, would use their youthful power to fly away from me, into the wind, which had the effect of gaining height, making them a better target for the boss who by now had picked his prey from high above. At that moment, I would stop still to be an onlooker at one of nature's best shows.

The falcon, rolling over to tip the air from under his wings, plummets to earth, only occasionally adjusting his trajectory with a half open tail or wing, and in what must be a split second of action – although, as in a motor crash, things seemed to happen much more slowly – whacks his target in a cloud of feathers. As the forlorn grouse or whatever falls to earth, the falcon zooms up for one last look at his handiwork, then drops upon it, and the grouse hits the heather with a bounce. I don't have the required literary skill to describe it better.

But the battle with the rooks wasn't such an elegant affair. Off on the wind they all went, climbing ever higher and out of sight. It was several days before I saw my hawk again. He was picked up near Huddersfield with several plucked-out feathers and two black eyes, courtesy of mixing it with a carrion crow. It didn't stop him from chasing crows and rooks. I eventually lost that particular bird, but he was well able to look after himself and the shows he put on were worth the £500, so I hope he had a happy life. I know field sports aren't to many people's taste these days, but in defence of them I would say that most of those involved are good conservationists at heart and, as a rule, put more back in than they take out. Of course, as in all walks of life, there's always the dickheads who give it all a bad name. But having seen the slaughter of domesticated stock and the despatch of wild birds and beasts in the field I know which I would prefer as an exit.

As the winter came in and the rain and blustery winds made it impossible to go hawking – still not fired up enough to resume my art work – I'd spend more and more of my time helping out my mum and dad. Slowly but surely becoming indispensable to them in their advancing years. I'd take time out for fishing or have days away in the lakes, walking, but my world was gradually shrinking around me. My earliest brush with the law happened a bit later. And it almost brought the wrath of Scotland Yard down on me 16 years earlier than was eventually the case.

During the late eighties and early nineties there was one of those cyclical booms you get in the art trade that ended, in typical fashion, a couple of years into the nineties with a big crash in prices. While it lasted, I'd noticed the gains made by the works of the Scottish Colourists. This fine group of painters was influenced chiefly by the French Impressionists. All of them were different in their style. My own favourite amongst them was Cadell whose work had a pleasing pastel quality to it. The other contenders were Peploe, Fergusson and Hunter. For my attempt, I decided on Peploe simply because his work was bringing the best prices.

Peploe's technique is a nice thing and has a fluid and immediate quality to it that's more difficult to do than first meets the eye. As I said before, producing believable oils on canvas is just about the most difficult thing in the faker's repertoire. Most people have an image of the art faker as a bewhiskered old codger slaving away patiently at his easel. But I've never been bewhiskered and I wouldn't know how to go about my work patiently. It's always a bit frantic in my workshop with things getting made and destroyed all the time. The 'Peploe' came through this process in one piece and then received its cobbled-together provenance, such as it was. I knew that one of my mum's relations had once been an art dealer with a shop in Edinburgh. So I used this story to explain how it had come into our possession.

The one abiding worry that many of the dealers I've known seem to have is of buying a stolen work of art. The law being what it is, I can sympathise with that, though I've sometimes wondered if that overriding concern is occasionally the reason for them taking their eye off the ball in matters of authenticity. Something must play on their minds for them to miss such glaringly obvious mistakes in many pieces sold as genuine by the trade. Not just my things. There are many others out there.

The 'Peploe' was my dad's first 'sale' and almost his and my last. By this time, he had been retired for six or seven years and was bored to death with his lot. I asked if he wanted to go down to London to flog a picture and he jumped at the chance to get out and about for a change. I can't recall when my dad became aware of my fakery, but he rarely asked what I was up to during the earlier years when I combined my copies, as they mostly were at the time, with my various jobs. So I never told him. He'd probably guessed before I realised he had. Dad had been a bit of a rogue himself in his earlier life, but never a bad person, despite what some arseholes have been allowed to say about him. All lesser men I'm sure. The inadequate always shout the loudest, don't they?

I'd already made a few enquiries as to who might be up for a 'Peploe' and we set off early to get into the capital by mid-morning, calling first on a dealer not too far from Harrods. Although keen to buy, he was a ditherer, and after lots of it, he upped his offer, but to nowhere near enough for a genuine Peploe. That said, I never expected to get a 'full' price for anything I did, especially not from dealers. After all, they have to make a living, too.

Having wasted a good part of the day on the ditherer, we set off into the West End and alighted on a shop near Duke Street. The only thing I knew of Duke Street was that it had been the London home of Brunel, so I half expected the whole street to be clad in plate iron and rivets. My dad was fired up to do his first sale, so off he toddled with the painting under his arm while I waited to see how things went. The whole experience was a new thing for me and a bit nerve-wracking. I prefer to do my own dirty work, if that is what selling those fakes is.

Listening later to the tape recording of my dad's deal – I always recorded my dealings with the art dealers on a Sony pocket recorder and remembered to slip one into my dad's pocket as he set off to flog his first fake – this dealer seemed taken with the picture from the start and expressed an interest in buying it. But before parting with his money, he wanted to subject it to an 'authenticity test'. From my dad's description of the process, I concluded it was nothing more than a raking UV lamp in a black box of tricks. This would show up any recent restoration and touch-ups. After pronouncing the picture genuine and a fine example of the artist's oeuvre, he entered into typical dealer mode, disparaging it for not being of a suitable dimension for his discerning clientele, and all that. However, he would like to make an offer of £20,000. My dad almost bit his hand off and agreed instantly. At that time, £20,000 for such a picture was daylight robbery. But seeing as how it was my dad's first deal, his enthusiasm was forgivable.

I've always kept a close eye on the prices of artwork and what's at the top of its cycle. Timing is quite important in getting things to market, especially with the long lead times of getting a thing authenticated and into a sale. It's something I've been aware of since making those first 'pot lids'. Those were the most desirable and rare things to come out of the bottle tips, so they brought the best prices.

Dad took a cheque for the picture and emerged into the street after about an hour looking very pleased with himself. The whole experience seemed to bring him back to life, especially the £20,000. In the boom years, Peploes at the top of the market were going for

£50,000 to £100,000. So I thought the dealer could have been more generous.

A few days after banking the cheque, we had a call from someone who identified himself as a detective from Scotland Yard's Art & Antiques Squad. They had apparently received a complaint from a West End dealer in connection with a 'Peploe' he'd bought from us. In the end, the Yardies failed to follow up this contact and we heard no more about it. I heard later that they were massively overstretched at the time, which, this being the art world, I can well believe. What was curious was that in the course of the detective's ramble on the telephone he described the work in question as being done in 'acrylic paints'. Apparently, the purchaser had taken the picture to restorer who told him it must be a fake as acrylics were unknown in Peploe's time, as indeed they were. This story was brought up again by the Yardies during their investigation in 2006. They again mentioned that the picture was a deliberate fake, done in acrylics, that it was a poor effort and had started to peel from the canvas.

This was a bit of a puzzle to me. I don't paint in acrylics and never have. What would be the point? But I didn't contradict them and went along with their description just for the peace of it. By that time, I'd had quite enough of their interrogations. All I can say now is that when I do a canvas, it ought to be good for at least a couple of centuries. So that little episode must remain a mystery. After the near miss with the Scottish picture, I turned away from modern art, as I call anything later than the mid-nineteenth century, and went back to doing sculpture and metalwork of an earlier and, for me, a more interesting time.

The only painterly exceptions to this were some fragmentary bits of fresco that I'd discovered were missing from an old collection. Years earlier, I'd done something similar for Monks – some fresco pieces 'rescued' from the burning of the Basilica of St Paul in Rome. These latest bits were supposedly taken from the demolition of old St Peter's itself when it was being 'remodelled' on the orders of Pope Julius II at the beginning of the sixteenth century. I always think it incredible that no less a building than the Basilica of St Peter, the centre of the Christian world, erected on the orders of the Emperor Constantine in the fourth century, could have been demolished so brutally. I know what stands in its place is a worthy successor, but the ruination of old St Peter's was a scandal in its time and caused great concern. I can't imagine Westminster Abbey, which is now approaching its millennium too, being torn down and replaced by a contemporary design. But that is what happened in Rome in the sixteenth century. If they do ever knock down the Abbey, it would most likely be replaced by a smoked glass and polished steel dildo-type construction, with no mention of God anywhere within. After all, the apologists of the venerable Church of England wouldn't want to offend anyone, would they?

The fragments of fresco from the walls of old St Peter's were done in a pre-Renaissance style. I've always been mesmerised by the great frescoes to be seen on the walls and ceilings of the fine churches of Florence and Rome. Buonarroti's work on the Sistine Chapel is known to all and out in front of everything else. But my own favourites are the Masaccio frescoes on the walls of the Brancacci Chapel in the Church of Santa Maria del Carmine at Florence. They've been topped and tailed by other fine painters – Masolino and Lippi – but in technique and vision Masaccio's work is outstanding and was recognised as such. Buonarroti and Raphael both went to look and learn from Masaccio's work. And they certainly knew quality when they saw it.

Fresco and tempera, the preferred materials of pre-Renaissance Italian art, were both water-based. Fresco is painted at a rapid rate onto drying lime plaster, laid patch by patch as the picture progresses. The bigger the patch, the greater the ability needed to finish it before it dries. As the paint sets, it reacts with the lime and is drawn into the plaster to make a permanent image. If you get the chance to see an old fresco fragment in cross section, it's similar to the effects of water being drawn into a dry sponge. The image is there in depth, so it lasts the ages. It also intensifies the colours to give fresco its unmistakable look.

Tempera was usually done on a smaller scale, the ground colours mixed with egg and water, but not exclusively so. Its effects are easier to fake than oil paints which superseded both techniques. A very fine example of Masaccio's work in tempera can be seen at the National Gallery in London, part of an altarpiece originally in the Carmine Church at Pisa. It's an outstanding example of painterly perspective of the early Renaissance and a beautiful work.

Oil painting came from the northern tradition of the Low Countries in the fifteenth century, but my favourite exponents of it are the Venetians, Bellini and his star pupil Titian. Titian took oil painting to a level that set the standard for all to follow. Even now, many of us can't keep up. In the next age, it would have to be my 'star' painters, Caravaggio and Rubens, then on to Rembrandt. These are the great artists of a great era. And they certainly don't make 'em like that any more.

I've always had a liking as well for views of ruined buildings – the watercolours of abbeys done by the English artists of the early nineteenth century and, especially, the even earlier views done by Piranesi of the ruins of ancient Rome. On my first trip there in the mid-seventies the 'souvenir shops' were full of modern repro-ductions of these things and I bought as many as I could afford. I would stare at their details for ages and imagine myself digging in the ruins and – hopefully – finding more than I ever found in those Victorian 'bottle tips' around Bolton. Knowing me, I'd most likely have ended up selling marbles 'just excavated from the ground' to the gullible of the Grand Tour. But I'm not the only pretender in the art world. Far from it.

Just for the record, I'll mention something else that happened to me, so you can see how oil paintings can occasionally effect remarkable transformations. The picture involved was a copy of one of my favourite artists, L. S. Lowry, a millscape, in typical Lowry style. I like doing them for themselves and have, in fact, only sold very few of them as possibly by Lowry. Mostly for un-Lowry prices. This particular one I took to a large provincial auctioneer for an initial appraisal and a hoped-for sale. When he clapped eyes on it, the valuer thought it to be 'right' and described himself as something of an authority on the works of L. S. Lowry. As usual, he asked if it would be possible for me to leave it for further investigation. So away I went with my scrap of paper as a receipt.

I know it's generally thought that Lowry painted his stuff on 'cardboard boxes', but he was painting for posterity and the works he produced were designed to last, something that's common to all serious artists. His technique in oil is a difficult thing to emulate, due mainly to his dry-brush impasto style. Laying on the paint as he did means it takes many years to fully harden, a must if it's going to be taken for something 80 or so years old, as most of his best works now are. He would start by laying on a thick layer of lead white, then leave this to 'go down', sometimes leaving this base coat for several years before even starting to put an image on it. Using all the right materials is crucial in any convincing copy and with Lowry it's impossible to take liberties. In all his work, throughout his long career, he only ever used three colours – yellow ochre, vermilion red and Prussian blue, along with lamp black and lead white. These are so distinct and unwavering that anyone even half familiar with his style would notice the slightest dab of a wrong colour.

Thanks to my time looking over the shoulder of Carol the restorer I could get round the 'age' problems. But it's a very involved process and, as I've said, I'm not known for my patience. Even with everything sorted, I couldn't resist putting in a few subtle skews to the perspective, all very un-Lowry like. His pictures may look simple, and even childlike to some, but that's the genius of them. The geometry and perspective is actually spot on.

None of these deliberate faults were picked up by the 'Lowry expert' at the auctioneers. A few weeks later, however, he rang to ask me to collect the picture – on account of it not being by Lowry after all! I thought he had taken a better look and spotted the mistakes. He was the 'expert' after all. But when I called to collect it, there in the frame sat a not very convincing copy of my copy, complete with all the faults I'd put in. Either he had copied it himself or he had got someone else to do it during those seven weeks it was with him. It wasn't even in the right colours! To overcome the long drying times inherent in oil paints, his crappy new picture had been done in acrylics.

I've been diddled many times by art dealers, but this guy must have been the cheekiest bugger I've ever encountered. With his deadpan expression, he would have made a great poker player. For obvious reasons I didn't want to cause a stir and took the acrylic away with me. After all, a fake of a fake would have been hard to explain to a policeman, wouldn't it? The art business is a dog-eat-dog world and, on that occasion, I was the dinner instead of the diner. Not for the first or last time.

My interest in painting seems to dip when it reaches the eighteenth century. I prefer the sculpture, architecture and, especially, the work of the silversmiths of that era. There's no particular reason for this. It's just a personal preference. I think the Renaissance and the baroque produced the best painting, though a couple of artists of the eighteenth century – Chardin and Watteau – do stick in the eye, especially Chardin.

By the late eighteenth century, until well into the twentieth, France was the artistic centre of the world, just as Italy had previously been. And although my own favourite was sculpture, with the likes of Houdon and Clodion, the thing I've done most of and like greatly is, as I said earlier, early eighteenth- and nineteenth-century watercolours. The English tradition is strongest here and I think they are what I do best, in paint at least.

One watercolour that made up part of the police investigation – not an English one in this case – was a small thing I did in the early nineties, a copy of the work of the nineteenth-century American landscape painter and fellow Boltonian, Thomas Moran. I like American painting – all of it. But Moran's style is something I find easy to copy. I'd done this little picture in a bit of a rush, along with a set of about 24 pencil sketches, all views of such places as the Yellowstone volcano, various ranges in the Rockies, the Grand Canyon in Arizona, everything scribbled in his style and signed, or at least initialled. I'd intended them for a London auctioneer and planned to take them down to London at the same time as the Gauguin Faun made around the same time, thus killing two birds for the price of one.

First, though, I took the picture to our art gallery here in Bolton. Not to sell it to them, but because the Bolton Museum had a few Morans and he had been born in the town. So I thought this would enable me to mention to the auctioneers that the museum had given it the thumbs up and that this might help it on its way.

I'd been to look at the Moran pictures in the Bolton Museum when I was a kid. At that time they were rarely if ever on show in the gallery and I would have to go 'back stage' to see them in store. In the inventory, I noticed a listing of a watercolour entitled 'Rainbow Over Yellowstone Lake', but the curator said it was unlocated. Where it had disappeared to, heaven knows. On seeing the Moran daub I'd done, not only was he interested to see it but he asked if he could apply for a grant to buy it! I know I shouldn't have gone along with that, but, being imperfect as I am, I did. The museum bought it with a grant from the V&A for £10,000, not a huge sum for a Moran watercolour, but £10,000 more than they should have had to pay. It's something I deeply regret. Bolton Museum has been one of my favourite places from my earliest memory. The drawings, meanwhile, went off to auction, along with that Gauguin sculpture. But I can't remember the details of the sale.

I have done quite a few paintings after nineteenth and twentieth-century American artists, though mostly avoiding the 'Western' stuff, which has been done to death and extensively faked over many years. Even in his own lifetime, Moran's work brought huge prices and his paintings were already being faked. Those fakes are now as old as the real paintings, so you need to be very careful when coughing up for one. Some years back, the Bolton Museum paid around two million for a large Moran painting, a panoramic landscape of the 'Cliffs of the Green River', a similar aspect and the same title as the little watercolour they bought from me some years earlier – only this one was genuine. It is a very nice painting and well worth its money.

The largest painting I ever did was an American scene by an artist of the Old West called Alfred Jacob Miller. During the early 1800s, he painted scenes of the Plains Indians, trappers and adventurers. This particular picture was something I'd known about for years. It had been the property of a Scottish aristocrat called William Drummond Stewart of Murthly Castle. I've fished the river Tay north of Perth, not far from this place, several times. Stewart was an adventurer who took Miller as his artist on a tour of the US in the 1820s. Murthly Castle was the home of a painting called 'The Trapper's Bride', of which several versions exist in museums and collections in the US. At over 10 foot by 8, the Murthly one was the largest. It was apparently sold at a London auctioneers in the 1870s and hadn't been seen since.

This was quite a common fate for many pictures. I recall another American masterpiece, once the prize possession of a Victorian industrialist, being rediscovered in a Manchester old folks' home. It was a huge oil by Frederic Edwin Church called 'The Icebergs'. The council flogged it and it went back to the US in the late 1970s. This was the background to my effort. Around the time, several American dealers were on the prowl in the North West, all hoping for a similar find. In 1979, another was made – a second American landscape just half a mile from where I lived at a cottage hospital in need of funds called Blair Hospital. It was just by the Last Drop Hotel, the watering hole of those detectives who came to visit me years later. I thought, if two such works can be found, why not three? Hence the return of 'The Trapper's Bride'.

It was some years before I had the wherewithal to make an attempt at it. The great size was the most difficult part. Carol's method of ageing the paint without buggering up the colour involved taking it down below freezing at several points in the picture's production. It wasn't necessary to hold it at a low temperature, just to get it there for crystallisation to occur locally. As a 10-foot freezer was a bit much to make, I knocked up a Heath Robinson affair using refreezable icepacks. The walk-in freezers at the Co-op would have been ideal, but ice, polystyrene and tin foil, in a plywood case, had to do. And they did the job OK.

I can't recall exactly what happened to 'The Trapper's Bride'. It's probably somewhere in North America. Most of my attempts at British art have been English watercolours, along with the occasional sculpture. Also, several Scottish artists whose works are first-class and can be seen in the Hunterian and Burrell collections in Glasgow – not my copies, the works that inspired them. As for continental stuff, I've avoided the French Impressionists for the same reason as the American 'Western' artists – they've been done to death and then some, and need a cast-iron provenance. Though even cast iron rusts, doesn't it?

My copies in paint cover a long period – from fragments of Egyptian tomb paintings of a few thousand years BC, to stuff of 1930s vintage. Not all of them were done in a convincing manner, of course. Some of them were terrible scrawls. But I mention them to give you an idea of what has interested me in the world of the painted image. Although painting has been a lifelong obsession, for sure, it's not something I've ever really considered my thing. I've tried to do the work to the best of my ability but it's all been in the style of others. If I try to be 'original', I'll stand back, see the hand of another, shake my head and pop it in the bin. So much for being an artist. Maybe 'parrot' would be a better description.

It was always a relief when a particular picture was finished, and for every moment of its creation its completion was uncertain. If it started to go 'wrong', or lacked the vital spark, back into the firmament it would go. Over the years, I must have binned a large proportion of my work. But those that went deserved their fate. They were crap.

At least the metalwork I've done could always be recycled. It's the only thing that could be brought back as something else. Paper, canvas, stone and pot are a total loss. Some of the objects I did in metal, though, had been four or five things before they went off as a saleable item.

I've had a go at a wide range of things from all ages. My earliest metal efforts were in bronze, crude unsophisticated copies of Bronze Age socket axes and daggers, cast in piece moulds of either cuttlefish bone or soapstone. I managed to sell a few of these things at local markets in my school days, but they were unlikely to fool anyone who knew what they were about. In those days, I knew little about the composition of ancient alloys. Two of my productions in metal were part of the Scotland Yard investigation into my wrongdoings. These were a copy of a late Roman silver plate, known as the Risley Lanx, and a small gilt Corpus Christi, supposedly found in the tomb of bad King John. These were made in 1990 and 1997, so at least they were made of the right stuff. I'd learnt my trade by then.

My interest in such things goes right back to my earliest memories, when I'd spend many days of my school holidays looking at the treasures in the museum or reading about how they were made in any book I could get hold of. Looking back, it was a wonder I never got badly injured at the time, though a few blisters and burnt-off eyebrows or singed hair weren't unknown.

I found out the hard way that most of what's written in the 'how to' books is written by people who have obviously never practised what they preach. Most likely, they have copied down things written by others who had equally little practical knowledge of their subject and so perpetuated the 'boolshit', as the foundry master from Turin used to say. The older I became, the more his words rang true. Many art books are in a similar vein – talking heads prattling on about this or that aspect or hidden meaning in a work that was probably cracked out in very little time with equally little thought by the artist who made it. After a couple of explosions and a fire that burnt down the front portion of my dad's garden shed I sorted how to do it and chucked all my 'how to' books away.

The study of early metalwork, especially the compositions of metals used around the world, is of interest to me and it's crucial not to overlook this in any fake. Especially the more valuable things which, for obvious reasons, come under closer scrutiny. Ingredients such as lead or arsenic are easily overlooked, but they can be a fine pointer to the origin of many early Bronze Age artefacts. Arsenic is, for example, present in fairly high concentrations in early eastern metalwork and also in pre-Columbian stuff.

The fantastic early Chinese bronzes of the Shang dynasty, of around 1200 BC, are a great example of the bronze caster's art. China, and indeed Japan, have a very fine tradition in metalwork and have produced many things which I admire. Shang bronzes are particularly high in arsenic. I have done a few of them. The best was a double-headed ceremonial axe head in the form of a winged dragon, complete with simulated corrosion and mineralisation of the surface. The fake age effects took longer than the making of the bronze, but it looked well for the effort. I sold it to a dealer who used to have a shop off Bond Street in London. I don't know how far it got. I haven't seen it since.

With arsenical bronze you can achieve a beautiful silvery sheen on the surface by slowing the cooling of the cast and through it the crystallisation of the metal. The arsenic is forced to the surface and, hey presto, it's something looked for in early Chinese work. I think the Shang probably arrived at the effect by accident. They used thick ceramic moulds as opposed to the clay or plaster ones with burnt-out organic matter used in the western tradition which draw in cold air and set the metal quickly. The thick ceramic moulds of the Shang would have caused a slower cooling, resulting in a high concentration of arsenic at the surface. It's just a thought.

British and Irish Bronze Age articles also contain lead, arsenic, antimony and such, and they occur in all old metalwork, too. The faking game is getting harder all the time, in all manner of ways. Some are due to better connoisseurship. But the most difficult to overcome are the advances in the lab. The Risley Lanx, one of my metal products investigated by the police, was thought to be of Roman-British manufacture of the fourth century. The silver for it came from Johnson Matthey on Vittoria Street in Birmingham's jewellery quarter, fine-casting grain, 12 pounds of it. The 1 per cent gold content came from the same place and cost not much less than the 98 per cent of silver. The other 1 per cent was made up of copper, lead and other typical trace elements from my scrap metal sack. But each part, small or large, is as important as any.

Most of the tiny proportions of such things as antimony, bismuth and arsenic, aren't readily available. I'd usually add them to the molten melt at the last minute in oxide form from my pottery supplies. Many are used in glaze and colour preparations, and it's surprising how the things used in one line of work overlap another, especially in metalwork, ceramics and paint colours. Arsenic isn't used in pottery, but, years earlier, when I was in my metal detecting phase, I found a golf ball-sized lump of this dull greyish stuff in a plough field. The old-timers gave arsenic to their horses to worm them, or so I've been told. This chunk probably fell from the ploughman's pocket – no doubt the same one in which he kept his lunch. In those days, toxicity wasn't something that was much bothered about, I imagine.

After adding the trace elements to the mix I would give the crucible a good stir with a graphite rod and pour the 'Roman' silver through a flame to avoid gas 'pick up'. Given the opportunity, molten metal soaks up oxygen like a sponge, making for poor casting and hammer work. With the Risley Lanx, I kept a soft reducing flame playing on the surface of the poured ingots until they had set. Then it was time to get on with the actual making of the silver plate.

The lost original had been found in 1729 ploughed up at a place called Risley Park on the border between Derbyshire and Nottinghamshire. I've been to see its find spot in a field by the M1 motorway. It's private land, so I only got to see the place from a distance – good farmland with the subtle humps and bumps of ancient earthworks all about. For some reason, none of these are marked on the Ordnance Survey. They may be figments of my imagination, but I don't think so.

My first 'discovery' of this lost Roman treasure was in a book I read in the Manchester Library on one of my unofficial away days from school in about 1973. It came back to mind in around 1990 when I heard of the recent discovery and legal wrangling over the great Roman silver of the 'Sevso Treasure'. This inspired me to try my hand at something similar to the Risley Lanx. I didn't want to replace the original which, I suspect, may still be around somewhere, at least in parts, probably lying around in a drawer or cupboard unrecognised for what it is. We'll all have to look out for it on the *Antiques Roadshow*.

A flawed copy, I thought, might be an interesting project, if only to see how far it would go. Some months before committing my cash to casting grain, I went to look at that book I'd first seen in 1973 to get a copy of the eighteenth-century engraving in it. The book was still there, gathering dust, probably untouched from when I'd laid it down 17 years earlier. It was in the same condition as I remembered – hardly ever read. I photocopied the page with the illustration and later, back home, photographed it and made a black and white enlargement to see the detail at actual size – a must if you can't go to see an original work.

I learned how to do my own developing and printing when I was about 14. It's come in handy with all my artwork over the years. Whenever I see an image appear on the paper in the developing tray it's still a magical sight to me, even though I know it's only basic chemistry – chemistry put to great effect.

After doing detailed drawings from the enlargement I set about filling in the substantial missing sections of the plate's design. It was found under the plough and was apparently in a brittle and oxidised state. The yokels who found it broke the old plate into pieces – that's if the tumble under the plough hadn't already done so – and made off with their plunder. The parts shown in the old engraving were the only bits recovered by the landowner. They were recorded for posterity in an engraving ordered to be done by the eminent antiquary of his day, William Stukeley. The illustration was less than 50 per cent complete, but after applying a little imagination, the plate was back with us as I thought it might originally have looked.

One of the glaring faults on the Risley Lanx copy that I made, plain to see without ever going near a laboratory, was never picked up by anyone who examined it. Or it wouldn't have spent a period in the British Museum as it did, would it? The most obvious fault is that the whole design is in an eighteenth-century style. The eighteenth-century engraver drew the fourth-century fragments not in fourth-century style, but in that of his own age. For example, if you've ever seen the Lanx, the large boar at bay in the central panel is distinctly un-Roman, more of a porker that wouldn't look out of place on a Hanoverian pig farm, the type of place frequented by old King 'Farmer' George of history. The whole thing is an eighteenth-century version of the way they saw ancient Rome.

All artists, of all ages, always put something of themselves and their time into their efforts. They just can't help themselves and are usually completely unaware of the process. In fakes, it's a dead giveaway. Something I have always been conscious of and paid particular attention to, though not always successfully. Looking at the details in the enlarged book illustration, I couldn't help but think that the original hadn't been in silver at all. Most likely, especially for a Romano-British work of the fourth century, it was done in high-tin pewter as a cast.

The best quality Roman silver, such as that seen in the Mildenhall Treasure and that from Kaiseraugst, wasn't cast, but beaten up from blanks with punch and chasing, and then given a repoussé-beaded border to finish off the effect. The Risley Lanx was somewhat simpler in its design and construction. This, along with the typical ridged beading of the border, made me as sure as I could be that if its original bits ever come to light, they will be found to be in pewter and not silver. However, the thing was described as being in silver. So silver it was to be.

The alloy I'd put together was high purity compared to today's sterling standard of 92.5 per cent, and more akin to the old Georgian Britannia standard. I'd settled on a 97 per cent silver content, with 1 per cent gold and the rest made up of the usual suspects. Overall, a typically high-quality Roman alloy. There remained the modelling of the bas-relief and this was done in white Plasticine on a cut-to-size white Formica panel bought from B&Q. First, the Plasticine was rolled into sheets about 1 millimetre thick, then these were patched together to cover the Formica. I then traced on the design I'd come up with, which included the original portions from the engraving, and cut out the individual figures, removing the unneeded bits. All that was required now was to model the detail and take a mould for casting in wax.

The mould was done in latex with a plaster-supporting case. After removing it from the model and pouring in the beeswax, out came a new Risley Lanx, although in wax rather than silver. It looked particularly good. At this point, I decided I would put in a fault so that at some time in the future it would be seen as a nice copy of the Risley Lanx and not the original. After all, that plate is a major British treasure and I wouldn't want the real thing to come to light and be dismissed on my account. Instead of casting the plate whole and breaking it up to be reassembled, I decided to cut up the wax pattern into separate parts and cast each one individually, about 20 in all. When all the parts were present and correct, without chasing up the detail on any of them, I assembled the whole with some very amateurish soldering. Under close scientific scrutiny, it would be seen that the crystalline structure of the metal in each piece didn't match its neighbour. So it couldn't be the original plate, just a nice copy, and not wholly in a fourth-century manner, courtesy of the Hanoverian pig and its pals.

For the casting materials I'd had to find a new supplier. The firm of F. L. Hunt of Salford, the place where I'd got my first bronze casting supplies in the seventies, had gone out of business by this time. So the moulds were made in something called Gold Star Investment Powder. It's used in the commercial jewellery business, as well as the dental industry. I cast it with the aid of my new furnace, a Kerr Maxi-Melt, a superb digitally controlled thing no bigger than an electric kettle, just as easy to use and in another world from my old coke contraption. Actually, my coke furnace wouldn't have looked out of place in Roman Britain. Swapping the coke for charcoal it would have been fully of the period.

My Kerr Maxi-Melt was used on a legion of things. Its exact temperature control and reducing atmosphere were ideal for producing the fine soldering of wire and granulation seen on much high-quality metalwork of ancient times. It worked a treat on all sorts of things. In my time with it, I burnt through two sets of elements – and they are built to last. I've also managed to do this type of work using the tools the ancients used – a brazier and blowpipe. But it takes lots of constant practice to do well. Where possible, I have always tried the old ways first and then found an easier path. It gives an appreciation of how good those old-timers were.

One example of something I did in silver in the original manner – with brazier, blowpipe, hammer and tongs – was a thing I'd made in my teens. I think I was 17 and just starting out on a serious attempt at ancient work. It was still with me when the Scotland Yardies took it away in 2006 – a small Anglo-Saxon reliquary of the martyred King Edmund in the shape of a church of the period, with wirework, granulation and a little gold cloisonné portrait of the king, set with a sapphire and crystal. It wasn't the most convincing of productions, but I did the best I could at the time, using fully traditional methods, something I still find difficult after years of practice. It's probably lying on a dusty shelf at the Yardies' HQ, so I won't be seeing that again, will I? Even though I never sold it to anyone or tried to.

The Lanx, now polished up, was photographed and I sent off its mug shot to a dealer I'd heard of. Some days later, he called in an excited state. I think I've still got the tape recording somewhere. He suggested that we meet privately at a motorway services halfway between London and our hometown. He immediately expressed an interest in buying it, and came straight out with an offer of many thousands of pounds, adding that he was prepared to take a risk on it with the proviso that if it turned out to be the real thing there could be no comeback from us. To be fair to him, he also added that if it was a copy, he would take the loss. I thought this was an excellent way of doing business – bold and to the point. This guy had guts and the courage of his own convictions. Something rare in the art world I knew.

My dad was involved in this deal and, much to his dismay, I suggested we take the thing no further. I've never done the fakes just for money, though it's always been welcome. The pursuit of art and money by others, the lengths they will go to, has always amused me. In the end, they leave it all here, as we all do, so why chase it? When I turned down the bold offer my dad almost swallowed his tongue and thought I'd lost my senses. Maybe I had. With hindsight, I should have taken the money. It would have made life simpler. But, as usual, my dad went along with my decision.

From my point of view, the Scotland Yardies always seemed to have it in for Dad during the time we were in their power – as if he had led me astray or something. In fact, no one would have been happier than my mum and dad if I'd done something proper with my life. Throughout my school days they both tried to get me to walk the right path, but to no avail. I'd been making and selling artwork, legitimate and not so legitimate, for decades before my dad became involved in my deals. It is a great regret to me that I ever did involve him, or my mum, in the things I did. Later on, their part in everything was bigged up for specific reasons. But I'll say no more on that.

The offer at the motorway services declined, it was agreed that I meet the dealer at his West End gallery. My dad had decided that he wanted to do the deal, especially as the previous deal he'd done with that Scottish daub had gone pear-shaped and almost brought the Yardies down on us. I wrapped the 10 pounds of silver that was the new Risley Lanx in an old tartan travelling rug, the type they used to have in almost every car when I was a kid, and we set off for London. Getting there early afternoon I popped the Sony recorder in my dad's top pocket and into the gallery he went, clutching the hoped-for cash cow. The upshot of that day was a new offer of £700,000, if it proved to be the original plate. I don't mind admitting that, at that moment, I wished I'd cast the damn thing in one piece and broken it up to make a believable object that would have passed much closer scrutiny.

The dealer had a couple of experts with him to see the plate – one, a former Keeper of Roman Antiquities at the British Museum – and from what I could hear from the tape they all thought the thing was real. It did look fairly convincing, at least to the unsuspecting eye. Dad handled himself well and in no time had the lot of them on the hook. Now to land them. As every angler knows, hooking a big fish is one thing, getting it onto the riverbank quite another. We left the plate with them for further research in return for a receipt, insurance for a million and a few books kindly given as gifts.

For some weeks after, that was that – except for my dad pestering them on the phone every other day. He's an impatient bugger, so at least I know where I've inherited that gene from. Apparently, the plate caused quite a stir in London and all sorts of experts had an opinion on it, all of them wrong as things turned out. The Lanx was variously described as something brought back from France after the battle of Agincourt and even as a recast made of melted down Roman silver coins. I dread to think how much that would have cost. To cut a long and boring story short, eventually, after the best part of a year of dithering by its hoped-for purchaser, my dad and I returned to London to take it back. Frankly, I'd had enough of the indecision.

Dad went in to collect it – well, that was the idea. What he actually did was flog it to them for £5,000 in cash! He thought he'd done a good deal, and I suppose £5,000 would have been a tidy sum when he was young. But I was none too pleased. By 1991, things had gone up a bit in price from the 1940s. I'd expended a lot of time on that project. Just the silver and the other materials to make it had cost over £1,000. But I wasn't going to fall out with my dad over a crappy bit of metal and a few thousand quid. The making of it was something I'd enjoyed and I had learnt a bit more into the bargain. So I let it go at that and split the cash with my dad.

The Risley Lanx's journey didn't end there. In 2006, when I was being questioned by the detectives from Scotland Yard, one of them suggested that the dealers who bought it had paid us £50,000. I obviously denied this, as it was plainly untrue. What I did know was that subsequent to our sale of it, it was sold on to the British Museum where it resided in the treasure room of the Roman gallery until 2006. A wealthy American philanthropist had been persuaded to stump up the cash. The dealers eventually admitted paying us £5,000 and not £50,000, mainly because the police had the original signed and dated receipt for the money. Dad had kept it as a souvenir.

My own favourite period of the silversmith's art is the eighteenth- and early nineteenth-century work of such fine craftsmen as Paul de Lamerie and Paul Storr, the King's smith. The ancients are definitely beaten back into second place by these men. Their works have always inspired me whenever I've had the privilege to see them. In design and skill of production they are in a class of their own and well beyond my ability. I've never made anything bearing English hallmarks, or coins of any type, or, for that matter, any work by a living artist. I wouldn't be party to any of that. All my works have either been imitations of people from ancient times or artists from our own age who've long since turned to dust.

My only other works in metal, apart from sculpture – which I've left to the last chapter – have been a few pewter patens and a small silver chalice in medieval style, the type of things found in monastic grave finds of the nineteenth century during the often overzealous Victorian 'restorations' of ecclesiastical buildings. The last of my silver productions was part of the police investigation. It was a small and insignificant thing – a 3-inch silver gilt Corpus Christi, or body of Christ, with a provenance that was rather interesting, and not wholly made up.

There is a famous and well-documented account of the opening of the tomb of King John – he of the Magna Carta, blubbery brother of Richard the Lionheart, that 'royal hero' who followed the line taken by many of our 'great leaders' in fighting hard for other people's causes whilst his own went without. His brother was even worse. Bad King John's tomb lies before the altar in the very fine cathedral at Worcester, laid by the banks of the river Severn, a great setting for a wonderful building. There, on top of the monument, is an effigy of the king in Purbeck marble, sadly knocked about a bit. The famous tomb opening took place in 1797 and the accounts of it are a fascinating read. Apparently, the royal body was laid out in a monk's habit with the cowl up over his head, complete with kingly regalia. This was always made of gilt copper and enamel 'repro', instead of actual precious metals. Nice stuff nevertheless – a crown, two sceptres, a jewelled sword belt with long sword and a 'gold spur on his foot'. There he still lies, decked out in his kingly apparel, all covered by a goodly monk's habit. He probably thought it would help him sneak past St Peter.

There was no mention of the gilt corpus. It was wholly my invention. The small Christ was modelled first in wax in a suitably twelfth-century English style. Then cast in a low-grade silver. After all, King John was known as a debaser of the coinage, wasn't he? The model was done with falling hair and a typical triangular frontal apron and belt. I've made quite a few crucifixes over many years, one of them, larger than the King John example, about 8 inches tall and in a sinewy early Gothic manner. It was one of my earliest casts in bronze, done when I was 13, and just about the only thing left of what I did in those times.

The gilding on the King John corpus was done in the traditional manner, something that can be very injurious to your health, so great care must be taken when practising it. Mercury, or 'fire gilding' as it was termed, has been used from ancient times until relatively recently when it was superseded by electroplating, though the modern method cannot match the quality of mercury gilding. It doesn't even come close.

Fire gilding, which is similar to lost wax casting, is something you can read how to do in 1,001 books. But I've never read anywhere how to do it properly. As far as I'm aware, it isn't practised anywhere in the UK any more. If you really need to see it done in the old style, go to Lahore in Pakistan. There are some very skilled decorative metalworkers there who are still working in the old ways. I dare say you could have a whole 'Roman treasure' put together in Lahore for not very much money. All you would then need is an old bronze vessel to put it in and a good story to back it up. Oops. That one may already have been done!

After I'd cast and gilded the little figure, and punched in the wound given to Christ on the cross by the centurion Longinus, I filled it with ground cinnabar – the pigment vermilion when used in painting – and then set about putting a story to it. I prefer the word 'story' to 'provenance'. As I may have said before, and I apologise for labouring a point, a provenance is an independently verifiable story. The corpus wasn't mentioned anywhere in historical literature, except on the vellum support carrying it, and that was something I made. There was no independent way of proving the tale, so it remained conjecture, not provenance.

The support was a folding cross-shaped piece of vellum I'd cut from a damaged eighteenth-century land deed, the whole folding neatly into a small packet with the corpus at its centre. The inscription detailed its finding in typically flowery Regency wording, describing it as coming from 'the tomb of King John of ancient memory' blah blah blah. I put in a suggestion that it had been presented to a young aristocrat called Henry Somerset, the future Marquess of Worcester, thereby making a Worcester connection even if it was a tenuous one. He had come to mind from my reading as a kid of the campaigns of the Duke of Wellington in the Peninsular War. Henry grew up to be Wellington's aide-de-camp in that campaign and so became the convenient young recipient of King John's Corpus Christi. I reasoned that he would be a suitably obscure figure who fitted the time window perfectly and who would give the thing a bit of whizz with the London trade. They do like a good tale, even more than a work of art.

Similar small gilt figures, though less historically important, had been bringing upwards of £100,000 in sales around that time. And a much corroded gilt bronze of St John of a similar size had recently brought three times as much. So I had high hopes for my little King

John bauble. Much to my disappointment, it fetched its reserve of £10,000 with a one and only bid at a leading London auction house.

During my questioning by the police in 2006, the corpus was only briefly hinted at and, as far as I can recall, never mentioned directly. This seemed strange to me for they made a great deal more of far less important things I'd made. One of the detectives told me it had been bought for the Royal Collection, and no one bids against that. That's why it only fetched its reserve. I don't know if this is so. But it's what I was told in the corridor of the police station in Bolton whilst waiting to be interviewed. I hope it isn't true, because even though I've done what I've done, I believe myself to be essentially a good citizen and would never wish to offend the sovereign.

I forgot to mention the fault with the corpus. It was made of silver, unoxidised, and so still soft and pliable, something 800-year-old low-grade silver can never be. In the auction catalogue, it was described by experts as being made of 'gilt lead'. Lead melts at 327°c, while mercury boils off at more than 356°c. So how the heck could anyone fire gild a piece of lead as tiny as that figure? It would have been a puddle in the gilder's flame in seconds. At the time, no one seemed to pick up on this. There's more to art than just art history. Those expert bodies probably need a few practical people on their staff, as well as academics. But who am I to suggest such things?

Whilst writing all these things down for this book, I'm wracking my brain, or what's left of it, to remember as many things as I can and it's a surprise to me how many there are. I can't remember them all without boring everyone to sleep, so I'll finish with the metalwork and end this chapter with a couple of ceramics that were also part of my undoing – the Gauguin Faun and the Hepworth Goose.

My work in ceramics has been a lifelong interest. I started on my own work early, thanks to my mum and dad buying me a 1 cubic foot electric top loader from a chap in Stoke-on-Trent. It lasted 30 years with just two new sets of elements. It was propped up in the corner of my dad's old shed, without its lid and full of bags of glazes and colours, the ones with which the detective decorated himself on the day he first came to see me. It's gone now.

I haven't only done fakes in pottery. Some of my pots of earlier times were to my own designs, though influenced by such people as Bernard Leach and Hans Coper. I know a bit about modern potters, unlike modern painters. I did manage to sell some of these, along with my watercolours, but never in enough numbers or at good enough prices to make a living. So eventually I abandoned them and made what sold well – fakes.

I also had a period making copies of old English porcelain – Chelsea, Bow and some of the other early makers. My first attempts at the Red Anchor ware of Chelsea were done whilst I was still at school. I'd read that the distinctive 'moons' seen in these pots – small patches of greater translucency – were a sure pointer to them being genuine. My solution to getting these 'moons' into my versions was to drill some holes in the drying clay, then fill them with a glaze and clay slip. After that, I'd sand the surface smooth and fire it in the normal way. Held up to the light, those glaze-filled holes appeared as brighter, more translucent spots – or 'moons' as they're known. Despite being fairly simple products, those early attempts were taken for the genuine article more times than you might think. I suppose the buyers must have read the same book as me: 'If the moons are present in Chelsea Red Anchor wares they must be genuine, because fakes never have them.' They do now.

One particular dealer who always seemed to like my pots was an old gentleman who had once been the curator of a well-known museum and was, by all accounts, a respected expert in the field of ceramics. By the early eighties, he had set up in business dealing in pottery of all ages and types. I used to visit his shop now and again to unload things that I thought had turned out well. Some of the rubbish I made wouldn't have had a chance of getting past him, so I only ever took my best work to his gallery.

His 'big test' for authenticity was quite unusual. I would go into the shop and plonk down my latest creation in its plastic carrier bag on the counter, and after carefully unwrapping the pot he would hold it to his ear and proceed to tap it with an antique silver paper knife, like a mad musician playing a xylophone. Usually to the accompaniment of his wife's commentary about how he could tell a fake from a real antique by the 'resonances', whatever they were. They reminded me of Jack Sprat and his wife, he being a small wiry fellow and she being very large and bossy. That's as kindly as I can put it.

I always felt a bit ashamed of myself for diddling the old-timer, although he must have done well enough out of the things I sold him because he was always ready for more. Like most of the people I sold stuff to, he probably did better out of them than I did. As he strummed away at those pots held close to his ear, I was tempted to say out loud, 'If you'd held that up to your ear last week, it would have burned your f****** ear off, you silly old fart.' But I didn't have the heart to disappoint. And fakes only disappoint when they're found out, don't they?

The good thing about ceramics, unlike pictures, and, for that matter, metalwork and stone, is that they don't ever seem to show their age. A little dust in the crevices, some discolouration to the foot ring – a five-minute job – and they're ready for market almost straight from the kiln. The materials are dirt-cheap as well. The downside is that due to the potentially high value of top-end ceramics and terracotta sculpture they come under very close scrutiny. So the materials and methods of production have to be absolutely spot on.

The most valuable pot I ever made was a piece of Chinese porcelain. Such things have been copied continuously over the ages ever since they were first made, most effectively by later generations of Chinese potters themselves. China has a very long and illustrious history in the world of ceramics, far in advance of the rest of the world, and only really came under pressure from Europe in the late eighteenth century, though it easily held its own against all comers, and does so to this day. This particular pot was a copy of a double gourd vase of the early Ming dynasty, though I can't recall which emperor's reign mark I put on it. The decoration was done in under-glaze peonies. I can't forget that – getting those things right was such a struggle. That pot was the most difficult thing I ever made in clay, besides being the most valuable.

The porcelain of the early Ming period was extremely fine and the very best pieces were made in the imperial workshops for the exclusive use of the Emperor and his court. The export wares of later years were always more heavily potted and crudely decorated. Luckily, I had access to some analytical papers on Ming period ceramics which I'd had since my days doing stuff for Carol and the restorers in the Cotswolds. Carol knew many people in the restoration business and because of my interest in all things ceramic she got me these documents which were invaluable to me over the years. They listed such things as the chemical make-up of all kinds of pottery, not just Chinese stuff. I read those papers over and again, until I knew them thoroughly.

There are as many recipes for porcelain as there are styles of pot. Basically, it's kaolin, or china clay, with something added that used to be known as 'petuntse'. This missing ingredient was the thing that stumped early European potters in their quest to make hard paste porcelain in the manner of the Chinese. They got round it, in a way, by using calcined animal bone and white ball clay, along with the kaolin. This is the stuff, known as soft paste, used by English makers such as Chelsea. It's quite distinct from porcelain proper as the bone ash renders the kaolin translucent at considerably lower temperatures than true porcelain. It was this poorly ground bone that formed the lumps which created those distinctive 'moons' in the porcelain I'd struggled with years earlier. Back then, I didn't know these things.

Petuntse was actually decomposed feldspar which doesn't only occur in China. In fact, the biggest deposits are now mined in the Americas. Today, all these raw materials can be bought cheaply from the potter's suppliers in Stoke. It's just a matter of knowing how much of each to add to the mix. Then you bung the lot through the pug mill and you're ready to go. We've got it much easier than the old-timers. They had to find it, dig it, refine it, before even making a start on a pot.

Increasing the percentage of petuntse to kaolin increases the translucency of the finished porcelain, but it also increases the temperature at which the clay matures. So, as in most things, it's a matter of balance. The double gourd vase I was making would most often have been decorated in blue, the easily recognised 'blue and white' of old pottery. For this, the Chinese, and indeed everyone else, used cobalt. Not the metal which is used today in such things as jet engines, but the oxide and carbonate of it. It's the carbonate that gives the best blues. My effort, though, was to be in 'iron red' – a colour that's more difficult to get right as the kiln has to be managed more carefully to recreate the quality of the best wares. But I like to do things that are difficult. Easy isn't a challenge, is it?

The hardest part of that project was painting the decoration. I'd decided to do it in an overall design of peony flowers – simple enough you would think. The expert painters of the Ming workshops would do this freehand in no time. But not being up to their standard, I struggled to get the balance and the flourish needed to make a convincing effort. You'd think a few flowers done in monochrome would be easy, but it took me longer to get my hand in at that work than almost any picture I've ever painted. After a lot of cock-ups, I had what I thought a fair effort, both in the pot and decoration. So into the kiln it went.

My electric kilns were useless for this job. At an element-busting maximum, they could reach 1200°c. But the 'Ming clay' I was using needed to be held at a higher temperature for a realistic attempt. So I had to build a 'home-made' gas kiln. I suppose I could have bought one, made properly, but the cost wasn't insignificant and I didn't intend making many of these imperial pots. They were too difficult. Not wanting to send myself to sleep prematurely with the toxic fumes – although there might be a few people who wish I had – I built the gas kiln on the outside wall of the concrete garage at the bottom of my dad's garden. The council demolished them in the early nineties, making most of my equipment homeless. From that time on, I would usually rent a small workshop here or there, whenever I needed to, but that was a bit of a pain. I seemed to spend more time moving between workshops than working on projects.

By the time everything was ready to go, the garden looked like a V-2 launch pad, with several large propane gas bottles piped up to a kiln that had been put together roughly with firebrick and cement. The kiln itself wasn't any larger than it needed to be and was a snug fit for the pot. But I over-ordered the gas supply, hence the launch pad look. As the firing cycle ended and the kiln was reducing in temperature, it was time to reduce the atmosphere, too. This was necessary to get the colour in the painted decoration to turn. That only occurs in a kiln atmosphere starved of oxygen. The timing is critical and needs to be done at around 800°c for the best results.

It's surprising how the eye, with practice, can judge temperature through the colour in the kiln. By this time, I'd had many years of practice estimating such things. To reduce my firings, I always use mothballs. You can use any combustible material, but most burn with some debris landing on the pot, causing imperfections. Mothballs splutter and vaporise instantly, starving the kiln of oxygen. After that, it's just a matter of waiting until it's completely cool before opening it to find a treasure – or a disaster. Disasters are more common. At least in my work they are.

I didn't attempt to pass off that pot as a genuine piece of Ming. Mainly because there have been so many good and not-so-good

Ming copies done over many centuries. The reign marks on all Chinese porcelain can never be relied upon as evidence of its age. Many of these copies weren't done to deceive, but more in an attempt to measure a potter's skill against the best. And porcelain made in China in the time of the Yuan and Ming dynasties was surely that. My effort was made in a similar spirit.

Some years later, I saw my 'Ming' pot in a sale. Those peonies I'd sweated over were unmistakably burnt into my memory, so I was fully confident it was mine. The odds of there being two done exactly the same way, several hundred years apart, were impossible. It sold for a very large price, but I'll not say how much. It lives in Hong Kong these days.

Some other things I made in my home-made gas kiln were a few copies of Persian lustreware. These were more complex than the lustrewares of the eighteenth-century English tradition, Sunderland Ware and such stuff. And more difficult to do. The lustre on Persian ceramics is developed in the glaze, rather than on it, as it was in Geordieland.

While I still had that kiln, I also made some attempts at a type of pot I'd been fascinated with as a kid – the products of the Martin Brothers pottery of Southall, which were very popular then and now. These weird and wonderful birds made in salt glaze stoneware are a tour de force of originality and design. I'm not sure exactly how the Martins themselves went about making them, but I would model them in solid clay, take a piece mould in plaster, press sheet clay into that mould, making sure to replicate a similar thickness of body to the originals, then model all the fine detail, freehand. Quite a lot of work. And each one had to show individual 'character', for that was what they did so well. I like those things very much. The Martin Bros' wacky birds.

For most of my ceramics a reducing atmosphere wasn't necessary. So the gas contraption didn't last long. I dismantled it along with its 'launch pad' to the relief of certain bystanders, my mum for one, who thought it looked rather sinister. My pottery works went on to range across a wide style, including such things as English delft, the tin-glazed earthenware named after the plates and tiles originally made in Holland. I usually stuck to the delftware described as English, not for any jingoistic reasons, but for mercenary ones. English delft brings better prices, probably due to the fact that there's far less of it. As the old saying goes, 'better to be hung for a sheep than a lamb'.

The white tin-glaze of Delft was an early attempt to simulate the porcelain of China, but much softer and more crudely done. I think the Ming and Ching potters, who were about when this stuff was being made in imitation of their wares, would have been amused at its primitive charm. The Emperor might not have been so forgiving. He would have had the potters' bollocks chopped off for their failures, I should imagine. The glaze itself is heavily leaded and toxic to work with, so my English delft pots weren't in production for long. I've seen many poor copies of this work. There are a lot about. The clay body is usually the first giveaway. It's too refined. In real pieces of delft, you can see debris in the clay, even without magnification, and the oxides and leaded glaze can't be imitated with anything but what they are. A good faker, just like a good artist, has to be a close observer, and for convincing results in clay work there is no option but to use original methods and materials. With no compromise.

One of my ceramics that was part of the police investigation was the Gauguin Faun mentioned earlier. I made it in 1993 and sold it in a London auction in 1994. I took it to London along with that set of drawings supposedly by the American artist Thomas Moran and left both with the auctioneer for appraisal. Details of the Gauguin were sent to the Wildenstein Institute in Paris, the official authenticator of such things. They identified it as a lost work by the artist. The Moran drawings were identified as late autograph reworks of Moran's western landscapes. If I remember rightly, the Morans brought about a thousand apiece. The Gauguin brought a disappointing £18,000. Not a bad hourly rate for the time it took to make, but I knew – as does the world and his wife – that original works by a major post-Impressionist artist of the calibre of Gauguin, even small charcoal sketches, sell for at least six figures, not five. Especially considering its provenance and previously recorded existence, to say nothing of its being thought completely genuine by the experts. I can't – at least not within the pages of this book – say why such a major work by such a regarded artist brought so little. There have been suggestions and I have my own ideas. But auctions, by their very nature, are a bit of a lottery, so perhaps we mustn't jump to conclusions.

The Gauguin was quite an awkward thing to make for several reasons. I'd first come across it in a sketchbook of the artist's doodles of the 1880s. Gauguin was never as well known for his sculpture and pottery as he was as a painter – a very good painter, but I think even he would admit he was not on the same level as his pal and great visionary, Vincent van Gogh. The first problem I encountered in doing the Faun was the fact that it was so poor an effort. I consider sculpture my best medium, though of course my ability falls well short of the artist–sculptors who have long been my inspiration. When I first spotted the thumbnail sketch in the 1880s sketchbook, I had ideas to do the Faun in a classical manner, something of the type, perhaps, of one of my favourite later sculptors, the Frenchman Clodion. But before getting on with things, I decided to familiarise myself with Gauguin's style in clay. I soon realised that to follow Clodion would have been the kiss of death for my Gauguin lump. He may have been a very fine painter, but his clay models, woodcarving and pottery were very weak.

I don't say this to insult an artist I hold in high regard, but if I'd known of the Faun when I was a 12-year-old doing those pot lids, I could have made that thing quite easily. It was surely the worst piece of sculpture I have made as an adult. All the time it was on the turntable being modelled, I had to restrain myself from doing it any better than I thought Gauguin would have done. It's very difficult to aim higher than you can achieve, but aiming lower is almost as difficult and certainly more awkward.

The modelling took a couple of weeks of frustrated effort. Eventually, having shaped it in what I thought a Gauguinesque manner, the next thing was to mould it in a good imitation of the distinctive clay body used by Gauguin on most of his pottery. I had decided to put a few faults into it, as I did on most of my later productions, in ever-greater numbers. But no matter how glaring they were, the more I did them, the less often they seemed to be picked up.

To be fair, the clay I cobbled together was a dead ringer for Gauguin's stuff and turned out far better than I had hoped. It was made of a commercial stoneware slip to which I added iron oxide and some iron rich clay which I dug from a deposit in the Jumbles Country Park close to my parents' home. I'd noticed Gauguin had used an unrefined clay in his works, with the telltale pinholes blown out in firing. These are caused by organic matter erupting onto the surface and look like tiny glazed craters or miniature volcanoes. You sometimes see similar things on delft. The clay deposit I used was dug up by the banks of a stream overhung with ferns, so I knew it would have the plant debris in it. Filling a carrier bag with the stuff, I took it home, sieved it for any large grit and added what I thought was the right amount to the stoneware slip I'd bought from my supplier in Stoke. And that was it.

There was a bit of trial and error with the firing temperature. The ball clay additions to the stoneware tended to make the resulting mix slump and bloat at high temperature. But at too low a temperature the colour development was poor. I must have used up at least half the clay on making tiles for trial firings before I got it right. Eventually, it was spot on. When the Yardies were trolling through the old stuff in my dad's garden shed, they picked up a handful of these tiles, all code numbered and of differing shades, but distinctly the stuff of the Gauguin Faun. They were stacked in a cardboard box, along with my set of glaze enamels which I used on my copies of English porcelain. They can't have recognised them for what they were, as they left them behind that day.

As far as the faults were concerned, the first 'mistake' was that the Faun itself was cast in three separate parts – something Gauguin didn't do. His stuff was slab-built, with modelled and cut detail, not cast in a plaster mould. I cast the upper torso in one, with the head slipped on as a separate piece, and also the arms. That was the first part. Next were the legs and the arse part, lacking the customary Faun's phallus, which was generally of stallion-like proportions. Incidentally, I left the Faun without tackle to suggest that the sculpture lacked balls, not for all the weird and wonderful theories and postulations suggested by the experts during its time in the spotlight.

After moulding the todger-less lower torso and legs, I slipped that part onto the dome on which it sat. Then I constructed the base which was slab-built in the proper manner as there was no other way to do it. As a last flourish, I scribbled a few goats and sheep in a pastoral setting on the band running around the base in a suitable Gauguin hand. Finally, I put on a signature of sorts – 'PGo'.

I now had three separate bits and fired them as such. After the firing, the three separate parts came out of the kiln looking just like the stuff Gauguin used for his ceramics, and a small part of me wished I had done the whole thing properly and fired the sculpture as a single piece. Instead, I glued them together with Araldite two-part epoxy resin. Anyone who can be bothered to look can plainly see the joins: one beneath the midriff belt around the Faun and the other between the dome on which he sits and the inscribed base. I never thought such glaring faults would be over-looked, but they were. The glue couldn't have been taken for repair by anyone half-familiar with ceramics. Each section was clearly an independent work, designed as such. Neither Gauguin nor anyone else would have done such a thing in an original work of art.

I can't really say more on this subject, except that during my first questionings by the police with regards to this item, they seemed under the impression that the Gauguin piece was an inscribed bowl rather than a sculpture! They said this was the mysterious description of it given to them by the auctioneers who sold it. All I know is that whoever bought it in the sale for £18,000 passed it on, and that it eventually made its way to the Chicago Art Institute. I suppose they paid a bit more for it than I got back in 1994. At the time, it was just one thing amongst many, done in a couple of weeks once I'd sorted out the problem of getting the right look to the clay and interspersed with other work of greater merit. It's only really a half-remembered thing and far from a best effort or a favourite memory.

The only other ceramic that was part of the police investigation was a small terracotta goose in the style of the twentieth-century British artist Barbara Hepworth.

The goose was modelled on a photo of a lost original I'd seen in one of the many sculpture books I used to own. I took it to the Henry Moore Institute at Leeds Art Gallery in 2002. It wasn't meant to be sold to that museum. I intended it to be an introduction to the London auctioneers for a much more important and valuable piece of twentieth-century British sculpture that had also been lost and that I planned to make later. But after the Leeds museum expressed an interest in buying it, I decided not to proceed with the major work. I didn't want the museum buying that as well. I do have a conscience, despite what some may think.

This goose was yet another thing that should really have been seen for what it was. I had only one angle to work from, as that was the only photo I could find of it. If my effort had been photographed from the same angle as the original and the image was then enlarged, the two images, original and fake, would easily have been seen not to be the same thing. No faker, however competent, can copy a three-dimensional object perfectly from a single angle two-dimensional image. Enlarging has the effect of exaggerating the discrepancies and shows up the tiniest variation of line. Though I must admit to using the enlargement comparison myself in doing copies. So it isn't exactly a cast-iron method of telling fact from fiction in fakes.

The museum offered £3,000. It's what they thought 'a fair market value'. In 2006, someone suggested it was valued at £70,000, quite a rise in price in just four years, eh? If they hadn't sought to buy it, I would certainly not have asked them to, but that doesn't make things right, does it?

Away from the twentieth-century copies of ceramics, the ancient pieces I've attempted – mostly for my own interest and with varying degrees of success – are such things as pre-Columbian pottery, made originally by craftsmen of outstanding ability, but ridiculously cheap nowadays. Probably because so much of it has been heavily faked, unconvincingly so in most cases. I've also copied, or tried to copy, Roman Samian ware, both for its press moulding and its finish.

The 'glaze' on these things isn't the glassy stuff of later pottery, but similar to the earlier Greek tradition on the red and black 'Attic vases' so beloved of the present-day antiquities dealer. It's achieved by applying a slip, or, as potters refer to it, an engobe. Making this is simple enough. Using the clay of which the pot is made, you grind it – and I do mean grind – for 24 hours in a ball mill. A good way to waste a week is to insist, instead, on doing it by hand. Next, dry the stuff and powder it through a fine sieve. Then add the powder to some water in a solution of about half a kilo to one litre, and let it settle in a tall thin vessel for about a week. After that time, you will see three distinct levels in your jar. Siphon off the top layer and sling it. Then collect the second layer. This is the one you use. The remaining layer can be recycled for the next effort which saves considerably on time. Now paint your sludge onto a 'Greeky' style amphora in a suitably 'Atticy' hand, fire it and out of the kiln will come a convincingly 'old pot' with just the right sheen that you see on originals. For sale, or just to admire.

I'll add one last thing to my ramble on ceramics – glass. Not strictly pottery, in fact not pottery at all. I've done bits of glasswork, though not the blown stuff. I've never had the facility to do any of that. My efforts have been in lost wax casting in the tradition of the French glassmakers Daum and Lalique. René Lalique was a remarkable artist crossed with a shrewd businessman. His fine and brilliant jewels, though done to his design, are actually the work of Japanese craftsmen. Lalique, Fabergé and others took advantage of the great skills of the Japanese and brought the best men over to Europe in the early twentieth century. Made of glass, but cast in the manner of the bronze caster, this is the type of stuff I tried to do.

One of my best successes in Lalique's style was a set of figures of the four seasons. Back in the late eighties, these were authenticated by a Paris museum, though I don't know what has happened to them now. Other things I've done have been bronze mounted vessels and a few weird and wonderful animal and bird figures. Glass casting is a fascinating hobby and quite difficult to do well. More often than not, a piece will emerge from the mould looking more like a jellyfish than what it was meant to be.

The only other glass I've done is something called gold glass, which was done best by the Romans in the Late Empire. They were originally glass bowls or beakers, but hardly any complete vessels of this type have survived, only the heavy bases of thickened glass with their gold inlay portraits. These are still around in fair numbers and are always a good seller. I once knew someone who would make me the bases in an authentic Roman glass mix and I would then set about turning them into something they were not. First, I'd beat out a sheet of 'Roman gold' whose ingredients I bought from Birmingham. When I'd got it to as fine a gauge as possible, using a hammer, it was sandwiched between two pieces of animal skin, preferably dog skin, and then beaten some more. Please don't send the RSPCA after me for saying that. Although dog skin was apparently the best stuff for the job of preparing gold leaf, I've never actually used it myself. I prefer dogs with their skins on.

Thus prepared, the gold leaf, which, incidentally, is much thicker than the stuff produced these days by electrolysis, is rubbed onto the inside of the glass base. On this is drawn a portrait, usually of the Roman nuclear family, Mater, Pater and Sprog. The background is then scratched away and an extra disc of glass, gently heated, is placed over the gold drawing and heeled in whilst it is still soft, sandwiching the gold for posterity.

The ageing of glass vessels with their much-looked-for iridescence is easy to replicate. I've always used a ceramic pot – a terracotta plant pot will do. Fill this with fine cinder ash dug from your local Victorian tip and bury your 'Roman' glass in it. Cover with a tile and fire the lot in the kiln. The temperature is the critical thing. But with a little trial and error, it soon comes right. The gases in the cinders cause a reducing atmosphere, and the chemical and metallic fumes that are given off corrode the glass surface and cause iridescence, or lustre.

If extra iridescence or corrosion is needed, simply dissolve some silver filings in nitric acid, evaporate the solution and add the resulting silver nitrate crystals to the cinders. This will give a beautiful pearlescent sheen to your glass vessel, making it look a couple of thousand years old at least. Crushed stone of a certain type, used similarly, will give the 'mineralised concretions' so beloved of antiquity experts. According to them, it's a definite feature of age that can't be reproduced and can only develop over time. A bit more subtlety is required to pass actual lab tests, but that's the general idea. The rest comes with practice and thought.

In the last chapter, I'll say something on the Amarna Princess and deal with my favourite subject – sculpture – from the Old

X.

The road to Amarna

S CULPTURE HAS ALWAYS been my thing. Some of my earliest
memories are of me with beeswax or Plasticine in hand, usually
covered in fluff and dog hair from rolling it around on the floor,
waiting for inspiration or a clout from my brother for getting under
his feet. Both the inspiration and the clout usually got me fired up.
I remember once modelling a very nice horse's head in wax after
my eldest brother flicked me with the elastic from his catapult. I
think I was about six at the time, so the horse head probably wasn't
as fine as my memory recalls. But I can still feel the sting from that
catapult. I think sculpture is the thing I do best and it's certainly
what I enjoy most.

I thought I'd start at the point where my interest begins to fade,
in the middle years of the twentieth century, then work back from
there through things that have intrigued me and that I've tried to
copy over the years. I've never followed a set chronology. Rather,
I've flipped from one period to another as something new took my
interest.

My knowledge of contemporary sculpture is like my understanding of contemporary painting – non-existent. I've only ever
attempted one 'sculpture' based on a found object – something by

the Dadaist and photographer Man Ray. It was one of his 'ready-mades' in plaster and wood. I recarved the wooden element in it and mounted it on a plaster base that I made. It was never sold. I didn't have the heart to take money for such crap. It was still kicking around at the bottom of a cupboard at my mum and dad's house in 2006 when the police came to visit, and taken into custody with all the other things.

I'd seen a photo of this 'found object' in a book along with the caption 'location unknown', which was always a tempting label for me. So I decided on a bit of surrealism of my own – Man Ray's found object, lost and refound by me. These concepts are the things I find difficult to understand in some modern and contemporary art. Maybe I'm just too thick to get it. I don't really consider myself an artist at all. I have the actual ability and am prepared to put in the hard effort that all good art requires. But I lack the artist's original vision. I think many in the field of contemporary art have this vision. But they lack the ability to put it down in a proper manner.

The best sculptor of the twentieth century, in Britain at least, would be the Russian-Polish-Yankee-Brit, Jacob Epstein. However, all his work is well-documented, which makes the opportunity for rediscovering lost originals very slight, if not impossible. I have had a go at one of Epstein's contemporaries, Eric Gill, also a very fine sculptor, whose work can be seen decorating the BBC's Broadcasting House in London, amongst other places.

Gill worked in the tradition of the stonecutters who were responsible for the gargoyles and religious figures decorating the great cathedrals. They worked directly into the stone, freehand, without first making detailed drawings and models to transfer to the block as happened in the classical tradition that re-emerged in the Renaissance, and went on beyond. Both methods require great skill to do well. But direct cutting leaves no room for error. In fairness, most of the works of Gill and his contemporaries were of a simple line. For pieces as complex as those of Bernini and co, it would have been nigh on impossible to keep the sculptures on track without any drawings or models for reference. You would just get lost in the stone block and knock bits off that were needed later.

Much of the work of such artists as Henry Moore would have been familiar to the sculptors of the Renaissance and baroque – not as finished works of art but as the first blockings done by assistants, or boasters, as I believe they were referred to. To an old-timer of that age, Henry Moore and his mates would have been considered craftsmen rather than artist–sculptors. But I like Moore's work and that of most of his contemporaries.

There are several early works by Moore that are still 'unlocated'. I have had a go at a few of these. They were not sold as fakes. But I don't know what happened to them later. I did make at least one in cast concrete, coloured black with manganese dioxide as used by Hans Coper to colour his ceramics. The old Delft potters also used it for the plummy colour seen on their stuff, the sponged-on foliage effects on chargers and the like. There are cheap commercial stains for colouring concrete, of course, but looking closely at the early concrete casts of Moore, I was convinced he used manganese. So I did as well. It has a definite purple sheen and polishes up very well. A similar effect is evident on some works by Käthe Kollwitz, whom I also rate highly as a sculptor.

Other twentieth-century sculpture I've done were such things as a near life-size limewood figure by the German expressionist Ernst Ludwig Kirchner. Many of these figures are missing, most probably destroyed in the time of the Nazi terror. The German expressionists produced many fine works of art, most of which were declared 'degenerate', along with anything else the knobheaded Nazis didn't understand or envied. They destroyed many master-pieces. But if you are the type of person who thought nothing of destroying human beings on an industrial scale, art wouldn't even register, would it? The most difficult part of that Kirchner figure was the painted finish. That took me longer to get right than the carving of the actual figure. I didn't get a full price for it, but some time later it turned up in a dealer's shop in Bonn with a new provenance by someone capable of great imaginings. I suppose most of those dealers have now decamped to the new Berlin. My statue was done before they knocked down the wall.

There are enough missing works from the efforts of twentieth-century artists to keep any faker busy for a lifetime. One of my favourite sculptors, Jacques Lipchitz, did many stone-cut sculptures. But by all accounts, Lipchitz didn't carve the stone pieces himself. He did the original model, then employed the services of a good mason. They were then produced in a bronze edition, most of which are well-documented and found today in many of the best collections around the world. However, a high percentage of the stone-cuts are still missing. I once did a rendition of a guitar player after one of these lost originals. Also a head that I only vaguely recall. I can't remember what happened to them.

Dad once tried to unload a few of my early attempts at modern stuff that had been hanging around in the garage for years. One was a poor copy of the great work by Otto Dix – the head of the philosopher Nietzsche, who looked for all the world like a baddie from a Buster Keaton film, but very well done under the hand of Dix. We took it to the Tate in Liverpool, along with a couple of copies of lost works by Brancusi – a blocked-out infant head and a wooden something or other. The chap we met expressed a desire to have the Brancusi for an upcoming exhibition at the Tate in London, or so he said. There was no mention of cash so my dad lost interest and we left.

Some weeks after, we received a letter from Vienna from a 'world-renowned expert' on Brancusi who offered to come and authenticate the sculpture that we'd taken to the Tate. The only catch was that he would require a payment of £17,000, first-class travel and hotel accommodation – all at our expense. That is what it would have taken to see if we possibly had a 'real' Brancusi. I'll not put down into words what my dad's verbal reaction to the letter was. Only to say that the expert never got an invite or a fee.

I've always thought it strange that art, unlike most professions or trades, has as its experts and explainers people who can't do that of which they speak. The medical profession is a wonderful example of how else to do things. As I understand it, no one can go on record giving medical opinion without actually having qualified to practise medicine. Even the various ball-whackers – footy, tennis and the like – always have retired or recognised practitioners of that sport gobbing off whenever their great skills are debated in the media. Perhaps the Royal Academy could form a trade guild, or trades union for artists, so as to let a few artists speak on art. It might make interesting listening. I haven't had a grumble for a few pages, so I hope you don't mind that one.

That expert I'd seen at the Tate Liverpool turned up years later amongst the gaggle of men who put Scotland Yard on my trail. On the day I went to the British Museum to collect that Assyrian relief panel in 2006, I arrived early and was waved in through security ahead of my appointment. On walking into the store unannounced, there, talking to the Keeper, was the man from the Tate. Having seen so many similarly suited and booted experts over the years, I didn't place his ugly mug for quite a while.

Getting back to sculpture, one of my favourite modern artists is Modigliani. In my teens, I'd read of his struggles to get the look he wanted in his work and how, in his frustration, he took a hammer to his sculptures and then dumped several years' worth of work into the canal at the bottom of his dad's garden at their family home in Leghorn. On reading this, I almost set off without delay for the said town to launch a salvage, until someone suggested that others had probably beaten me to it in the intervening 70 years. So that trip didn't happen.

In a similar vein, but planned several years earlier, when I was about 11, I hatched a plot to go to Hamilton in Scotland to relieve one of the old Dukes of Hamilton of a fine schist sarcophagus from ancient Egypt. I'd read somewhere that he'd been buried in this thing in a grand sandstone mausoleum in the grounds of Hamilton Palace. I later learnt that they'd knocked the whole palace down in the 1920s and carted off all the occupants of the mausoleum to a graveyard in town, sarcophagus and all. Graveyards and 11-year-olds with vivid imaginations don't really mix, do they? So that mad expedition was also dead and buried. How I would have carried off a several ton sarcophagus or, for that matter, unseated its ducal occupant, never occurred to me. Just reading of how the thing had been carved in the image of an Egyptian princess and was covered from head to toe in hieroglyphics, was enough for me to decide I must have it for my collection. The mausoleum of the Dukes of Hamilton can still be seen, by the way, by the side of the motorway between Hamilton and Motherwell. Its sleeping lions are much finer works than the ones that grace Bolton Town Hall.

Other twentieth-century sculpture that appeals and which I have copied are works by the Russian constructivists. I believe they embody the fiery spirit of revolution, so they can't be without merit if only for that reason. I did at least one after Tatlin, another in white painted plywood by Rodchenko and a few attempts as well at the porcelain of the period, made in the former imperial factories after they were 'revolutionised'. These were bits of desk furniture and the like, in the Malevich suprematist style, a black and red geometric pattern on a white ground, much simpler and easier to do than Chinese or English porcelain of earlier times, and in some cases more valuable too.

Whilst I was doing stuff for Monks and his band of pirates in the eighties I also did several American sculptures. One of them sticks in the memory. I was given several black and white photos of this particular work and asked to copy it to the nth degree. It was a plaster model, a third life-size, for a planned monument to President Abraham Lincoln – an unmounted saddle horse, 'Lincoln's

Horse', made, photographed and lost to posterity by the artist Thomas Eakins. It needed to be exact in every detail, except that the signature wasn't to be included. After all, Monks's client wasn't into fakery, was he? He merely wanted an honest copy to put on his mantelpiece.

My only other American things have been the works of the early nineteenth-century neoclassical sculptors Hiram Powers and Horatio Greenough. The first of these was a small bust by Powers after a lost original. The sitter was the sister of his contemporary, Horatio Greenough – a very pretty girl, something that always helps sell a work. After all, who wants to look at an ugly mug, even one in stone? Beauty in art is always much harder to capture than ugliness, but I suppose that's the same in life for real, isn't it?

I also did two sculptures in the manner of Greenough himself. Both of them were part of the police investigation. One was a terracotta bust of the third president of the US, Thomas Jefferson, and the other was a plaster of John Adams, president number two. I've always liked sculpture done in the neoclassical style of the late eighteenth and early nineteenth centuries. There's something distant and cold about it. It's always immaculately cut and finished, and much more austere than the classical sculpture that inspired it.

Greenough's sculptures, especially the later works, are well recorded, and this is always a problem for anyone hoping to fake them. Unrecorded pieces, new to market, aren't readily accepted no matter how well they're done. One solution is – or was – to do early works, usually things alluded to in print or other fitting circumstances. This was the route I took in doing the Jefferson bust in 1998.

I'd become aware of the sculptures of Greenough and Powers years earlier through a general interest in neoclassical art and architecture. This was long before trying my hand at such things in stone. It was known that Greenough, whilst a student at Harvard, and before he set off for Italy to continue his studies and improve his hand, had carved a 'chalk' likeness of John Adams, one of the founding fathers of the American Republic. By then, Adams was an old man in retirement, though still a very great one. During a period when I was doing some portrait sculpture practice, just for my own interest and with nothing particularly in mind, I decided to do this John Adams bust.

Some years earlier, I had done the Hiram Powers sculpture of Greenough's sister which I cut in the finest grade Carrara marble. Even back then, the block cost a few hundred quid. But it's always worth the cost when you see the results. I'd visited the quarries at Carrara years earlier and hope to do so again, life permitting. I prefer Carrara marble to the Greek marbles – the stuff from Mount Penteli and Mount Hymettus, near Athens, which was used to build the fine monuments of that great and ancient city, including the Parthenon itself, along with the many fine sculptures and reliefs that can mostly be found in the British Museum. Carrara, however, cuts better and is less granular. The Greek marbles can be difficult to work due to the amount of dirt inclusions in the coloured veins. For fine portrait sculpture, it has to be the stone dug in Carrara.

The bust of John Adams never made it into a marble version. I modelled the likeness in clay and then moulded a plaster from that which was worked over with chisel and rifflers to give it a 'cut look'. Being fairly busy at the time, this was the quickest and simplest way to go. That bust hung about in the garage for a good few years before it went off to market, and only then because the Jefferson terracotta bust, made later, managed to sell almost straight from the kiln.

This terracotta bust of Thomas Jefferson, supposedly by Greenough, was made by me in 1998 and loosely modelled on a well-known bust by one of the best portrait sculptors of any time, the Frenchman Houdon. He produced many fine portraits of the most eminent people of the age, including a life-size statue of George Washington, done from life sittings, copies of which are dotted all over the US, though the original is fittingly preserved in Washington DC. My terracotta was to be an unrecorded early work by Greenough who, I reasoned, would have been familiar with Houdon's works and may have based his study on the bust of Jefferson in a high-collar coat cut by Houdon.

My own method for modelling busts, fairly unconventional due to my lack of proper art instruction, is to draw as good a profile as possible onto 1-millimetre card, cut this out, set it into position on a plywood and wire frame, then quickly plaster the thing in clay, getting the nose right first, then along the forehead up to the hairline and across the brows. If I can get this quickly, the rest follows. Once the likeness is there, the head is eased apart gently along the now damp and softened card profile. The said card is removed, the two halves of the head pressed together again and the seam gone over to remove any trace of it. I know it's pretty unconventional, but it works for me. To get a really good likeness when the thing has to be readily recognisable, this is the quickest and surest way to go. Greek or Roman stuff is much easier. They just need to look godlike or of their period. And since no one to my knowledge knows the face of the 'gods', any old fizzog will do, as long as it's in balance.

After modelling the Jefferson bust, I took a plaster piece mould of it and into this I laid sheet clay of about a half-inch thickness. After carefully slipping the individual parts, the plaster mould was reassembled and then taken apart again to reveal the hollow sheet clay bust. Then it was just a matter of throwing the socle, or circular base, on the potter's wheel, sticking both parts together and putting in the finer details by hand – eyes, ears, hair and the like. It was then left for a week or so before going into the kiln for an overnight firing.

I wasn't really satisfied with the look of that bust. Most of my sculptural ceramics were made in the clay in which the Hepworth Goose was made – a superb buff earthenware, with a wide firing range, which, after a little surface treatment, gave a convincing eighteenth-century look. Unfortunately, by the time I made the Jefferson head, my supply of this stuff had dried up. So it was made in a 'bog-standard' red earthenware body bought in Stoke. Because of this, I never expected that bust to pass as a work of the 1820s. When it emerged from the kiln, it looked brand new. I even buffed it up with 'Mr Sheen' spray polish instead of giving it the careful weathering and wear pattern it needed. A week later, it was in London being catalogued for a sale.

The buff clay which I had hoped to use was a thing I'd bought since my teens from a country pottery situated a few miles from where I lived in a remote spot on the road from Haslingden to Darwen. I was familiar with it as this was also the Sunday race venue of my teenage years, the place for taking on the lard-arse coppers of the traffic division on their equally overweight and sluggish Hondas and Nortons. This pottery had been a thriving business for over 100 years, but by the time I became a regular customer it was a shadow of its former self, and run by an old lady and her husband. Due to the health and safety führers and their tangle of red tape, they had mostly given up trying to make a living out of pottery and clay digging, and survived by running the place as a tearoom for the passing trade, and the occasional coach party on its way to Pendle Witch Country, not far away.

Their storeroom held an ever-dwindling supply of 25-pound bags of clay which had been dug years ago from the pits all about. Their prices were years out of date, too. I mentioned this to the old-timer and suggested he hike his prices, but he never did. I could get six bags of good stuff from them for the price of one bag of crappy stuff from Stoke. As a way of easing my conscience about ripping them off, whenever I bought a new supply of clay I would always try to spend a little more on some craft pottery they sold on commission for local potters, along with a few sticky buns and several cups of coffee from the tearooms.

Almost the last time I called in, the place had been ransacked by a bunch of yobbos. The old lady passed away not long after, followed soon by her husband, and with them went my best supply of the best stuff for my ceramic ventures. All around that pottery there will be hundreds of thousands of tons of good clay under the fields. But I suppose everyone's too tired to dig it these days. After all, we can import it more cheaply, can't we? Until the inheritance runs out. As we all know, money doesn't last forever. Not unless you're a banker or a politician, or even an unworthy aristocrat sitting on a large slice of the nation's land bank and riding the gravy train.

Getting back to sculpture, the other nineteenth-century stuff to look at is the great body of work done by Auguste Rodin, inspired by the art of Buonarroti whose hand runs through everything Rodin did. There is so much of Rodin's work that the odd fake being passed off as a Rodin original isn't unknown.

Some of my favourite nineteenth-century sculptures, mostly bronzes, are by the group of British artists known as the 'New Sculpture' movement. These are very fine works inspired by the Florentine sculptors of old – Donatello, Ghiberti and all – but done in a contemporary way – for the 1870s – by such artists as Hamo Thornycroft, George Frampton, Alfred Gilbert and Lord Leighton. I once did a large terracotta group after Frampton, an unlocated figure of a 'Rustic and Child with Scythe'. It was similar to a piece featured in a well-known Manchester exhibition of the 1900s, but I can't remember which one.

Around the time of doing that Frampton work, I produced my only Impressionist sculpture. To be sure, there's not much of it about, just a few ballerinas and one or two old nags by Degas, and that's almost it. This particular work was a head of Diana, the mythological huntress, done by Renoir of all people. I'd read somewhere of these sculptures, a lone group done by Renoir late in his career and not repeated. The Diana head was about life-size and done as an exact copy from the photo of the original, but unsigned. It was sold to Monks in the mid-eighties. I haven't seen it since.

With the brand-new-looking Jefferson head, after I'd fired and spray-polished it, I took it to the London auctioneers where the Gauguin thing had been sold some years earlier. It almost came a cropper straight away. I carried it into the auctioneers covered in a bin liner wrapped in the messy old tartan travelling rug and duly misjudged the placing of it onto the table in reception. It hit the table with a boom and rang like a bell for several seconds. Luckily, due to its thickness being on a par with a few other skulls in the vicinity, no harm was done. The bust was catalogued as of Jefferson, by Greenough, and sold several months later for £48,000.

After that success, if that is what it was, I decided to send off that grumpy-looking plaster bust of John Adams that had been hanging around in a cupboard for years. It was known that around the time Greenough would have been making it, old Adams had suffered a debilitating stroke, so I tried to show this in his face, not very successfully. It was bought by someone who outbid the buyer of the terracotta Jefferson of the previous year, and paid what I thought was an over-the-top price into the bargain of £110,000.

I later heard that questions were raised about its authenticity and it couldn't be moved on at that price. The catalogues are quite plain on this – buyers must satisfy themselves on questions of attribution and the auctioneer's opinion is just that, an opinion. The legal jargon is more entangling than my simple mind can cope with, but that's how I interpret the small print. In this case, the purchaser kicked up a fuss, so I refunded his money. For obvious reasons I didn't want to draw attention and there would always be another day for shearing, or so I thought.

If the distinguished gentleman who bought the Jefferson had also been successful in buying the Adams then I think I would most probably have heard nothing more about that affair until my run-in with the Yardies in 2006. During my dealings with them, and with my solicitor in 2007, I was informed that the purchaser of the Jefferson bust was no less a person than another recent president of the United States. Out of the great respect I hold for that office and country, I'll say no more on that. I do hope that – at least for the time he believed it to be by Greenough, and not by Greenhalgh – it brought this other Jefferson pleasure. I also hope he doesn't send round the secret service to duff me up.

Probably the best known and certainly the finest sculptor of the neoclassical period would be Antonio Canova. Most will be familiar with him through the much-publicised public purchase some years back of his rendition of the Three Graces. Not by any means his best work. He also carved Napoleon's sister, reclining in the buff as the goddess Venus, a sculpture that's now in the Villa Borghese in Rome. To my eye, there doesn't seem to be much of a family resemblance. The fat little Corsican corporal doesn't look anything like her, or she like him.

At one time, I had Canova's thumbprint and several of his fingerprints in silicon rubber. Tom the antique dealer gave them to me. He reckoned they were taken from some terracottas lodged in the National Museum of Scotland in Edinburgh that had once belonged to the Earls of Carlisle. How Tom came to get a set of fingerprints off them I have no idea. That's assuming they really were the 'dabs' of Canova.

I've done a few Canova-inspired bozzetti, or working models, but his marbles would need a large workshop and a few strong assistants to complete. Fine sculptors such as Canova produced hundreds of working models, most of which haven't survived or have been lost, so these things are always a more realistic proposition for people such as me to do. To have the fingerprints of the master upon them is a bonus.

Going back through the ages, the period before Canova and co is more interesting as the age of scientific experimentation and discovery than it is in art. The Age of Enlightenment is a fascinating epoch, a time when much of the modern world was first formulated in the minds of men and women. But most of its artistic endeavour, excepting the work of the silversmith and the potter, does little to impress. The rococo is generally unremarkable. As far as I'm concerned, the kinds of thing bigged up at the court of the French kings are more showbiz than serious art.

The first Renaissance sculptures I ever saw, as a kid of about seven, were the bronze casts on the tomb of Henry VII and his queen at Westminster Abbey. These were the work of the Italian Pietro Torrigiano. I can well recall standing there to get a closer look at them with my nose pressed hard up against the superb wrought-iron grill that surrounds them, feeling like a piece of cheese going through the grater. The figures of Henry and his missus, cast and chased in copper and then gilded, with surrounding putti and heraldic devices in the best hand, is a very impressive piece of metalwork. I don't know their history, but I would imagine they would have been cast in the King's Armoury at the Tower. That's if they were cast in England at all.

At that time, the technical requirement for such large casts, moulds and all, would have needed the resources of the cannon makers and their foundries. Much of the bronze work of the Renaissance was produced in them – such as Donatello's great equestrian statue of the soldier Gattamelata. I hope I've spelled his name right. It's a bit of a mouthful, isn't it? Not a good thing for a soldier, I would imagine. Before you could shout, 'Duck Gattamelata!' he'd have been decapitated by a cannonball. The statue is in Padua and apparently took Donatello and his star pupil, Bellano, along with a gaggle of assistants, nine years to make.

The cannon factories would have been familiar places for the geniuses of the Renaissance, men such as Leonardo, working for the great patrons and warmongers of the age. There's nothing like a war to fill a place with monuments, is there? After all, the cannon makers needed something to do in the peace. Giambologna's equally impressive equestrian statue of Duke Ferdinando, the bronzes of Ghiberti, Cellini's 'Perseus with the Head of Medusa' would all go hand in hand with the workshops dedicated to the production of the machinery of war.

My most convincing sculpture of this period was done in the mid-eighties when I was doing my best work. It was a bronze cast of a piece by the Venetian sculptor Alessandro Vittoria, done in the mannerist style, which requires that the sculpture has a balanced overall design and that all the viewpoints are equally important in the manner of the ancients. It's different from, say, Bernini's style, the baroque style, where the works were designed to have a 'best side', like a Hollywood film star, though I personally can't find a bad side in any of Bernini's proper sculptures.

Vittoria's work can be seen all over Venice. He is one of that city's greatest artists and anyone familiar with the art treasures of Venice will know that is quite something. Most small Renaissance bronzes were cast in editions of just a few copies. Unlike modern editions, which often run into thousands, they were only done in small numbers for rich and self-important patrons. The casts themselves were always subtly different from each other in pose and finish, which gives a certain latitude in remaking them, though any weakness in design is easily picked up by a good expert, so you have to be on top of your game in doing them. I settled on a bronze, of some 20-odd inches, in the form of a St Sebastian in the usual and popular pose for the time – a semi-naked self-pitying wimp, tied to a tree stump, shot through with arrows.

I found as many illustrations of Vittoria's work as possible and, when I'd soaked up as much from these as I could, I went off to see some of his art in the flesh before setting to work on my own effort. Starting with a set of detailed measured drawings, done from four viewpoints, I then constructed the wire armature and, over a period of about three weeks, modelled the clay figure to a satisfactory state of finish. Next came the rubber mould. This was then filled with molten beeswax. It isn't necessary to fill the mould to the brim, just a quarter full. Then you slosh the wax about carefully to build up a skin of wax as the stuff cools, making sure to keep building layers of constant thickness throughout the design. The more uniform the thickness of wax in the model, the better the resulting cast.

In Vittoria's time, the moulders charged with reproducing his sculptures wouldn't have had the convenience of rubber moulds. Instead, they would have used gelatine supported in plaster. Gelatine doesn't wear well with hot wax, and I would imagine the process was very frustrating and laborious. This is what causes each wax pattern to differ so from its neighbour and resulted in the variations seen today in so many Renaissance casts.

To allow a good and fluid flow of metal through the mould, the figure needs to be hollow and well designed, and this, combined with the aesthetic of the pose, is where the artistry, combined with a knowledge of foundry practice, sorts the wheat from the chaff when the finished article goes to market. The St Sebastian was at my outer limits, both in artistic ability and as a bronze caster. I've done one or two similar-size Benin plaques at 20 inches or so, but they were cast flat, so the mould wasn't subject to as much pressure. To a commercial foundry, a 2-foot bronze is small fry. But for a back garden effort, done single-handed, it's a challenge, especially when pouring the molten bronze into a red-hot mould without getting frazzled or filling your boots with the stuff if the mould bursts. Quite a few Heath Robinson contraptions were needed to bring that one off. For me, though, that's all part of the interest in doing these crackpot ideas.

The mould ended up looking like a large artillery shell, 10 inches in diameter, 28 inches tall and weighing I know not what. I always cast my metalwork in a sheet steel case, which I cut, roll and fix with bolts. This is then lowered over the wax pattern already fitted out with runners and risers, all looking like a plumber's nightmare.

The steel case allows the use of a vacuum pump, which helps avoid the pockets of trapped air that would disfigure the cast. As a one-man band, I find that easier to do than the old method of building up a mould with layers of plaster and ludo. Those ludo moulds need really careful handling and assistance, and I'm always in favour of modern shortcuts if they are more convenient and don't lower standards.

The Sebastian mould was placed in the kiln upside down, then raised to 200°c to melt out as much of the wax pattern as possible. The first awkward bit was to manhandle the scaldingly hot steel case, and turn it the right way up for the burnout and pour, something I never managed to do without raising a few blisters, despite fireproof gauntlets and an apron. The mould was then raised slowly to 600°c. Any more and the binders in the gypsum start to degrade, weakening the sides. Any lower and the heated oxygen fails to scavenge out the remaining carbon deposits in the wax residue, resulting in tiny pockets of gas in the metal and a bronze that looks like bubbling chocolate. So the temperature and duration need to be carefully controlled.

That large mould remained at soak for the remains of the day and most of the next night, until, in the early hours of the morning, I decided it was 'baked'. To pour it, I'd gone to the trouble of jacking up the kiln on bricks to waist height and fitting a loose floor. When the mould was ready, I could remove the chocks holding the floor in place and lower it on a small hydraulic pump truck, the type used in warehouses to handle pallets. As it descended from the bottom of the red-hot kiln, it looked like a being from another world – sparkling and glowing cherry-red in the early morning half-light.

I wheeled it over to the furnace as quickly as possible, knocked away the iron band holding the fireclay plug in the bottom of the crucible, and out poured the molten bronze, down the home-made fireclay chute and straight into the mould at a rapid but steady flow.

The whole thing worked as planned and I had hardly strained a muscle, though I did overestimate the amount of metal needed, so it overflowed and almost got me.

After cooling the mould, the bronze statuette, complete with its tangle of runners, was broken out and the most laborious part of its manufacture began. This involved cutting away the runners and filing then chasing the surface until no visible trace remained of its method of production. That done, all that was left was to colour or patinate the bronze, a crucial part, and one that can make or break a fake. Most modern copies of period bronzes, no matter how well cast, are usually given away by an obviously fake finish, crudely done with acid and sulphur. There are loads of ancient and modern recipes for colouring bronze statues. Most work well enough. But to get something that looks as if it has slowly developed over hundreds of years isn't easy.

The St Sebastian, in my own opinion, was my very best work in bronze. Many bronzes of antiquity and pre-seventeenth century have been 'authenticated' by subjecting their ceramic core material to thermoluminescence dating, in much the same way as the pottery I mentioned earlier. The experts and their gullible patrons seem to set great store by 'authenticity certificates' and take pleasure in waving them in the face of doubters. It doesn't seem to occur to them that the acquisition of some simple pot shards or wall plaster of a suitable vintage, grinding them to a slurry, then pouring the slurry into the cavity of the bronze, might upset the thermoluminescence data quoted on their bulletproof certificate. So I wouldn't set too much store by certificates, no matter who's signed them. Look at the artwork and enjoy it for itself.

I never managed to do any convincing stone sculpture of the sixteenth and seventeenth centuries. It's just too difficult and on too grand a scale. Given a few assistants to do the donkey work, and a patron with very deep pockets, I'd have given it a go, for sure. The very best sculpture of the period, or of any other, is undoubtedly Buonarroti's first 'Pietà', which he cut in his early twenties and which now resides in St Peter's at Rome. It is a stupendous achievement in both design and virtuoso carving. If there was ever a better work than this, I would want to see it. In bronze, it would have to be Cellini's 'Perseus with the Head of Medusa', Donatello's 'David' in the Bargello and last, but by all means first, the east doors of the Baptistery by Ghiberti. All three in Florence.

Sculpture, particularly for anyone with an eye on the market, becomes less of a commercial proposition as we leave the fifteenth century and go back further in time through Gothic, Norman, and the various styles and fashions of the continental states that emerged in the Dark Ages following the collapse of the Western Roman Empire. Even the sculptural wares of the Byzantines aren't that popular compared with earlier and later periods, though the carved gems and enamels do bring bigger prices. Which is not to say that all this is somehow inferior. The great Gothic and earlier churches are spectacular monuments to their masons and craftsmen. But for the people I mostly dealt with, none of it was very commercial. Which is just as well really. Having gangs of neo-Cromwellian Puritans or the aristocratic descendants of Henry VIII's corporate raider chums sacking the cathedrals and flogging off the treasures again wouldn't be a good thing, would it?

The art of the Middle Ages hasn't featured much in my own work either, if you discount the King John thing and the few Nottingham alabasters I did in my youth. These were made in a rather crude manner in an opaque gypsum alabaster, as opposed to the translucent calcite alabaster favoured by the ancient Egyptians. One was a fragmentary relief of the nativity, fitted into a 'Victorian Gothic' oak frame. The other was a figure in the round, a seated God the Father holding the crucified Christ in his lap, as seen in 101 representations to be found in church art of the period. They had tiny traces of colour, done in tempera, and were fairly convincing.

My favourite artist of the age, although many of them were anonymous, is Pisano. His reliefs on the pulpit and font of Pisa Cathedral are the first spark of the Renaissance and what was to come from it, yet they were done 100 years before Donatello picked up a pencil. Other things to look at would be the enamels of Nicholas of Verdun, mini masterpieces of design and skill, and pointers to the way ahead.

In terms of saleable sculpture, however, especially over the last 20 years, the period is best represented by the works of the Indian subcontinent, something which, I suspect, can only get stronger – though I'm no longer in a position to put it to the test. India is covered in exceptional architecture and sculptures. My own efforts in this respect were done a few years ago. Two of the best, though still not done to a satisfactory level, were a couple of heads from statues cut in fine-grain yellow and red sandstone. One was about life-size, the other twice that.

Although carving in sandstone is physically simpler than marble cutting, it's easier to mess up and requires a lighter touch. I sold both of them to a dealer who specialised in eastern art, though not exclusively. He didn't pay proper prices for them and I think he thought his efforts in acquiring them were a real steal. But in the end they didn't seem to bring him much luck. If I'd put them into auction perhaps they would have done better, though that opens them up to a wide field of experts, so it's a tougher path to follow for the faker. Dealers, on the other hand, who think they can rip off any unsuspecting novice, are a much easier audience to convince.

With the Indian heads, the provenance for them or, more accurately, the story, for they weren't backed up by any material proof, was that they had once been in the collection of a certain Captain T. S. Burt, a Victorian soldier in the Bengal Engineers. I'd read somewhere of his rediscoveries of the great temple complex at Khajuraho in North-Central India in 1838, all overgrown and lost in the forests. Khajuraho is about 180 miles south-east of Agra where stands the Taj Mahal in its sparkling white marble and *pietra dura* decoration – something, incidentally, brought to its construction by the artists and craftsmen of Florence at the time of its construction in the seventeenth century. Many of the Khajuraho temples have survived in good condition from the time of their building in the tenth century. But there are also some ruinous ones which have been plundered. Some for building stone, others for sculptures. So Capt Burt's collection of Indian pieces was a possibility.

The two heads were quite different. One was supposedly from a nymph or Apsara. These are invariably depicted in the buff, except for some jewellery, and usually sport a pair of knockers worthy of the best imaginings of a Californian plastic surgeon. The head was life-size, cut in a fairly hard yellow sandstone, typical of most of the carvings at Khajuraho, complete with a high-piled elaborate hairdo. The Indian sculptors, over many centuries and into the present, are extremely fine artists and craftsmen. All their work is impressive on the eye.

The other piece was of an earlier time and, to my mind, a better effort. It was in the style of the much-collected Gandhara sculpture of about AD 200–300, showing strong classical roots of the Greek type in both proportion and detail, courtesy of the arrival on the banks of the Indus of Alexander the Great. A head of the Buddha, in red sandstone and over life-size, wasn't meant to turn out so large. The clay model was on a similar scale to the Apsara. But in my enthusiasm it got enlarged times two and took on the proportions of a sack of potatoes, so heavy that it became too difficult to lift single-handedly. This is what I was referring to when I said those heads didn't bring much luck to the dealer who bought them. The Buddha, I heard, rolled over onto his foot, breaking some bones. In his panic to lift it, he apparently strained a bollock as well. So these days, he's probably singing soprano at the Royal Opera House, in between art deals. I do know that his gallery is now a fast-food shop, at least it was the last time I passed by. I don't know what happened to the stone heads.

Some time before doing the Indian stuff, while I was still in touch with Frank Monks, I'd worked on at least one relief panel of pre-Columbian type – a depiction of 'the divine ruler of the underworld'. I know it sounds like something out of Doctor Who but the stone carvings of the Maya and their remarkable civilisation are of great interest. The stone slab for this one was supplied by one of Tom's associates and was of a type unfamiliar to me. The subject was a disjointed figure, surrounded by glyphs, quite a difficult thing to make. In the end, it looked a bit cobbled together to my eye, but I later heard that it was thought right by an eminent scholar who I believe came from Cambridge. I once saw a similar piece hanging on a gallery wall. The dealer was displaying it upside down and probably had as little knowledge of the art of the Maya as I did. But I believe he managed to flog it for a fortune, all the same.

Some of the art of pre-Columbian civilisation is really top-drawer stuff. The giant Olmec heads are particularly impressive. And look startlingly African in origin. The reclining figures of the Aztec were a big influence on the sculptors of twentieth-century British art, in particular Henry Moore. Some of his early work is almost a direct rip-off of it. The goldwork of the period is also very good, but it's something I haven't tried. Under magnification, it's quite distinctive, due to the particular inclusions found in the placer deposits utilised by Aztec goldsmiths. Though not impossible to fake, it always encourages close scrutiny as it's been extensively copied over many years. As have the jades and ceramics of those times. So it was something to pass over.

The Maya panel's 'story' was that it had come from the old home of a notable explorer of the Victorian age. Anyone who knows anything of pre-Columbian art will know that two of its earliest rediscoverers were the American explorer John Lloyd Stephens, and a British photographer, Fred Catherwood. Tom knew where

Catherwood's home had been, somewhere in North London if I remember rightly. Catherwood died there in 1854 and the panel was supposed to have come from this address in the 1930s when the house was being demolished. This tall tale had nothing to do with me. It was concocted by the West End dealers and their pet expert, and only came to my ears second-hand. It was yet another example of the type of 'inspiration' that gave me the ideas for the Amarna Princess later on. In art, it's always best to use your eyes instead of your ears. As someone once said, I think it was Walter Sickert, 'Never believe what an artist says, only what he does.'

With the Gandhara works of the early centuries AD, we go back into the classical world. Two of my best efforts in Roman-style sculpture were one that was definitely recorded, though lost – the Blundell Lion I referred to earlier – and another that I started in my teens and finished almost 20 years later. I suppose it was my poor equal of Ghiberti's 'Doors of Paradise' in Florence. At least it took me as long to do, though the effects weren't quite the same. I'll deal with the Blundell Lion first. It was cut in the piece of *rosso antico*, or antique red, that I'd bought cheaply in Ireland, and fitted the description of a lost work previously in the collection of Henry Blundell of Ince Blundell Hall, north of Liverpool. Rosso marble is an easy stone to work, but care is needed in the design. To achieve the best effects, the facial features or telling bits of anatomy have to avoid the heavy veining in the marble. A large lump of stone is, therefore, required for even a relatively small work.

In copying anything of an earlier time, the first thing to get right is the scale or measurement of the period. This is often over-looked in planning fakes. After carefully drawing the lion design in Roman proportions, I modelled it in clay at the actual size to be cut in stone. This was then cast in plaster. Then it was just a matter of transferring what I saw before me to the marble block – about a month's work. Carving is always the most pleasurable part of doing any sculpture. Where it gets soul-destroying is in the polishing and finishing. Proper sculptors would always leave this mundane work to assistants, but seeing as how I've never had any assistants I had to do the whole thing myself. I didn't mind. Leaving things to others has never been my style and even for great artists it can cause problems. The 'Risen Christ' by Buonarroti is a case in point. The sculpture, which stands in the church of Santa Maria sopra Minerva at Rome, was famously overdone in the finishing. Although still a great work, well beyond most, the overenthusiastic clean-up buggered up what it was meant to be. It could almost pass for a Canova now.

After carving and polishing, the next thing the poor forger has to do is put time in reverse and undo all their hard work by degrading the surface of the stone to simulate the wear and weathering of time. Who'd be a forger, right? Early on, I took great care in the weathering and mineralising of my sculptures, but over the years it dawned on me that most of my efforts were pointless. The experts were always far more impressed by a good 'story' than a good work of art or its telling finish. That was the last thing they looked at. And sometimes not at all. Gradually I gave up trying to impress and just sloshed any old muck on the stone. It rarely concerned those charged with identifying them.

Ageing stone sculpture is something I never fully perfected. I've tried many things, but time is always of the essence in forgery and most of my efforts were drawn-out affairs. There's just no other way to do a convincing job. This is particularly important in ageing the harder metamorphic and igneous rocks, which, due to their hardness, weather less. The subtle effects that are needed are, on the other hand, more difficult to get right.

To degrade the stone, I'd first soak strips of cotton rag in nothing more than water. These were placed strategically on the surface of the sculpture. After donning apron and visor, I would then pour liquefied gas onto them. The resulting mini explosions would erupt on the surface in pre-arranged wear patterns blowing off a fine layer of the stone's texture in a way that looked like natural weathering under magnification.

The next process was to mineralise the pitted surfaces. So in came another of my home-made contraptions. It consisted of a plywood and polystyrene case, fitted with a Hippo water pump, spray nozzle, dryer and automatic timer, most of which I would buy from B&Q and the Maplin home electronics store in Bolton. I'd pop the sculpture into this case and switch on the gubbins. The actual way it was done was a bit more complicated than I've put down here, but that's the principle of it. As the eyes of the experts became ever more unseeing, so my contraption became ever more redundant.

The Blundell Lion, made when I still thought such things were important, was one of the things subjected to my attack with liquefied gas and the ageing machine. I don't recall where it ended up. The other Roman-style sculpture I did – which I consider to be the best thing I ever made – was also the hardest work. I started it in the late seventies when I was still flush with money from the sale of that now far-off Impressionist drawing and blissfully ignorant of the problems involved in attempting such a difficult work. It was an imitation of a Roman bust of the fourth century, done in a very hard stone called Imperial Porphyry. This stone, which all comes from a single site in Egypt, was the reserve of the Imperial family and only used in their architectural monuments, sarcophagi and portraiture. It's really hard to find, but I discovered a block of it in a stoneyard in Scotland in 1978, where it cost me the princely sum of £2,000. I know it doesn't seem a lot these days, but to put it into context, one of my mates was getting married at the time and he managed to buy a two-bed corner terrace for himself and his beloved for a similar amount.

Janey was with me when I found that stone. She thought I'd lost my senses to pay such a price for 'just a rock'. The owner told us that it had once been set into the wall of a Roman basilica and brought to Scotland by one of his relatives in the thirties when the ancient building was demolished in the remodelling of Rome under the dictator Mussolini. I don't know if this was true or just an early example of me being taken in by a fake provenance. But it was a very fine piece of Imperial Porphyry and I just had to have it. So I paid up there and then, never thinking of what I was going to do with it.

The bust took almost two decades of intermittent work to finish. It was based on a porphyry bust in the Cairo Museum, thought to be of the Emperor Galerius, though I added a pillbox hat to it as seen on the small but impressive group of the four Tetrarchs built into the wall of St Mark's in Venice. The features were modelled as a dumpier, box-headed fizzog of Emperor Maxentius. When it was finally finished, I stood there looking at it and remembered back to the day when I'd first seen it as a faceless block in that stone yard, 19 years earlier. Half of my lifetime ago. Suddenly the thing seemed full of sad memories. Janey had been right. It was 'just a rock'. So I hit it on the crown of its head as hard as I could with a 20-pound sledgehammer. It burst into several pieces and a thousand flying fragments. I'd proved to myself that I could do it and by 1997 the reason I'd started it no longer existed. So neither would the bust. Later, I put its shattered remains in a sack and dumped them beneath the Forge Weir at Caton on the river Lune, where I used to go fishing. I presume they will still be there.

Porphyry is like granite, only more difficult to work. It can only be fashioned on the diamond saw and burrs, more in the manner of the lapidary than the sculptor. Consequently, it can only be carved with a thousand cuts, not bludgeoned into form with a drill, mallet and points, as with marble. I've read many accounts written by experts of how the ancient Egyptian granite cutters and their descendants would fashion porphyry sculpture for their Roman masters using nothing more than diorite pounders. Banging one rock on another, they would hammer the surface to powder, slowly shaping 20-ton blocks of granite into the likeness of a pharaoh.

I'd like to see someone try this. Not just the few powdering blows on a boulder demonstrated by a talking head on a telly programme, but the actual fashioning of the delicate parts of an Egyptian masterpiece, the fine facial features you always see or the internal corners of a quartzite sarcophagus. No one could do that with a rock. It isn't possible. I reckon they used copper wheels powered by some kind of lathe. It was either water-powered or, more likely, a man-powered hamster wheel contraption. I know there is no evidence in archaeology for this idea, but the great products of Egyptian stonework, the fine features and precise undercutting on most of their hardstones – to say nothing of the thin slices used in their goldwork – are just too good to have been achieved by banging one stone on another. So wheel-cutting was surely the way to go.

Even the works of the Greeks and Romans, done mostly in marble, so a doddle to work compared with the hardstones favoured by the Egyptians, are not for the faint-hearted. Cutting any stone is more graft than art. Marble is a metamorphic rock, much softer than granite or porphyry. And in Roman times it was mostly of Greek origin. Many of the best sculptors of Rome were also Greeks, or others trained in that tradition. I prefer the archaic sculptures of Greece – pre-fifth century – to the later classical stuff. The large standing figures are similar to the statuary of Egypt, which has obviously been their inspiration, and the proportions of many of them are very close to Egyptian work of the later dynasties.

Although the monuments of Athens and the ruined temples seen all over Greece are a fine sight, my own favourite, like many of the best Greek sculptures, is not in Greece at all. About 60 miles south of Naples is the ruined city of Paestum, founded and built by the Greeks, and known to them as the city of Poseidon. The temples are mostly of the sixth and fifth centuries BC, and done in the best order, Doric. Compared to what came later, Doric seems plain, but for me that austere look adds to the grandeur of the architecture. As in most things, and certainly in architecture, less is more.

The temples in Poseidon have all been robbed of their sculptures, whatever they were. I think they featured in the old *Jason and the Argonauts* film, the one with the seven-headed hydra and the fighting skeletons. One of those skeletons was a dead ringer for my physics teacher at school. And I think the hydra taught religious education there too. But I can't exactly recall their names.

I've only done Greek sculpture as fragments, usually accompanied by old-style inscriptions detailing made-up find-spots of late eighteenth- and early nineteenth-century date. Nothing too specific. Some of the sculptural fragments were none too convincing. The heads were usually mounted on buff terracotta socles that I'd throw on the wheel. The fragmentary bits of relief – torsos, bits of centaurs, that type of thing – I'd mount in old unglazed picture frames or plain oak banding.

I did at least one copy of an early Cycladic figure, the ones that look as if they could be the product of Brancusi's workshop in AD 1913 rather than 3000 BC, which is their actual date. The Neolithic burial grounds on Naxos and other islands of the Greek Cyclades were plundered for these sculptures in the 1960s. So with the massive prices they were bringing in the 1980s there are a lot of fakes about. These are easily spotted, made in haste by amateurs out for a fast buck. Many are aged by 'blowlamping' the marble to degrade it. Or acid bathing. Or shot-blasting. Or combinations of all three. And whatever else could be dreamt up by the nutters who made them. One or two are better, but they still lack the correct proportions and working techniques. As with many 'childlike' modern works of art, the real sculptures are more sophisticated than first meets the eye. Putting on 4,000 years of age is always a problem. I suppose they filled a gap in supply. And for their owners to be lumbered with a dud for their cash serves them right. Most knew that many of the genuine pieces coming to market have been tomb-robbed, with much of the detail of the burial lost in the ransacking. So I've no sympathy for them. And I know they've little for the likes of me.

Those Cycladic figures are the oldest things I've tried to copy in sculpture. If you go back any further, there are only the very early civilisations of Mesopotamia, and then it's cave paintings or the occasional fat-bottomed earth mother in stone or mammoth ivory – all too rare for fakery. On the subject of mammoth ivory, some years ago I bought a piece of it, quite legitimately, from a dealer who'd advertised it in a gem and mineral quarterly I used to get. This magazine was the place to buy the uncut gems and rare stones I sometimes needed for my projects, and having rung the ivory dealer and paid for a piece of the stuff, I waited in vain for it to wing its way over the Atlantic from Alaska.

He apparently got his supplies from the permafrost diggers in the high Arctic tundra where mammoth remains survive in top condition. You can easily get mammoth teeth and ivory from the stuff dredged up in the North Sea, but it's all badly degraded. The ivory supplied by this Alaskan dealer was as good as new elephant ivory. But after a month, it hadn't arrived. So I rang him, called him a twister and demanded a refund. As things turned out, he hadn't twisted me at all. The next week I received a snotty letter from HM Customs and Excise telling me I owed them 50 quid. The piece of mammoth ivory had been impounded at Heathrow and sent to the Natural History Museum in London for identification. The letter went on to say that it had, indeed, been identified as mammoth ivory by the NHM experts, but had it been elephant tusk I would have been prosecuted. Something of which I was well aware. They may as well have informed a holidaymaker that if the tin of talc in their luggage had been cocaine they would have been arrested for drug dealing. Or if I had been born on Mars I would be a Martian.

Power to the elephant protectors. They do need all the help they can get. But I can't help thinking that the 50 quid didn't get spent on protecting jumbos. Anyway, I paid up and by the time the ivory arrived, I'd forgotten what I'd wanted it for. I think it winged its way back to London in 2006 with the haul the Yardies took.

That brings me to the end of the things I've made over the last 40 years, except that Assyrian panel I've already told you about – the one that finally did for me – and another sculpture I carved in alabaster that seemed to complete my lifelong obsession with all things Egyptian. The so-called Amarna Princess.

The history and art of ancient Egypt – from the archaic period of around 5,000 years ago, through to the glory years of the New Kingdom pharaohs, then on to the rule of the Greeks and Romans, and even the rediscoveries and adventures of Napoleon's expedition with the deciphering of the hieroglyphics by Champollion and others – is a fascinating story. By my mid-teens, I had tried a lot of sculptural styles, but I always seemed to end up back with the Egyptians. Most of the things I did in the early days couldn't be termed sculpture in its proper sense. It was mostly clay and wax modelling. A few things in stone that might perhaps be counted were some small relief heads in lapis or jasper, the type of thing the Egyptians would set into gilded furniture and suchlike. I struggled to cut these heads with the cheap diamond burrs I could afford then, and it was usually a race to finish the cut before the diamond grit wore away. Even today, the best cutting wheels and burrs for hardstone cutting are very expensive and don't last long if you put them to hard work.

One of those early heads, not very convincingly done, was found by the Yardies in my dad's desk in 2006 and taken away by them to I don't know where. I'd never tried to sell it. I gave it to my dad as a birthday present in 1972 and he must have hung onto it. I would occasionally give the stuff I made as gifts to the family. They were received with varying amounts of pleasure or displeasure, depending on who the recipient was. Mum and Dad liked them. But my older brothers usually took them with a grunt or a sigh. I wasn't a skinflint or anything like that, but saving money on a present was always handy in affording more art materials.

The Egyptians used many interesting stones in their works

and this has always been something I liked about them. The gold jewellery they made was set with a wide range of semi-precious stones, all expertly worked. The intense blue lapis lazuli which they used in abundance was, and still is, sourced in Afghanistan. These days, a lot of it comes from Russia and there are loads of synthetics about, so you have to be doubly careful in sourcing stone, especially for fakes. This goes for powder colours, too, for painting. Many of those are minerals ground from these same stones.

In medieval and Renaissance Europe, the best Afghan lapis was more valuable, weight for weight, than gold. Even the Egyptians often substituted it with blue glazed steatite. And they weren't known for being stingy with themselves when it came to preparing for eternity, so it must have been costly back then as well. Other stones they used in jewellery were turquoise, carnelian, the black volcanic glass called obsidian and the two jaspers, red depicting the male anatomy and yellow depicting the female. All of them are very difficult stones to work that only yield with any ease to the diamond saw.

About 20 years ago I managed to get hold of a large lump of the best-quality yellow jasper and out of it I cut a set of small plaques and a couple of rings in New Kingdom style, with royal titles on them of a king I can't recall, only to have them identified as being made of plastic of all things. And this by a respected international authority on all things Egyptian. Whether this was done in the hope of acquiring them for buttons or out of ignorance, I don't know. But ignorance on this scale for such a person would be unusual, wouldn't it?

One nice thing on which I used a bit of that yellow jasper was a thing called a 'kohl pot'. These were usually small, 2 or 3 inches tall, in the form of a bulbous body with a broad flat rim. They were the containers for the black eyeliner used by male and female Egyptians alike that's so familiar in depictions of them. The one I made was designed to be an upmarket version. I cut and polished the main body in calcite as a lotus bud, and topped and tailed it in sheet gold with repoussé hieroglyphs, finishing the effect with a yellow jasper stopper inlaid with the name of a Ramesside princess. The whole effect looked quite good, though I say so myself.

My first proper Egyptian sculpture was a portrait in limestone of an Old Kingdom type who wouldn't have looked out of place in a modern art gallery – a fat, middle-aged, balding man with painted skin tone and black eyeliner. I carved this head, along with the poor attempt at a seated scribe that didn't turn out as I wanted, when I was 17 and working at the reclamation yard. Monks's place was across the way and I sold it to him as my first deal in anything stone-cut.

Since then I've done a number of Egyptian-style sculptures, the best-known of which is the calcite Amarna Princess, which wasn't my best effort, even if it did bring the best price. Other things that may be of interest (if I'm getting boring flip on a few pages) were a couple of sets of canopic jars, one in calcite and two in fine white limestone. These things, just like the ushabtis, have been extensively faked for many years, but almost always badly. What generally gives them away is that they don't follow the canon of Egyptian proportions. The Egyptians were boringly predictable in their representational art and their style, excepting the Amarna blip we're about to come to, barely changed or developed through-out their long history, though subtle stylistic differences do occur in different dynasties.

Canopic jars, always four in number, representing the cardinal points, held the body's internal organs. Besides wrong proportions, most fake canopic jars are too small for this purpose. They were supposed to hold the liver, lungs, stomach or intestines – and a human intestine is a fair bucketful of guts. Especially the beer-bellied and well-fed upper classes depicted in Egyptian art. I think some of their guts would fill a beer barrel, let alone a small stone jar. So size is everything, as they say.

I've also had a go at granite cutting, though I cheated in this and used my 10-inch diamond saw and burrs, something the ancient Egyptians didn't have. Or did they? The distinctive Aswan granite, with its large feldspar flakes, is a very beautiful stone but a bugger to work. I can recall one of the Met detectives picking up one of my unfinished granite statuettes from the floor of the garden shed at my parents' home and putting it down again, seemingly unrecognised. It was a small New Kingdom statuette in Aswan granite, plainly of Egyptian inspiration, and needing only some final shaping with a diamond burr and the cutting of the fine detail. They left it behind whilst taking minor things of no significance. So that's a bit of a mystery.

They also missed a half life-size torso in sandstone. That was carved as a bit of an experimental work in the mid-eighties. Later, I removed the head and mounted it as a separate piece. It was supposed to be a representation of the heretic king Akhenaten, one of the most interesting and original thinkers of the whole of Egyptian civilisation. When I did it, I strayed a little from the proportions and carving style of genuine works, and the overall effect wasn't too convincing. So it remained in the garden, unsold, for almost 20 years. The torso was in full view, standing in the flower border of the back garden. Its head, mounted on a wooden block, was taken by the detectives from the shed. I suppose it now rests with the other stuff somewhere in the bowels of New Scotland Yard.

One of the stones used to great effect in the Amarna Period is a stone called indurated limestone, a very hard and difficult stone to work. It's actually common sedimentary limestone that's been subjected to heat and pressure in the earth's crust, like all the other metamorphic rock we learn about in school if we can stay awake long enough to listen. This stuff must get an extra squeeze and bake because it's harder than marble and fractures with a conchoidal break, like hard igneous rocks such as jasper, rather than the linear and granular fracture patterns of the marbles. These days, it's quite difficult to source. But if you can get it, and work it, it makes very believable sculptures.

The material I used to make the Amarna Princess was the opposite of granite and indurated limestone. It was alabaster, a stone that's just about as soft as it's possible to find. Cutting it requires less effort than cutting a similar work in hard wood. The artists of Amarna used this soft stone in abundance, and their new art and society has always interested me. In historical terms, it's only the blink of an eye, but I think it produced the first artistic revolution.

Over many years, I've done several alabasters. The detectives took a couple away with them in 2006 having found them lurking at the back of a cupboard. During the time I was 'helping them with their enquiries', I remember one of the Yardies from the Art & Antiques Squad pointing out that, in his expert opinion, I'd got them wrong. 'The neck's too long and thin,' said he. As I was in no mood for an aesthetic debate on the subject of proportion and form in Egyptian sculpture, I left him with his expert views.

In fact, the art of the Amarna Period was very experimental. And in the works made around the same time as the sandstone torso in the garden I'd taken this aspect further. That was the reason why the alabasters found in the cupboard looked that way. They were never intended for sale and were made over 20 years earlier. The one I sold to the Bolton Museum was made in my dad's garden shed in the winter of 1999, a few weeks before the millennium. At the time, it was just another thing amongst many and not of any particular significance.

It was supposed to be an alabaster torso representing a daughter or wife of the king, dressed in a fine diaphanous pleated gown. Or at least what was left of her. Her head had gone, and so had her feet and arms. My inspiration for her was a beautiful red granite version in the Louvre. Rather than being hammered, like other stones, alabaster is best done in a woodworking technique. If you hit it with any force, it bruises and becomes opaque. The way I did this carving was to mark it out first in profile on all four sides of a block using carefully prepared drawings, then cutting down to that profile in quarter-inch slices – similar to how I cut the granite pieces. But instead of a diamond saw doing the work, all that was needed for alabaster was a B&Q wood saw and a bit of elbow grease. The profiled figure was then rounded and shaped with gouges and rasps, before having the fine pleats of the robe cut with my best set of woodworking chisels. After careful sanding and a low polish, it was only a matter of putting on the 3,000-year-old patina and she was ready for her debut.

The provenance came from a catalogue I'd bought in the late nineties from a dealer in old documents – paper, vellum and the like – with whom I had dealt for some years. This sale catalogue listed the contents of a country house, the property of one George Wyndham, described as 'the last Earl of Egremont'. Not quite true. I believe the earls of E are still batting and reside at the family pile at Petworth in Sussex. One of their number was a major patron of the painter Turner and a noted collector of sculpture. The catalogue stood out as it included two Egyptian mummies for sale amongst the contents of the house. It was only a few pounds. So I bought it out of a slight interest. I didn't get it with an eye to using it later for a provenance. That only came to mind a year after I'd acquired the catalogue and started work on the Amarna figure.

It was soon finished and in the spring of 2000 I took that figure along to the Stockport offices of a London auctioneers. As a sculpture, it was of little significance and not worth a trip to London, hence putting it in at their nearest collection point. I left it with them for 'identification' and off it went to London in their in-house transport. There it rested until the autumn without much thought from me. One Friday morning, on returning with the weekly shop from the supermarket, my dad mentioned that the auctioneers had been on the phone and sounded very keen. At first, I didn't connect this call to the half-forgotten alabaster. Until Dad said it was in connection with an Amarna Period statuette, a thing he wasn't even aware I'd made, let alone attempted to sell. Apparently, they'd had an expert look at it and, though not fully committing themselves to its worth, suggested it could be 'very valuable'. What's more, it was going to be entered in their December sale in London. And most likely featured on the front of the sale catalogue. Great, thought I.

Two weeks later, I took a call from their 'Egyptian expert' who rang with the bad news that it wasn't an Amarna statue, after all, but, nevertheless, he could get us at least £500 for it. Although only '100 years old' it was a nice thing for interior decor and, he quickly added, he could pop the cheque for the £500 in the post today. All that was highly irregular practice for fine art auctioneers. In all my dealings with them, it's the only time any of them have offered payment for an item entered for sale. I thanked him for his trouble and asked for its return.

During the next few weeks, he rang several times trying to persuade us to part with the statue. Over the period of his pestering, the price rose to £1,500. Eventually my dad threatened to call his boss and we heard no more from him. A couple of weeks later, I collected it from the Stockport office and into storage it went at the back of the cupboard, along with the earlier 'wrong 'uns' identified as such by the expert detective a few years later. There it stayed, forgotten, gathering dust, for another 18 months. Which is where the Bolton Museum enters the picture. Or should I say re-enters, because I'd sold them a small watercolour in 1993, supposedly by Thomas Moran, but done by me. I wasn't proud of it then. And I'm not proud of it now. Though it's a bit late for regrets.

The Bolton Museum has an internationally important collection of Egyptian art. I should know. It's somewhere I've been more times than I care to recall. Once, when I was about six, I got into trouble for leaving a family trip to the Odeon cinema. We had all gone there as a treat one Saturday afternoon to see *Doctor Who and the Daleks*. Halfway through, I left, unnoticed, and went off on a short walk to see the mummies in the museum. I was found there by my brother, in the Egyptian gallery, and got a good slapping for my trouble. I've rarely been to the cinema since. I suppose I've also paid my last visit to the Bolton Museum. These days, they'd probably have me horsewhipped from the premises as an undesirable, and I wouldn't really blame them.

My dad rang the museum in the spring of 2002 after seeing a thing in the papers about something Egyptian bringing a high price. This type of report always seemed to catch my dad's eye and he reminded me of that alabaster gathering dust in the cupboard. By then, I was completely fed up with being ripped off by the trade and reluctant to put it back in front of the auctioneers. So Dad suggested he show it to the museum staff, seeing as how they didn't have a financial axe to grind. We could get an unbiased opinion on it. And if it was positive, put the piece back into auction with the backing of expert opinion, sidestepping the type of person we had dealt with the year before. I could see the logic in this and can honestly say that in the beginning of that episode, it was never our intention to unload the Amarna Princess on the museum. Looking back, I suppose that outcome was always a possibility.

A few days after my dad called the museum to ask if they would like to give us an opinion on a statue we thought might be Egyptian, the Egyptologist arrived. On seeing the statuette, she identified it as an Amarna Period torso of a princess, as signified by the fact that the remains of a side wig, worn only by female members of the royal court, were still visible on the right shoulder. The lady from the Bolton Museum was very knowledgeable on all things Egyptian and obviously aware of the manner in which the trade works. We told her of our dealings with the auctioneers of the previous year and how they had offered to buy it for £500. Her response was to suggest they were 'most likely trying to rip you off'. After several minutes, she asked if it would be possible to take the sculpture away for further examination and left with the work in exchange for a receipt.

For a few weeks, I thought that would be that. But on a day I was away, the lady from the museum returned. She told my dad that the sculpture was indeed a rare survivor from the Amarna Period and went on to ask him if it would be all right for the museum to make an application to buy it. This was quickly followed by a suggestion that he should 'ask a quarter of a million for it' and, seconds later, 'No, ask half a million. I'm confident we can secure that amount.' If anyone doubts that turn of events, I think I may be able to furnish them with an audio recording of it.

What do you say to that kind of temptation? What would you say? My dad was 82 at the time and had worked damn hard all his life for far less. Despite what has been said of them, both my parents worked all their lives up to retirement, and my mum is especially proud of the fact that she had never spent a day 'on the sick' or unemployed in her whole life, despite having seven children and the tragic loss of one in infancy.

Also, while I'm about it, certain scumbags have tried to rubbish my dad's war record. My dad volunteered from a reserved occupation to fight for his country. He didn't need to go at all, but he did. As a last word on this, I would point to the fact that he's had a war pension since his twenties. The war pension is only awarded to soldiers injured in the service of their country. My dad was injured whilst serving in Italy and, as he has told me on occasion, he may not be able to wave about an empty sleeve or trouser leg, but injuries you can't obviously see are just as debilitating, aren't they? Amongst all the people I've had the displeasure to deal with in this distasteful affair, and there have been quite a few, I'd take very long odds on not one of them – defence, prosecution, detectives, crap journalists and others – ever having shed their blood in as noble a cause as the one for which my dad took up arms. None of them seemed to me to have the spine for such endeavour.

That's definitely my last moan in this book. So I'll get back to the story.

My dad succumbed to temptation. But I take full responsibility for that sculpture's eventual sale to the museum. It was my work, my idea, and I could have stopped it at any time. But I didn't. So I would like to offer my sincere apologies to the Bolton Museum, for what it's worth.

Over the next 18 months, the statuette went to and fro between the Bolton Museum and several establishments in London, the British Museum, and various labs and experts. I was surprised that its faults were not picked up in these examinations. It was never destined for such close scrutiny. I'd intended it for a quick auction sale, most likely bought cheaply by one of the barracudas of the London trade. On picking up his 'steal', he would have come unstuck trying to pass it on for a big price hike and the closer scrutiny that involves. Then he'd know that he'd been had.

The experts, the labs, and everyone who saw the Amarna torso, seemed blinded by its 'provenance'. All I can think is that they failed to look at the work closely enough. It certainly wouldn't be the first time that has happened to stuff I've made. Having said that, the British Museum staff and their labs are a very competent bunch. So how that little sculpture evaded detection – if not as a fake, then at least as an un-genuine copy – is still a bit of a mystery to me.

As far as its provenance was concerned, only two lots in that old catalogue were described as Egyptian. The two mummy cases and 'a group of Egyptian statuettes', all without description or dimensions. If that basic description can be construed as a provenance for such a valuable article then I think there's a failure somewhere to understand the meaning of 'provenance'. Nowhere in the catalogue did it mention an Amarna Princess, a name given to it not by me but by the expert opinion in London. If that alabaster could have been found to be recorded in the archives of the sculpture collection at the seat of the Earls of Egremont at Petworth House then that is what I would call a provenance – independent proof of its existence, irrespective of an old sale catalogue, not reliant on others connecting the two and presuming it had been bought at that sale.

The first problem with the Amarna figure was that it was not done to a proper proportion, something fundamental in all ancient Egyptian sculpture, even with the radical designs of the court of Akhenaten. Although their figural anatomy was exaggerated compared to earlier and later styles, the underlying proportion of design still follows the traditional canon of more than 1,000 years. All Egyptian sculpture is designed on a standard grid, unerring in its form, each point of anatomy corresponding to a particular point on that grid. If I'd been tasked with identifying that thing, this would have been my first step – making sure it conformed to the very strict rules of ancient Egyptian geometry and proportion. It didn't. Admittedly, the figure was fragmentary, missing both feet and head, but it would have been a simple enough thing to photograph it, draw in those missing elements and check the scale of the sculpture before doing anything else.

The actual carving didn't measure up either. The left arm, or what's left of it, was cut ovoid in section, which is again un-Egyptian. Part of the robe extending into the negative space to the figure's left is also totally wrong. Unforgiveably so for Egyptian art. The carver would have been carted off to the quarry for that blunder. This time around, he was merely sent off to Walton Gaol. One other mistake about it was that I put a 'contrapposto' into the torso that was totally out of place. That's the slightly slouchy pose you first see in Greek art of the classical period, post-fifth century BC. It isn't found at all in Egyptian sculpture. At the time of the Amarna Period it was more than 800 years into the future. It's like seeing Stephenson's Rocket chugging away in the background of the Bayeux Tapestry, a thing definitely out of its place in time.

These faults in design and style could be overlooked by many people, I suppose. But I was very surprised they didn't shoot the thing down when it went off to London, as it did several times over the period from early 2002 until late 2003, around 18 months in total, enough time not to have to make a rush decision. The lab reports were even more surprising. We were told that it had been scientifically examined at least twice. But a child armed with nothing more than a cheap microscope and a piece of litmus paper could have detected the things wrong with that alabaster.

When you look at the Amarna Princess, it's obvious there is a fracture in the stone running from the figure's left hip, through the waist, to the right breast. This is from when I dropped the block from which it was subsequently carved, and it split along a fault in the stone and fell into two halves. So I glued it back together with Araldite Rapid, the stuff with which, years earlier, I'd glued the parts of the Gauguin Faun. When I'd finished cutting the figure out of it, the glue line was exposed at the surface, and a quick look at this, even under very low magnification, would have shown it to be cut through in design rather than a later repair. I even coated the glue line in the overall sludge of the applied patina and this, too, was missed.

Over the years, I've concocted many recipes for convincing patinas of age on all sorts of things, but I eventually realised that nobody was looking closely enough to tell the difference. In the end, I just put on a crappy coat that only took a day to do. This was the patina I put on the Amarna Princess, just a bath in a strong corrosive alkali, with some staining. I didn't even neutralise the pH, so a dab with some litmus paper would quickly have shown her 'old coat' to be a very new one.

I made and sold the Amarna figure, but I don't think I'm the only one responsible for it ending up in a glass case in a museum. The fact is, such a botched job should have fallen at the first fence and should never have been identified as a 3,000-year-old artefact, no matter what 'provenance' it had. Even a cast-iron provenance can't protect such a thing, can it? I just hope people focus less on the label in future, and take more notice of the art. But I wouldn't bet on it.

In late October 2003, we were paid half a million for the Amarna Princess, less taxes. So £440,000. For some time after I didn't do much in the way of art. Despite some of the things that have been said about me, I'm not a total bastard and I wasn't at all comfortable with the outcome of that sale to the Bolton Museum. That's why most of the money was untouched and returned. For three years, it was on display at the museum, sometimes lent out to prestigious exhibitions. One thing that did stick in the craw was how, as time went by, the increased valuations put on the sculpture were parroted by certain people as a kind of victory over the 'simple old fellow' who sold it.

The next piece I made was the Assyrian relief which the British Museum was interested in and which I've already told you about. That's when the detectives from Scotland Yard came to visit and where this tale started, with that knock at the door. So now you know the rest.

Some people have condemned me for deceiving the art establishment with works such as the Amarna Princess, and probably rightly so, though being referred to in print as 'infamous', a description meaning, as I understand it, wicked or abominable, is a bit over the top. Perhaps those journalists have led very sheltered lives. There are worse things in the world than selling fakes. A few weeks in Walton would show them that.

Art – original, copy or fake – isn't of any importance in the real world. People are important, not inanimate objects. Even the best of art can only ever be a distraction. That's its nature after all. In their own time, most artefacts now looked upon as works of art were only ever functional or devotional objects, usually made for very different reasons to those ascribed to them today by the 'art elite'. But these days, bigging things up has become quite an art in itself, hasn't it?

The next time you visit a gallery, look at the artwork before you read the label and don't believe either, just enjoy the sight. Does it really matter who made it or when? And if some don't think that way, then we are at cross purposes. I'm talking of art, and they of money.

That's how I see things, for what it's worth.

Postscript

Since leaving prison, life has been pretty uneventful. A couple of years ago, I thought to have a go at 'modern art' and tried flogging it on a website, but binned that idea almost straight away. My heart wasn't in it and I felt more guilty taking money for such crap than selling the fakes of yesteryear.

Although no longer tempted to get back to my old ways, I still like to follow the art market just as a personal interest. And one or two of the things I used to make have surfaced. First, I would like to say that I don't mention them here to cause embarrassment to anyone. That's never been my intention. They were not sold by me as fakes all those years ago, and whatever labels have been attached to them since by others is none of my doing. So here goes.

A few years ago, a supposed piece of Chelsea porcelain made the news as a rare and valuable discovery by a leading London auction house. People were saying it was going to break the world record for a piece of English porcelain at auction. Since then, the thing seems to have sunk without trace, so I can only presume better-seeing eyes prevailed in the end. It was something I did in the early eighties – a head of a child in early 'triangle' period paste. The composition of the clay body was as exact as it could be – something I made up from a recipe given to me from someone who worked at the British Museum. Well, at their lab, which used to be on some premises in Savile Row.

It was based on a beautiful and genuine work you can see in the Ashmolean Museum in Oxford. I was always fascinated by Chelsea, and other early porcelain. As much by the struggles of such men as the Huguenot Nicholas Sprimont – a silversmith by trade and the founder of the Chelsea factory – to work out the formulas for the stuff from which his works were made, as by the actual pieces of decoration coming out of the kilns. The head in Oxford is supposed to be a depiction of the daughter of Sprimont's friend, the great sculptor Roubiliac. Sprimont was her godfather and Roubiliac is said to have done the original modelling. I think this must be so, as his hand can definitely be seen in the work, although it would obviously be at second-hand. The chap who formed it in porcelain from a plaster mould would have been a craft potter rather than a great artist, but still someone possessing valuable skill.

The most difficult part in making the copy was modelling the actual clay head at the required enlargement. Anyone could take a plaster mould from the original – that's if you could get the opportunity to do so, and I couldn't! The problem would be that after moulding and firing it, the new head would be significantly smaller than the original and so be seen as a cast by anyone half-familiar with ceramics – something the ceramics experts at the London auctioneers certainly are. Chelsea paste is particularly difficult to fire. It needs a very slow cooling to avoid dunting or cracking. Without wanting to be boring, soft paste porcelain in particular warps and cracks very easily if you rush the firing. Rapid increases in temperature warp it. Rapid cooling cracks it.

I managed to get a full set of good photos of the Oxford head, enlarged them by about 12 per cent – this being the approximate amount of shrinkage you get in early Chelsea ware, though it does vary slightly depending on the water content of the clay. After a few weeks of intermittent effort, the head was there, and after taking some careful measurements to make sure it was a good likeness, I took the plaster mould of it. The head came out of the kiln at the first attempt, complete and without damage, quite unusual for my stuff. After a bit of scuffing and wear, it was done.

The original in Oxford is coloured up in enamels and this was something quite difficult to achieve. I was a bit unsure of the composition of a couple of these enamels, and as the head turned out much better than I imagined it would, I decided to leave it 'in the white', a common enough thing in Chelsea porcelain. In fact, being undecorated was seen as a mark of excellence in early English porcelain. Getting a piece out of the kiln without blemish was a rare event and many objects were only enamelled to hide a pinhole or a glaze defect.

The head was sold in 1984 to a dealer in London. I never saw it again until it turned up in the news a couple of years ago. If you take very careful measurements of the curls in the hair, they don't exactly follow the trajectory of those on the original piece. As I said, it was an interesting project not a deliberate fake, and never sold as such.

Another of my things came to my attention recently in a very curious way. Since 2010, someone unknown to me has been sending art books to my dad's home, addressed to me. They bear a London postmark and some of them are rather expensive, but I'm not complaining. Though it's all a bit strange, isn't it? I received one such book recently, second-hand but interesting. Opening the parcel – hoping it wasn't a bomb sent by a disgruntled former customer! – the picture on the cover was immediately familiar, but better-looking than I remembered it.

Seeing some of my works from back in the early eighties and late seventies, a time when I think I did some of my best stuff, even though I was still quite young, is always a pleasure. They always look better than I remembered them. A typical example is something I saw some time ago, in 2002, I think. Back then, the Bolton

Museum bought a great Moran oil and held an opening exhibition of it, along with other loaned works. I called in to have a look and amongst the things hanging on the wall was a pastel loaned by a celebrity TV cook, a panoramic view of the Yellowstone Park. It had been reframed in some style and, at first, I was unsure it was one of mine. Though I say so myself, it looked too good for me.

Along the bottom, though, was a dedication in black shellac ink, in my hand, to a person called William Henry Jackson. This fellow was a real person, the photographer of the expeditions Moran was part of in the 1870s. I'd done this in 1983 and sold it in a dark oak frame at Sotheby's, Chester. It brought £150, as a copy. I don't know its subsequent history but I imagine it now has a fancy provenance and that Mr G probably paid more than 150 quid for it. The dedication along the bottom, worded as I wrote it, and a little eagle exactly in the spot where I put it in the sky, showed me it was my work. It made me feel, not for the first or last time, that I had misused and wasted my ability, such as it is.

Anyway, getting back to the book that was sent to me, its title was rather grand and pompous – *La Bella Principessa* – the beautiful princess. Or, as I knew her, 'Bossy Sally from the Co-op'. I'm a bit unsure of how to talk of this because the book was written by an eminent Oxford professor and must have been quite an effort. I don't want to ruffle any feathers or cause problems but I nearly swallowed my tongue on reading of its supposed value – £150 million! It would be crazy for any public body to pay such a sum. So I feel the need to say something about it.

The drawing is thought by some to be a work by Leonardo da Vinci, but it does divide opinion and wasn't included in the National Gallery's Leonardo show of 2011, a show which I saw and thought really well-done except for it being staged 'underground' in the Sainsbury Wing basement. Leonardo was a creature of the light if he was anything and I would have preferred to see his work in daylight. Apologies for that little moan.

I drew this picture in 1978 when I worked at the Co-op. The 'sitter' was based on a girl called Sally who worked on the check-outs in the retail store bolted onto the front of the warehouse where I also worked. Despite her humble position, she was a bossy little bugger and very self-important. If you believe in reincarnation, she may well once have been a Renaissance princess – she certainly had the attitude and self-belief of such a person.

It was done on vellum, quite a large piece to find unfolded and without crease lines. I did it on vellum because at that time I couldn't make old paper yet and I wanted to try my hand at an 'Old Master drawing'. Not particularly a 'Leonardo', just a thing in the style of those times, a pretty girl in a fancy frock. The piece of vellum I got from a local antiques shop called The Lantern – we always referred to the grumpy chap who ran it as 'the lantern man'. Most pieces of old vellum that are easily obtained are rather small. Even quite large eighteenth-century land and property deeds are usually folded quite small, which is OK for miniatures but that's about all. The Sally vellum was part of an old document, dated 1587, which had been scrolled rather than folded, so probably a local or national government legal document. It was very cheap because it had been badly burnt at one end. Maybe some old-time politician had been smoking it!

The first thing to do was to sand off the writing with 600-grit wet and dry paper. That done, it looked too new for anything old to look right on it, so I turned it over and did the drawing on the other side. That is why the drawing is done on the 'hair side' of the vellum instead of the much preferred 'flesh side'. The texture of the sanding should still be seen on its reverse.

As I said, the face is of 1970s vintage, and I think that shows in the drawing – a glazed and bored girl at the supermarket checkout and not a Latin princess at all, but still nice to know. The drawings of Leonardo and Holbein especially have always impressed me with their fineness of line and detail, and in my view they must

355

have been done under some magnification. I decided to do Sally in typical Milanese court dress of the late fifteenth century, which I think is the most elegant style, though not based on any particular work. The initial drawing was practised several times on cartridge paper to get everything clear and correct. Then it was ready to put down on the vellum.

The vellum is mounted on an oak board and if you look at the back, under some staining, you can see runs of old black writing ink. I disguised these stains a little to make the ink less prominent and to blur its source. It is actually part of an old Victorian school desk lid. At Bolton Tech, where my dad worked, there was a storeroom full of such stuff and he got this for me. Just for a bit of mischief, I even put a few butterfly braces into it to suggest it was older than its years, something I learnt from our excellent woodwork master in school days, Mr Young. Then a 'papering in' around the edges, similar to how I sometimes framed my 'old pictures', and that was the support sorted.

Before drawing on it, the vellum was stuck to the backboard with cabinetmaker's pearl glue, so it needed to be under a weighted press for a while to allow the glue to go off without 'cockling' the vellum. 'Cockling' is the effect you see on paper when you try to paint a watercolour without soaking and stretching the paper first. On vellum, the dampness looks like blisters or a cockle bed on the shore. It's caused by the water content of the glue, so the thing needs to be under a heavy press to dry it flat.

As a bit of experimentation, and just to prove a point to myself, I lightly traced the drawing I'd invented onto the vellum (I'm sure the graphite can still be detected) and started to draw the image in hard black chalk – carbon black in gum arabic – using a pair of jeweller's magnifying glasses. It took some time to get used to working like that and I had to go back to practising on paper for a while so as not to bugger things up. The drawing was a difficult thing to do and I almost abandoned it more than once, but it came out after a lot of detailed effort and, looking at it now, seems to be amongst my best efforts of those times.

It was done in just three colours – black, white and red – all earth pigments based in gum arabic, with the carbon black mostly gone over with oak gall ink. To be a bit Leonardo-like, or even Holbein-like – they were both left-handers – I put in a left-hander's slant to it. I'm not good with my left hand, but that is of no matter when imitating left-handed hatching. The Leonardo book seems to put great store by the apparent leftyness of the drawing, but it can be shown up very easily. With the face on the vellum facing left, just turn the drawing clockwise to face her skyward and hatch strokes from the profile outwards in a normal right-handed manner to lift the portrait from its background. Then turn it back to its original orientation and the hatching looks for all the world to be left-handed. Try it yourself.

There's a little more to it so as not to be detected, but I will leave that out. I don't want to encourage anyone. Incidentally, the book points out a palm print on the neck area, just the spot a right-hander doing an impersonation of a left-hander might rest their hand whilst doing the background hatching.

Although I am no Oxford professor, I could list umpteen reasons for not thinking this drawing to be by Leonardo. A glaring one is the standard of the interlace pattern on the leading edge of the caul, or hairnet. It is not perfectly regular in size or pattern as it recedes in perspective. Leonardo was a stickler in such matters. If you look at the patterning on, for example, 'Cecilia Gallerani' or, my favourite work by Leonardo, 'La Belle Ferronnière' – who looks like she's busting to laugh whilst holding a straight face – the patterning on both paintings is faultless, as you would expect of Leonardo.

Another weakness is the modelling of the suggested ear beneath the hair. It's rubbish, but my best effort. I couldn't match how Leonardo would have rendered it. But I do have a good excuse. He is he and I'm just me. The drawing was fixed with a misting of gum arabic in alcohol – to evaporate quickly and not cockle the vellum, which water easily does – and that was that.

The book mentions several holes on one margin as evidence that it had once been bound into a volume and also mentions some 'later restoration'. I did not do these things, and don't know who did, or where it went on its later travels. Looking closely at the picture in the book, it looks to have had the left margin peeled back an inch or so and been restuck, not very well, especially at bottom left. Could this be from when the left margin was pierced and roughly re-cut by someone else?

I sold it for less than the effort that went into it to a dealer in Harrogate in late 1978 – not as a fake or by ever claiming it was something it wasn't. I can't really say any more on it. At least it may now be known for what it is.

*

For my last words in print, I would just like to add that in between first writing all this down in my prison cell more than eight years ago and it finally ending up as you have just read it, a few things have changed in my life. The most significant of which is the loss of my parents along the way.

My dad died in the autumn of 2014 at the Bolton hospital, although he had been unwell at home for some time. My dear mum passed away at home, as she had always wanted, at the end of spring 2016. Both at the age of 91. They are laid to rest together in the churchyard.

Although I could go rambling on about how I thought my mum and dad were treated and portrayed in all that fakery stuff, my regrets and great remembrances of them, I think I have made that plain in what's already been written. Thank you for taking the time to read it.

So, finally, I dedicate my effort in this book to their memory.

Glossary

A

ALKALINE GLAZES   Brightly coloured glazes with a high concentration of alkali used extensively in ancient Egypt and Persia.

AMARNA PERIOD   An era of Egyptian history when the royal residence of the pharaoh and his queen was shifted to Amarna, and the sun god Aten was worshipped over all other gods.

AMPHORA   A tall ancient Greek jar with two handles and a narrow neck.

ANNEALING   A heat process in which a metal is heated to a specific temperature then allowed to cool slowly to soften it.

ARMILLA   An armband awarded as a military decoration in ancient Rome.

B

BALL CLAY   A type of clay that contains very few mineral impurities. Ball clays cannot be used by themselves due to their excessive shrinkage during drying and firing.

BALL MILL	A type of grinder used to grind materials into extremely fine powder.
BAS-RELIEF	A carving in which the figures are raised a few inches from a flat background to give a three-dimensional effect.
BENIN	A West African kingdom situated in modern-day Nigeria.
BRAZING	A process for joining metals with an alloy of copper and zinc at high temperature.
BURNOUT	A period of prolonged heating that removes the last traces of wax from a mould.

C

CALCINED	Heated to a high temperature to cause oxidisation, reduction or loss of water.
CALCITE	A colourless or white mineral found in stalagmites and stalactites.
CAMERA OBSCURA	An optical device for projecting images onto glass.
CANOPIC JAR	A covered urn used in ancient Egyptian burials to hold the organs from an embalmed body.
CARNELIAN	A brownish-red mineral commonly used as a semi-precious gemstone.
CARRARA MARBLE	The finest white Italian marble, as used by Michelangelo, mined in the quarries of Carrara in Tuscany.
CHAMPLEVÉ	An enamelling technique in which shapes are cut into a metal base and filled with enamel colours.
CHARGER	A large plate used during full-course dinners.

CHOCK	A wedge or block placed against an object to stop it moving.
CLAY BODY	The actual clay mixture used in forming an object.
COIN DIE	A metallic rod used to strike a coin.
CONCHOIDAL BREAK	The way brittle materials break or fracture when they do not follow any natural planes of separation.
CONTRAPPOSTO	An Italian term used in the visual arts to describe a figure standing with most of its weight on one foot.
CORPUS CHRISTI	A carved body of Christ in the crucifixion pose.
CRAQUELURE	The fine pattern of dense 'cracking' formed on the surface of old paintings.
CRAZE	To produce a network of fine cracks in a surface or glaze.
CRUCIBLE	A ceramic or metal container in which metals or other substances may be melted or subjected to very high temperatures.
CRYSTAL WAX	Wax in crystal form that brings an extra shine.
CUBIT PROPORTIONS	A system of proportions used in the ancient world based on the Egyptian cubit.

D

DECKLE	A removable wooden frame used in manual papermaking.
DEDICATORY	An inscription in tribute to a person or cause.
DELFTWARE	Tin-glazed earthenware, typically decorated in blue on a white background. Originally made in Delft in Holland.

DIAMOND BURR   A rotary device that contains diamond
                particles and is used as an abrasive.

DIORITE   A grey igneous rock.

DUNTING   Cracking caused by excessive cooling.

E

EARTHENWARE   Pottery made from a porous clay that is fired
                at relatively low temperatures. Faience, delft
                and majolica are examples of earthenware.

ENGOBE   A white or coloured clay slip coating applied
                to a ceramic body to give it decorative colour
                or improve its texture.

F

FAUN   A lustful forest god of Roman mythology who
                is half man, half goat.

FELDSPAR   An abundant rock-forming mineral typically
                occurring as colourless crystals.

FIRECLAY   A type of clay that is able to withstand intense
                heat.

FIRING   The process of bringing a kiln to maturity.

FIZZOG   Urban slang for a strange or ugly face. As in
                'Look at the fizzog on him.'

FOUND OBJECT   Or 'ready-made'. An ordinary object which
                the artist has selected or modified.

FRESCO   A type of wall painting done rapidly on wet
                plaster.

FRIT   A ceramic mixture of ground glass used in
                enamels and glazes.

G

GESSO
: A preparation of plaster of Paris and glue used as a surface for painting.

GLAZE
: A coating of coloured, opaque or transparent material applied to ceramics before firing.

GLYPH
: A symbolic figure that is usually engraved or incised.

GOLDEN RIVET
: Navy slang for a homosexual.

GORGET
: A piece of armour that protects the throat.

GRISAILLE
: A painting executed entirely in monochrome, usually in shades of grey.

GROUND
: A coating that serves as a surface for a painting.

H

HARDSTONES
: A range of semi-precious stones used in jewellery and sculpture.

HIPPO WATER PUMP
: A submersible water pump used for fountains and ponds.

I

IMPASTO
: Thick paint.

INDURATED LIMESTONE
: Hardened limestone.

INTAGLIO
: A design engraved or incised into a stone or other hard material.

IN THE ROUND
: A freestanding figure, carved or moulded in three dimensions.

J

JASPER   An opaque reddish-brown semi-precious stone.

K

KAOLIN   A very pure clay best known for its use in porcelain.

L

LANX   A large ancient Roman serving platter.

LAPIDARY   A person who cuts, polishes or engraves gems.

LAPIS LAZULI   A deep blue semi-precious stone prized since antiquity for its intense colour. Sometimes abbreviated to lapis.

LIBATION PAIL   A vessel for carrying ritual liquid as an offering to a god.

LOST WAX   A process used in metal casting that consists of making a wax model, coating it with a material that can withstand high temperatures to form a mould, heating until the wax melts and runs out of the mould, and then pouring metal into the vacant mould.

LUDO   Crushed material from earlier moulds used in bronze casting.

LUSTREWARE   Pottery or porcelain with an iridescent metallic glaze.

M

MAJOLICA   Earthenware pottery decorated with brightly coloured lead glazes.

| METAMORPHIC ROCK | A rock created from the transformation of existing rock types in a process called metamorphism, which means 'change in form'. |

N

| NIELLO | A black metallic alloy of copper, silver and lead sulphides, used as an inlay on engraved or etched metal. |

O

OBSIDIAN	A black, naturally occurring volcanic glass formed in igneous rock.
OLD KINGDOM	The name commonly given to the period in the third millennium BC when Egypt attained its first peak of civilisation.
OVERGLAZE ENAMELS	Enamel decoration on the surface of a glaze that has already been fired.

P

PATINA	A film or encrustation than forms on the surface of metals over time.
PATINATE	To furnish with a patina.
PATTERN	A form used to make a mould.
PEARL GLUE	A naturally derived gelatinous glue extracted from animal skins and bones.
PETUNTSE	Powdered feldspar, kaolin or quartz, used in the manufacture of porcelain.
PIECE MOULD	A sculptor's mould, most often of plaster of Paris, that can be removed from the cast in pieces.
PIETRA DURA	An inlay technique using cut and fitted coloured stones to create images.

PINHOLE	A glaze defect in which the glaze comes out of the kiln with pits in its surface. Pinholes are the smallest of these pits.
PITTING	A glaze defect that results in pits on a ceramic surface.
PLACER DEPOSITS	An accumulation of valuable minerals formed by gravity separation during sedimentary processes.
POINTS	Tools used in stone carving to measure points on a model and transfer them to a copy.
POUNDER	An implement for pounding rocks.
PRESS MOULDING	The pressing of soft clay into or onto a mould for shaping.
PROFILE	A shape cut out from a blank.
PUG MILL	A machine for mixing clay.
PUNCH AND CHASING	A way of decorating metal with a hammer and a punch that results in an effect similar to embossing.

Q

QUARTZITE	A hard rock which was originally pure quartz sandstone.
QUENCHING	The cooling of a hot metal by plunging it into water.

R

RAMESSIDE	An epoch in Egyptian history named after 11 kings with the name Ramesses.
RASP	A woodworking tool for smoothing out rough surfaces.

READY-MADE	A mass-produced object selected by an artist and displayed as a work of art.
REDUCING ATMOSPHERE	An atmospheric condition needed to achieve specific ceramic effects, in which oxidation is prevented by the removal of oxygen.
RELIEF	A shallow sculpture that projects from a two-dimensional background.
REPOUSSÉ	Shaped or decorated with patterns formed by hammering and pressing on the reverse side.
RIFFLER	A file with a curved face for filing concave surfaces.
ROSSO ANTICO	A fine-grain, pink to deep red marble, with occasionally thin black veins and white markings.
ROUTER	A woodworking machine used to shape wood.
RUNNERS AND RISERS	Connections needed to cast bronze when using the lost wax method. Runners are channels for the molten bronze to go down. Risers are escapes for the gases.

S

SALAMANDER CRUCIBLE	A particularly fine make of crucible named after the mythical lizard that was supposed to live in fire.
SALT GLAZE	A hard glaze with a pitted surface produced on stoneware by adding salt to the kiln during firing.
SANGUINE	A reddish-brown chalk that resembles the colour of dried blood.
SHEET CLAY	Clay rolled into sheets for handy use.
SHEET GOLD	Gold hammered into thin sheets.
SHRINKAGE	The change in size of clay when it is fired.

SILICOSIS	A lung disease caused by inhalation of silica dust, also called 'grinder's asthma'.
SILVERPOINT	The art of drawing with a silver-pointed instrument on paper prepared with a coating of powdered bone or zinc white.
SIZE	A glue put on a canvas before priming to protect it from the oil in oil paint.
SLAB-BUILDING	A way of making pottery by modelling a single lump of clay.
SLIP	A suspension of clay particles in water. Usually the consistency of heavy cream, it is often used in decoration.
SLURRY	A thin sloppy mud or cement.
SOAK	A period of high-temperature heating in the kiln.
SOAPSTONE	A type of metamorphic rock that's soft to the touch and largely composed of the mineral talc.
SOCLE	A short plinth used to support a sculpture.
STEATITE	A mineral talc, known as soapstone in its consolidated form.
STEP CUT	A carving process in which the stone is removed in thin slices.
STONEWARE	A type of clay greatly affected by the manner of its firing.
STUCCO	A fine plaster used for moulding into architectural decorations.

T

TANGO	An orange-flavoured soft drink launched by Corona in 1950.

TERRACOTTA	A type of fired clay, typically of a brownish red colour and unglazed, from the Italian *terra cotta*, 'baked earth'.
TESSERA	A small block of glass used in the construction of a mosaic.
TETRARCH	One of the four rulers of Rome in the system of government instituted in the time of Diocletian.
THERMOLUMIN-ESCENCE DATING	A method of dating archaeological specimens by measuring the radiation given off by ceramic materials as they are heated.
TIN GLAZE	An opaque glaze made of tin oxide.
T-MATERIAL	A high-quality clay with a very low shrinkage, popularised by Hans Coper.

U

USHABTIS	Small funerary figurines buried with the deceased to act as workers in the afterworld.